A History of the South Yorkshire Countryside

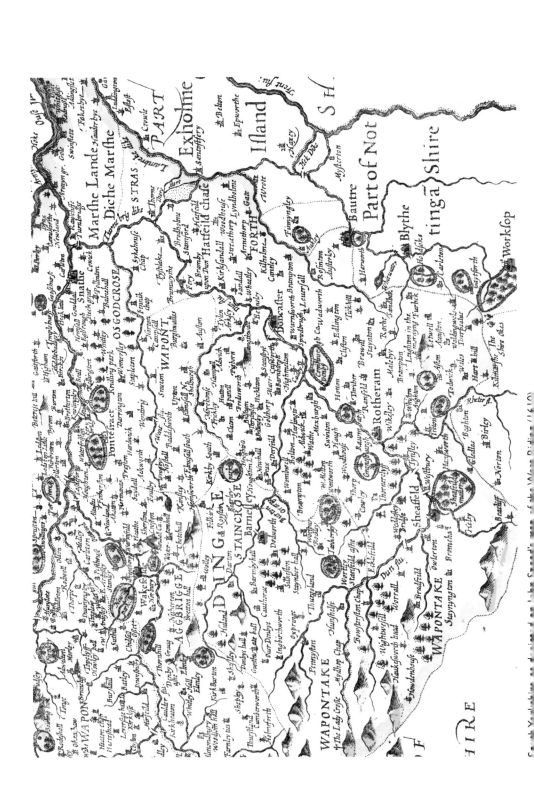

South Yorkshire, as depicted on John Speed's map of the West Riding (1610)

A History of the South Yorkshire Countryside

David Hey

Pen & Sword
LOCAL

First published in Great Britain in 2015 by
Pen & Sword Local
an imprint of
Pen & Sword Books Ltd
47 Church Street
Barnsley
South Yorkshire
S70 2AS

ISBN 978 1 47383 435 4

A CIP catalogue record for this book is available from the British
Library

Typeset in Ehrhardt by
Mac Style, Bridlington, East Yorkshire
Printed and bound in the UK by CPI Group (UK) Ltd, Croydon,
CRO 4YY

Pen & Sword Books Ltd incorporates the imprints of Pen & Sword
Archaeology, Atlas, Aviation, Battleground, Discovery, Family History,
History, Maritime, Military, Naval, Politics, Railways, Select,
Social History, Transport, True Crime, and Claymore Press,
Frontline Books, Leo Cooper, Praetorian Press, Remember When,
Seaforth Publishing and Wharncliffe.

For a complete list of Pen & Sword titles please contact
PEN & SWORD BOOKS LIMITED
47 Church Street, Barnsley, South Yorkshire, S70 2AS, England
E-mail: enquiries@pen-and-sword.co.uk
Website: www.pen-and-sword.co.uk

Contents

Preface

These twenty essays look at how our ancestors shaped the South Yorkshire countryside over the centuries. They deal not only with castles, country houses, churches and monasteries, but also with the houses and barns of peasant farmers, navigable rivers and industrial buildings, intriguing place-names such as Lindrick, and with fields, woods and moorland. Together, they tell the story of how the human landscape was created.

The book draws upon studies that I have made over the last fifty years. Some of my photographs were taken in the late 1960s and 1970s and are now historic documents in their own right. Parts of the text are based on articles that have appeared over the years in journals that are not readily accessible beyond specialist libraries. Occasionally, these articles were written with joint authors. I particularly wish to acknowledge the contributions and warm friendship of John Rodwell, formerly Professor of Plant Ecology at Lancaster University, who wrote two articles with me in the journal, *Landscapes*, the first on his native township of Wombwell and the second on the King's Wood in Lindrick. The publications of other friends, many of whom have accompanied me on visits to South Yorkshire's numerous historic sites over the years, are acknowledged in the footnotes.

This book, then, is about 'history on the ground'. Documentary research in the archives is an integral part of any historical study, but local and family historians combine the written evidence with what they see all around them, and they welcome the contributions of other specialists, including archaeologists, architects, botanists, geographers, place-name scholars, and aerial photographers.

I would particularly like to thank an old friend, Brian Elliott, for doing the editorial work and Matt Jones at Pen & Sword for overseeing the production process.

David Hey
July 2014

Chapter 1

The Oldest Parish Churches

As a general rule, the oldest building in a village is the parish church. Indeed, some South Yorkshire churches have architecture or sculpture that is more than a thousand years old. In many of our ancient villages the parish church was even more dominant in the Middle Ages than it is today, for it was usually the only building that was constructed of stone. But, as with many rules, there are exceptions. Today's villages may once have been just small places within large parishes whose church stood a few miles away. In other cases the medieval church has been rebuilt so thoroughly that nothing of the earlier work survives.

The oldest surviving building in South Yorkshire is St Peter's church, Conisbrough, the great minster church that served the royal estate of the kingdom of Northumbria near its southern boundary. Conisbrough means 'the king's stronghold'. Its territory stretched as far south as Harthill on the county boundary and as far east as the lowland moors beyond Thorne. The church is much older than the Norman castle across the valley, but as it was extended and enlarged from the twelfth century onwards the ancient part is now hidden from external view. On entering the building through the south door, however, we can see immediately that the outer walls of the nave have large corner stones (quoins) laid in the 'side-alternate' manner that was typical of the Northumbrian method of building. The lofty, rather narrow proportions of the nave are also typical of this early style.

The Normans enlarged the original church by constructing arches in the walls and by creating aisles. The remains of three pre-Conquest windows and a narrow, blocked opening that Peter Ryder suggested led into a side-chapel known as a *porticus* can be detected above the arches.[1] The lower part of the west tower also dates from before the Norman Conquest. Although we do not know exactly how old the original church is, it was certainly built during the Anglo-Scandinavian era, that long period when the Angles and the Vikings were dominant in the North.

The Normans enlarged the Anglo-Scandinavian church by creating arches through the original external walls in order to create aisles. The side-alternate arrangement of the quoins and the blocked feature above the Norman arches provide evidence of a pre-Conquest building.

Two other early churches at Bolton-upon-Dearne and Laughton-en-le-Morthen were built in a style that is associated with the midland kingdom of Mercia from the ninth to the eleventh centuries. In particular, the quoins of some of the walls were arranged in a distinctive 'long-and-short' manner. At St Andrew's church, Bolton such quoins can be seen at the corners of the tall, box-shaped nave and an original round-headed window can be spotted near the centre of the south wall between two blocked arches. These arches once served as doors, with the eastern one perhaps leading into a porticus. A church and a priest were recorded at Bolton in Domesday Book.

Domesday Book also notes that in 1066 Earl Edwin of Mercia owned a hall at Laughton. The only plausible site is that where the Norman lord of the newly created Honour of Tickhill erected a motte-and-bailey castle immediately to the west of All Saints church. It is not clear how much, if any, of the remains pre-date the Norman Conquest. A linear earthwork that is aligned on the castle bailey stretches across the northern part of the churchyard and may have enclosed the church within the hall's defences.[2] When All Saints was rebuilt in two stages in the twelfth and fourteenth centuries, the doorway and part of the walls of the former porticus on the north side of the earlier building were left intact, perhaps as a conscious reminder of past importance. The original church was built in Rotherham red sandstone, which stands out vividly against the magnesian limestone of the later building. As the lower part of the chancel walls and the gable-headed piscina inside the chancel are of the same reddish sandstone, it seems likely that they were constructed of re-used material from the early church, which must have been a building of considerable proportions.

The church of St Helen, Burghwallis can also be dated in part to the Anglo-Scandinavian era. The village of Burghwallis has shrunk since the Middle Ages, so the parishioners never needed to extend their church by providing aisles. The eleventh-century nave and chancel and the slightly later tower provide an excellent example of a typical parish church at either

St Helen's church, Burghwallis, has the largest amount of herringbone masonry of any church in South Yorkshire. This section forms part of the south wall of the nave. It dates from the eleventh century.

side of the Norman Conquest, but the large quoin stones of the nave and chancel are arranged in the side-alternate style that suggests their re-use from an earlier building. The south walls of the nave and the lower part of the north wall, together with the western part of the chancel walls, were built in a striking display of herringbone masonry, whose stones of different hues glint attractively in the sun. The combination of large side-alternate quoins with eleventh-century herringboning is unique. The tower was erected after the Norman Conquest but the workmanship was in the same tradition, a style known to architectural historians as the 'Saxo-Norman overlap'.

Peter Ryder has identified several examples of local churches that were built in the 'overlap' style of the eleventh century. At Brodsworth, where St Michael's church was recorded in Domesday Book, the aisleless nave, chancel and west tower date from this period, though they were remodelled in the twelfth century. The west tower of St Bartholomew's church, Maltby is 'overlap' in style, though the nave and chancel were rebuilt in 1869. Herringbone patterns can also be seen on the walls of the nave and chancel at Marr, the west gable of the nave at Owston, and on the west wall at Kirk Sandall. The lower section of the tower at Darfield, which contains an earlier piece of sculpture, the tall nave with thin walls at High Melton, the north walls at Wath-upon-Dearne, and the nave walls that were constructed of Rotherham red sandstone at Todwick also seem to be eleventh-century work.

After the Norman Conquest several old churches were rebuilt and many new ones were erected. A small Norman church without aisles or clerestories, which must once have been typical of its type, can be found at St John's, Adwick-upon-Dearne. Joseph Hunter described it as the purest specimen in the deanery of Doncaster of an original village church.[3] Adwick was a small parish with an absentee landlord in later times, so its church was neither enlarged in the later Middle Ages nor 'improved' by a Victorian squire. In 1911 Joseph Morris delivered a harsh verdict when he wrote in his *Little Guide to the West Riding* that 'the humble, unrestored little church is pink-washed, mouldy, and not worth a visit'.[4] Now, it is disguised by drab pebbledash and a blue-slate roof and by lancet windows that were added in the thirteenth century. The Norman bell-cote, however, is a rare survival from the time when many parish churches did not have a tower.

The bellcote of the small Norman church of St Helen, Austerfield is Victorian and so is that at St Mary's, Armthorpe, whose original Norman church can be recognized from its shape, its slit windows and plain chancel arch after the drastic restoration and extensions that were made for Lord Auckland of Edenthorpe in 1885. In Hunter's time St Mary's was a 'small building of one pace, with two bells hanging in a kind of pent-house on the roof … a fair specimen of what the original churches of the smaller country parishes must have been'.[5] Armthorpe was a chapel-of-ease within Kirk Sandall parish until 1202.

The Norman chapel at what is now a solitary farm at Thorpe-in-Balne on the opposite side of the river from the parish church at Barnby Dun fell into disuse long ago, but survives in part as a barn. The farmstead, its outbuildings and its medieval fishponds are enclosed within a very large moat, which once stretched well beyond the present road. The nave of the chapel was still standing when Joseph Hunter wrote about it in 1828, but now only the chancel survives as a barn that still retains some original windows and a doorway, with later Gothic windows and a thirteenth-century piscina. The chapel seems to have been founded by Otto de Tilli in the mid twelfth century.[6]

The church of St John the Baptist, Wales was originally a chapel-of-ease in the large parish of Laughton-en-le-Morthen. It was greatly enlarged in

A notable feature of the original Norman chancel arch of St John the Baptist's church at Wales is a smiling head with circular eyes.

1897 when the original building was reduced to the status of a north aisle and the Norman doorway was reset in the wall of the new south aisle. The tympanum above this door is decorated with a chequer pattern within an arched band of lozenges and the arch above is decorated with crude beakhead decoration, now much damaged and worn.

The Normans introduced architectural carvings such as this (as distinct from the sculptured standing stones of the Anglo-Scandinavians) into certain parts of their churches. St Helen's, Austerfield, which was originally a chapel-of-ease within the parish of Blyth, has a striking depiction of a dragon with a tail shaped like an arrow in the tympanum over its plain Norman south door. It dates from the first half of the twelfth century, when monsters and fabulous animals were regarded as figures of evil that served as a warning to everyone who entered a church. The tympanum above the south door at St James's, Braithwell has a less dramatic arrangement of rosettes and other simple motifs.

In the second half of the twelfth century itinerant craftsmen were commissioned to make much more satisfying sculptures. St Peter's, Thorpe Salvin, which was originally a chapel-of-ease of Laughton, has an outstanding Norman font, whose carvings depict a baptism scene and the four seasons: sowing, harvesting, hunting and sitting in front of the fire in winter. It ranks amongst the finest Romanesque sculptures in England. A member of the Salvin family, who owned a knight's fee here within the Honour of Tickhill, must have commissioned both the font and the elaborately carved south doorway.

Further north, St Peter's, Edlington has a series of carved heads acting as an external corbel table on the south side of the nave and chancel, though they are now badly weathered. Most of the church fell into disuse and was in danger of collapse until its restoration by the Friends of Friendless Churches in 1975–76. The Norman work is seen from the outside in the lower parts of the tower, nave and chancel, and in the north and south doorways. The south doorway is decorated with zigzag and beakhead on the jambs. Inside the church, the chancel arch, which is also adorned with zigzag decoration, rises from shafts that start about 4 feet 6 inches above the ground, perhaps because a screen once stood below. All these architectural features seem to date from the third quarter of the twelfth century after Theobald Walter acquired the manor of Edlington upon his marriage to Maud Vavasour. He held the office of the great butler of Ireland and his brother was Archbishop of Canterbury.

The present appearance of many other South Yorkshire churches disguises the fact that they are basically Norman in character or that they retain Norman features. The churches at Adwick-le-Street, Frickley, Harthill, Kirk Bramwith, Penistone, Stainton and Whiston each have Norman interiors. At Hooton Pagnell the lower stages of the tower, the nave and its north aisle, and the original short chancel are all of the twelfth century and the south doorway is carved with mysterious symbols. At Wath the lower part of the tower, the northern arcade of the nave, and the chapel to the north of the chancel are also recognizable as Norman. The twelfth-century church of St Michael, Rossington was largely intact in Hunter's day except for the addition of a tower. It still retains its Norman chancel arch, decorated with zigzag and other mouldings, and its south doorway with mouldings of nail-head and raven-beak.

At St Lawrence's, Hatfield the local boulders and cobbles that were used for the wall around the Norman door and the slit window at the west end make a poor contrast to the ashlar stone of the fifteenth-century Perpendicular Gothic church that was imported from quarries on the magnesian limestone belt. At Wadworth blank arcading adorns the south aisle and porch of the original Norman church, while the northern nave arcade and aisle were erected in the transitional period between Norman and Gothic. The lords of Wadworth, within the Honour of Tickhill, were the Chaworths, a Norman family with great estates in Nottinghamshire and Derbyshire who were benefactors of Beauchief abbey.

Some of the finest Norman work in South Yorkshire is found in the eastern lowlands. All Saints, Arksey is a large, cruciform church that was built in two stages during the twelfth century, with later additions in the Perpendicular Gothic style. Built of mellow magnesian limestone, it is one of the most aesthetically satisfying of our local churches. During the late Norman period the crossing was remodelled, aisles were added to the nave, and the chancel was rebuilt and lengthened.

About the same time, a start was made on the cruciform church of St Mary Magdalene, Campsall, a few miles to the north, but the original plan was soon abandoned in favour of a western tower, faced with ashlar stone, that Sir Nikolaus Pevsner called 'a piece of high display … the most ambitious Norman west tower of any parish church in the West Riding'.[7] The tower has twin bell-openings, a shafted window, a blank gallery of arches and a doorway decorated with zigzag. The right to present rectors at Campsall was shared between the Lacis, the Norman barons of Pontefract castle, and their knights, the Renevilles, so this striking display was probably a deliberate statement of the power and wealth of the leading families in the Honour of Pontefract.

Rita Wood has shown that a talented group of craftsmen who had worked at Malmesbury abbey in Wiltshire built the Cluniac priory that the Lacis founded at Pontefract and then stayed in Yorkshire to work on a number of commissions at parish churches.[8] The quality of their work matches that of western French sculpture and architecture. Of the 30 or so Yorkshire churches that have twelfth-century doorways with decorative sculpture the finest is at St Cuthbert's church, Fishlake, which formed part of the lordship of Conisbrough

The west tower of St Mary Magdalene's church, Campsall is the finest surviving example of Norman architecture in South Yorkshire. It replaced an earlier Norman cruciform tower.

and so was dependent on the Cluniac priory that Willaim de Warenne had founded at Lewes, Sussex. The Cluniacs were the only monastic order to make elaborate use of the arts in their buildings, so it seems probable that the designer of the south doorway at St Cuthbert's, Fishlake was a Cluniac monk who wished to illustrate the Christian message. The carved medallions of the four orders of the doorway contain pairs of seated and standing figures, animals, leaves and human heads, which depict the church interior as Paradise and represent the past, present and future in the history of salvation.

A larger quantity of Norman sculpture survives at St Peter's, Conisbrough despite the replacement of the twelfth-century chancel. The carvings on the capitals of the nave arcades are earlier than the sculpture in the castle, which dates from around 1180. Earl Hamelin Plantagenet, the builder of the castle, was the husband of Isabella, the widowed daughter of William de Warenne

III, who had been killed on the Second Crusade in 1148. Rita Wood thinks that Isabella was responsible for commissioning the remarkable tomb chest in the church as a memorial to her father. She has argued that, as the design includes fighting and two themes from the *Chanson de Roland*, the dense, irregular decoration and the disorderly richness of the carving had a special significance that was related to death on crusade. A standing bishop, a man fighting a dragon, a man lying below a dragon, two knights on horseback in combat, animals in medallions, signs of the Zodiac, and Adam and Eve with a serpent in the tree can all be identified. The medallions link the tomb chest to the sculptures at Fishlake and other Yorkshire churches, but the simple figures of the bishop, knight and dragon belong to an older, local tradition; the dragon's head is very like that at Austerfield. The rectors of Conisbrough church were the Cluniacs of Lewes priory; Pontefract priory was re-dedicated in 1149, when the work was complete. Was Conisbrough the next job for these travelling craftsmen before they moved on to Fishlake?

South Yorkshire's Norman heritage is impressive, but we need to remember that much contemporary work was lost in later times when churches were enlarged and refashioned. The evidence that survives from old illustrations or which has been discovered from limited excavations hint at the former existence of large Norman churches at Rotherham and Doncaster and of small Norman churches or chapels-of-ease at Barnsley, Hickleton, Stainborough, Swinton, Tinsley, Warmsworth, Wombwell and Wickersley. It seems that the Normans left few, if any, of South Yorkshire's earliest churches in the state that they were before 1066.

Chapter 2

The King's Wood and Lindrick[1]

Roche Abbey

Roche Abbey is famous among architectural historians well beyond the borders of South Yorkshire because its ruined transepts that date from the 1170s and 1180s rank with parts of the cathedrals of Canterbury and Wells as the earliest surviving examples of the Gothic style that was introduced into England from France. In 1147 two neighbouring lords, Richard de Busli, lord of Maltby, and Richard, son of Turgis, lord of Hooton Levitt, gave land and woods on the edges of their estates to found a Cistercian monastery. All Cistercian abbeys were dedicated to St Mary, but this one took its distinctive name – St Mary de la Roche – from a huge rock on the north side of the magnesian limestone gorge that was thought to resemble a massive cross-head and which became an object of pilgrimage.

In time, the name Roche was softened in local speech to 'Roach', in the same way that the famous Cistercian abbey at Rievaulx in North Yorkshire became known locally as 'Rivis'. The original buildings at Roche were wooden ones, but from the 1170s most of them were replaced in local stone that was quarried on the hillside to the north. By the late 1180s the monks were in great debt to Jewish money lenders. To their relief, but to their shame, in the 1190s, at the height of the Crusades and anti-Jewish feeling, King Richard I released them from a debt of 1,300 marks (roughly £866), an enormous sum in those days.

Woods

The abbey's foundation charter included Roger de Busli's grant of 'a wood called North Wood' (the present Nor Wood), which descended to the Maltby Dike, and the allowance of:

Roche Abbey was built in a woodland clearing on the boundary between Maltby and Hooton Levitt. The ruined transepts date from the 1170s and still reach to their full height.

sufficient timber from his wood of Maltby for the completion of their buildings, and they were to have for ever eight wain-loads of timber every year for building purposes, and for making fences.

From Richard, the son of Turgis, the monks received 'the whole wood as the middle way goes from Eilrichethorpe to Lowthorpe and so as far as the water which divides Maltby and Hooton'. This is the present Grange Wood. At some unknown date the monks also acquired the nearby Hell Wood and in 1241 Idonea de Busli, Richard's granddaughter, gave them the Sandbeck estate. By then, the monks owned the whole of the eastern half of the parish of Maltby.[2]

King Henry II (1154–89) granted the monks the much larger wood to the south of the confluence of the Laughton and Maltby Dikes that is now known as the King's Wood. In 1184, when Pope Urban III confirmed the grant, the wood was said to measure 100 acres. Today, King's Wood covers 160 acres, but the discrepancy might be partly explained by the round figure of 100 and by the use of a traditional measurement known as the long hundred of 120. A 1731 survey of the Sandbeck estate, where the woodland is noted as 'Roch Wood', gave its area as 145 acres.[3] In confirmation charters of 1219 and 1232 the wood was described as 'bounded by a ditch'. This ditch can still be traced on all sides except the west, where the present jagged edge of the wood perhaps still marks piecemeal clearances in order to extend the fields of Laughton.

The existing outline of the wood is very similar to that marked on Joseph Dickenson's map of the Sandbeck estate in 1724 that now adorns Lord Scarbrough's study, also on Thomas Jeffreys's map of Yorkshire in 1771–72, the Laughton enclosure award of 1771, and on the first edition of the six-inch Ordnance Survey map of 1855. However, within this ancient boundary, there were extensive fellings of the south-eastern and western sections of King's Wood before or during the Second World War, and afterwards the eleventh Earl of Scarbrough began substantial replantings on this ground.

The King's Wood is noted for its extraordinary abundance, along with occasional small-leaved lime, of large-leaved lime (*Tilia platyphyllos*). At this

The native large-leaved limes in King's Wood produce new trunks from ancient stools. They grow in abundance close to the Cistercian abbey.

site, the biggest large-leaved limes, including some especially massive trees, are to be found growing from the cliffs above the abbey ruins and on craggy ground within the wood itself. John Rodwell has observed that some of these trees are five metres or more in girth at breast height, a size that suggests an age of around 500 years. Especially big groups of trunks growing from single stools on the crags are also of this size measured around the very base, though this is a less reliable reflection of their age. There are also substantial numbers of bigger large-leaved limes surviving on the bank along King's Wood Lane, the ancient boundary of the wood to the south and east. Native limes are also found in Anston Stones Wood and, in smaller numbers, in some of the other woodlands in the south-eastern corner of South Yorkshire. John Newbould recorded the locations of a total of 119 mature large-leaved limes in this area.[4]

Coppicing

At the dissolution of Roche Abbey in 1538, when the woods on the Maltby side of the manor and parish boundary were sold by King Henry VIII to Henry Tyrrell, gentleman, they were managed on the coppice-with-standards system, with a regular cycle of fellings.[5] It seems likely that the King's Wood on the opposite bank of the boundary stream was also managed in this way.

The Sandbeck Estate Archives provide only occasional information about King's Wood after the dissolution, but enough records survive to provide a general picture of changing uses. A survey of 'Roche wood' in 1593 complained of poor management, but showed that at least some of the oaks were grown for timber, that the wood was divided into falls, and that the summer grazing of ten horses was allowed in part. One complaint of the surveyors was that the wood was 'unfenced & unsevered from the common which was in tymes paste walled rounde'. The verdict of the jury that was empanelled at Tickhill found that 'there hath bene great spoile of woode & three hundrethe Timber Ockes sould by Mr Eyre', the lessee.[6]

During the seventeenth and eighteenth centuries, the principal use of the woodlands throughout the South Yorkshire lowlands, extending from the magnesian limestone belt on to the extensive coal-measure sandstones and shales, was to supply timber and coppice fuel for the local charcoal iron industry. In 1719, for example, the felling of extensive woodlands on the estate belonging to the Duke of Leeds around Harthill, Anston,

Wales, Lindrick, Todwick and Kiveton Park raised £15,000. The estates
of gentry families in other magnesian limestone townships at Dinnington,
Gildingwells, Edlington, Wadworth and Sprotbrough also supplied large
amounts of timber and underwood. Amongst the most magnificent woods
were those of the Scarbrough estate in and around Maltby, which in 1724
covered 770 acres.[7]

The great value of these woods encouraged the leading ironmasters of
south-west Yorkshire – William Simpson and Francis Barlow (two Sheffield
attorneys who owned Chapel Furnace and Attercliffe Forge) and Dennis
Hayford of Wortley Forge – to build a forge at Stone, just downstream
from Roche Abbey, well to the east of their ironstone mines. On 20 April
1681 these three ironmasters purchased 2,170 'Oake, Ash or other Trees' in
Sandbeck Park and adjoining places, including Grange Wood and Hell Wood
and hedgerows, 'alsoe one hundred yews in Sandbecke Parke', to 'stubb &
carrie away Together with the bark Topps bodyes roots boughs Timber cord
wood & Ramill'.[8]

Stone Forge or the Roche Abbey Forge, as it was known alternatively, was
one of the smaller ones, with an annual production of sixty tons of pig iron.
It probably did not last beyond the mid-eighteenth century and in 1802 it
was converted into a corn mill.[9] The industrial demand for charcoal fell
sharply when coke became the established fuel. In the nineteenth century
coppicing declined and the woods were valued more for their timber and for
the cover they provided for game, particularly pheasants.

Accounts of regular, but small sales of timber to local builders or joiners
and carpenters survive from the middle years of the nineteenth century. On
27 February 1851, for instance, Isaac Allsop of Worksop, a regular customer,
bought '776 feet of Lime Tree from King's Wood', for £32.6s.8d., together
with small purchases of yew, elm, dutch elm, and cherry. In the same year,
another regular customer, Joseph Garside of Worksop, bought '708 feet of
Oak from King's Wood', with other oaks, ash, elm, beech, dutch elm, birch
and 'syrup', which seems to have been sycamore. Accounts that survive for
1878–98 show a similar modest annual return from sales under the direction
of a woodman.[10]

By far the most informative document for our purposes in the Sandbeck
Estate Archives is a printed catalogue headed:

To Sell by Auction on Thursday the 23rd Day of June 1870, At the
Scarbrough Arms Inn, Tickhill, The Following Valuable Lots of

Timber and Poles, Living in King's Wood, Numbered and Crossed with a Scrieve Iron. Most of the Lots are of large dimension, and well grown. The Beech and Limes are adapted for the Sheffield trade, and other Manufacturing purpose, and the whole well worth the attention of Timber Merchants, Colliery Owners, Contractors, Wheelwrights, Carpenters, &c.[11]

The reference to 'the Sheffield trade' is explained by the common use of beech for a variety of tool handles and of lime for the wooden patterns to make the moulds for cast iron decorative fireplaces, such as those manufactured by Hoole's Green Lane Works.[12]

The sale was divided into sixteen lots, with no striking variation between the mixture of trees in each lot and no specialised compartments. In most cases these are listed in two columns, giving the totals of each type of tree. The first columns are headed 'numbered trees' and the second 'crossed poles', suitable for coopers, fencing and crate makers, or for making bobbins. The overall totals for the numbered trees are: Oak 235, Ash 54, Elm 134, Lime 197, Beech 95, Holly 10, Crab 2, Service 16, Maple 6, Cherry 4, Mountain Ash 1, Birch 17. Those for the crossed poles are: Oak 278, Ash 185, Elm 425, Lime 124, Beech 18, Holly 35, Thorn 19, Maple 81, Cherry 7, Mountain Ash 34, Service 23, Birch 18, Crab 4. Of course, we do not know how many trees were left unmarked or were not for sale, nor whether all the above trees and poles were actually sold. No yews were felled and it is noticeable that sycamores receive no mention. Nevertheless, this list of trees indicates an assemblage with very much the same basic character as the woodland today, essentially

The boundary stream between Maltby and Hooton Levitt acted as a latrine. The King's Wood, or 'the wood of Lindrick' rises beyond.

of the semi-natural type characteristic of this terrain. The value of the information contained in such notices of auction is immediately apparent; they are a prime source for woodland historians to establish the character of a wood in the Victorian period and to relate it to what survives today.

The Limes and Lindrick

The King's Wood or Roche Wood had yet another ancient name. In the Middle Ages it was always referred to as 'the wood of Lindrick'. King Henry II's original charter does not survive, but the monks' ownership of the wood is mentioned in several confirmations. The earliest of these was issued in 1184, when Pope Urban III confirmed 'the gift of Lord King Henry II of one hundred acres in Lindric, near the said abbey'. In 1219 Alice, or Adelicia, Countess of Eu, in a deed executed at Tickhill Castle, confirmed the site of the abbey, the grange of Aggecroft, 'and the wood of Lindric as it is bounded by a ditch'.[13]

On 21 January 1232 an 'inspeximus and confirmation' of a charter of King Richard I (1189–99) to the monks of Roche Abbey noted the properties in Maltby and Hooton Levitt, followed immediately by 'the wood of Lindric next to the said abbey, just as the ditch encloses'.[14] The same words appear in a confirmation of 1329. Upon the dissolution of the abbey, the Ministers' Accounts of 1540 recorded amongst its possessions 'the wood called Laughton Lyndrek', estimated at 100 acres, close to the 'Firth alias Grange Wood' and Northwood.[15]

The etymology of Lindrick is thought to be 'lime-tree ridge', a compound of an unrecorded word *ric* with Old English *lind* 'lime-tree', as in linden, the old name for a lime. Margaret Gelling noted that **ric* is not a common place-name element, and that it is liable to be replaced by *hrycg* in modern forms.[16] Lindrick or Lindridge names are minor ones that are scattered thinly but widely in different parts of the country. In South Yorkshire and north Nottinghamshire, however, Lindrick is a district name. This is made clear from the name of the village of Carlton-in-Lindrick, just inside the Nottinghamshire border, which is so-called to distinguish it from Carlton-on-Trent, three miles north of Newark. The name means the 'settlement of the churls' or free peasants and it can be identified with South Carlton, that part of the village that contains the parish church with its late Anglo-Saxon tower, for Domesday Book also recorded the separate manor of Kingston, now known as North Carlton. The 'king's tun' and the 'churls' tun' probably once formed part of a royal estate.

After the Norman Conquest Carlton-in-Lindrick was included within the Honour of Tickhill, which straddled the Yorkshire-Nottinghamshire border; it was recorded as Carlton in Lindric in 1227.

About 1144 its lord, Ralph de Chevrolcourt, founded a Benedictine nunnery within his park at Wallingwells on the western border of his manor. His foundation grant included the gift of 'all the woodland of Sicam to be brought into cultivation, which is situate in length from the cultivated land of Rustoch as far as the ditch of Lindrick, and in breadth from the park as far as the assart of Theobald'.[17] These names are lost to us, so the location of the ditch remains elusive, but it seems to be related to the large bite that was taken out of Yorkshire at this point by Wallingwells Park, defined by the Owlands Wood Dike. Another piece of documentary evidence is contained in King Henry II's confirmation to the Benedictine monks of Blyth Priory, three miles north-east of Carlton and within the Honour of Tickhill, of 'all their Customs in the wood of `Lindric', without specifying where this wood lay.[18]

No other Lindrick names are recorded in Nottinghamshire; all the rest are from immediately across the South Yorkshire border. A cluster of Lindrick names is found within the township of Anston, which lay within the southern part of the soke and parish of Laughton-en-le-Morthen. Anston Brook winds its way through the deep magnesian limestone gorge of Lindrick Dale, with Anston Stones Wood climbing up the steep slopes on either side. This ancient wood contains numerous native limes. The brook forms the western boundary of Lindrick Common (now a golf course), whose northern limit is marked by Lindrick Hill Farm and Lindrick House. The next settlement to the north is Woodsetts 'the folds in the wood', first recorded in 1324.[19] In 1200 King John confirmed a grant to Nycol Salsarius of land in Anston and Dinnington, within the lordship centred on Tickhill Castle, but retained 'seven bovates of land with appurtenances in Lindrick'.[20] A bovate (or oxgang) varied in size from ten to eighteen acres.

Lindrick is also the name of the tranquil part of the medieval town of Tickhill that lies immediately south of the castle. Lindrick House appeared there on Jeffreys's map of Yorkshire in 1771–72, and Lindrick Villa, Lindrick Square, and Lindrick Lane leading to Woolthwaite are marked on the first edition six-inch Ordnance Survey map of 1855. The Thomas de Lindric, who in the early thirteenth century granted ten acres to Blyth Priory in his furlong within the fields of Tickhill, probably lived here;[21] likewise the William de Lindric who witnessed a charter of Maud de Lovetot, the former wife of Gerard de Furnival and lady of the manors of Worksop and Sheffield, in the second quarter of the thirteenth century.[22] At the present time, this part of Lindrick lies well inside Yorkshire, for the county boundary follows that of Tickhill parish in the low-lying former marshy area to the east, but it was originally one of several tiny settlements that were situated on the 50-foot contour line around the huge swamp which stretched northwards as far as the Isle of Axholme to form a nearly impassable barrier between Yorkshire and Nottinghamshire. The settlement name suggests that the wider district of Lindrick followed the western edge of this swamp and that Roger de Busli built his Norman castle directly on the border as a matter of deliberate policy. The major part of his new Honour of Tickhill lay in north Nottinghamshire, where Blyth acted as a rival centre at the other side of the swamp. Lindrick remains separated from the rest of Tickhill by a stream known as the Paper Mill Dike, which winds its way east of the castle before flowing northwards into the River Torne near Limpool Farm, a name recorded in 1263 which means 'lime-tree pool'. The farm stands just inside the Nottinghamshire parish of Harworth, the 'boundary farm or estate'.

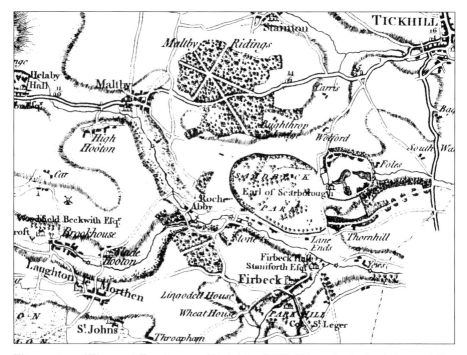

This section of Thomas Jeffreys's map of Yorkshire (1771–72) marks Roche Abbey and The King's Wood close to the Earl of Scarbrough's park at Sandbeck.

The present boundary between Yorkshire and Nottinghamshire was not determined until after the Norman Conquest. North of Tickhill, the original line was that of the River Torne, but then Bawtry, Austerfield and Rossington were brought within Yorkshire, though for church purposes they continued to form part of the deanery of Retford.[23] In 1828 Joseph Hunter, the great South Yorkshire antiquary, pondered on whether or not the Yorkshire boundary further south had also been extended in an easterly direction. He observed that Firbeck, Letwell, Gildingwells and Woodsetts 'seem to partake in their natural features more of the Nottinghamshire than the Yorkshire character', for they occupy sandy soils.[24] It is possible that all of Lindrick lay within Nottinghamshire before the Conquest.

It seems that Lindrick referred to the whole of the narrow but distinctive magnesian limestone belt in the Laughton - Tickhill - Carlton district. Its lengthy scarp is a dramatic feature on the skyline to the east of the coal-measure sandstones and shales, and with the remarkable concentration of ancient native large-leaved limes. Lindrick seems to be one of those enigmatic district names that originated long before the Norman Conquest and whose memory was preserved by later place-names. The virtual absence of pre-Conquest documentary sources for this district means that we will never know exactly when the name came into existence, but it is likely to be early in the Anglo-Saxon period.

Further north, the memory of the British kingdom of Elmet, which was conquered in 617, is preserved by Barwick-in-Elmet and Sherburn-in-Elmet on its former eastern boundaries. In the Yorkshire Dales, Craven is still a well-known district name that originated as that of a British kingdom and which comes from the Celtic word for 'wild garlic'.[25] If Craven could be named after a plant, then it is plausible that Lindrick could be named after its lime trees. Pre-Conquest districts close to Lindrick were named in a similar way: Ashfield (Nottinghamshire; Kirkby-in-Ashfield and Sutton-in-Ashfield) after the ash tree, and Hatfield (both sides of the Nottinghamshire and Yorkshire border) after heath-land.

The exact identity of Lindrick remains mysterious, but the numerous ancient lime trees in King's Wood - perhaps more than in any other English wood of its size - and in other, smaller woods near by, combined with local place-names that were recorded in the Middle Ages and which are still used locally, suggests that this district had an ancient unity that was symbolized by the exceptional number of native limes.

Chapter 3

Tickhill: a Country Town

I t is hard to realize now that Tickhill was once the second most important town in South Yorkshire. In the Middle Ages only Doncaster surpassed it in wealth and population. In 1295 Tickhill had two Members of Parliament.[1] It is now hardly more than a large village, but when we start to explore it on the ground and delve into its history we soon find plenty of evidence about its former prominence.

Tickhill takes its name from an Old English personal name, Tica, but this was not the name by which the place was known before the Norman Conquest. Domesday Book refers instead to Dadesley, a name that is commemorated by Dadsley Well Farm at the northern junction of Dadsley Road and Northgate.[2] In this lowland landscape even slight rises or knolls were called hills. In the absence of any other candidate, Tica's hill must be the natural lower third of the motte of Tickhill Castle. The only other hills in or around Tickhill are that named after the site of the church of All Hallows, which served as the original parish church near Dadesley, and Spital Hill, where a leper hospital was founded. So, all three 'hills' in this low-lying district were used as historic sites.

At the time of the Norman Conquest the most important place in South Yorkshire was Conisbrough, the southernmost royal estate in the kingdom of Northumbria. It occupied a site of strategic importance, where the ancient highway running north along the magnesian limestone belt crossed the river Don at Strafford Sands, the meeting place of the Viking wapentake. In 1086 the great lordship, or 'fee', of Conisbrough contained 28 townships to the south of the river. After the Norman Conquest William the Conqueror gave the fee of Conisbrough to one of his most trusted warriors, Wiliam de Warenne from Varenne in Normandy. In 1086 this William held land in thirteen English counties and had castles at Lewes (Sussex) and Castle Acre (Norfolk). In the 1170s Earl Hameline Plantagenet, who had married Isabel, the last of the Warennes, built the impressive castle that still dominates Conisbrough.

The hostility that William the Conqueror met with in Yorkshire led him to strengthen his position there by creating new lordships, or 'honours', alongside the ancient ones and placing some of his leading barons in command. In the southern part of the county, the Honour of Pontefract was created to act as a pair with the manor of Wakefield, whose castle was at Sandall, and the Honour of Tickhill was given to Roger de Busli to accompany Warenne's lordship of Conisbrough.

Only a third of the possessions of the new Honour of Tickhill lay within South Yorkshire. The rest were in Nottinghamshire, Derbyshire, Lincolnshire and Leicestershire, with one outlier in Devon. The Yorkshire manors to the south of the River Don were intermingled with those of the Conisbrough fee, while a group to the north of the river stretched from Wentworth in the west to Barnby Dun in the east. Motte-and-bailey castles were soon erected within the honour at Tickhill, Laughton-en-le-Morthen, Mexborough and Kimberworth, but Tickhill castle was the only one of these that was converted later into a substantial stone fortress.[3]

The great motte of the Norman castle stands apart from the town that grew alongside it. The parish church was a later addition, at the edge of the settlement. *Photo: M. Dolby*

Little is known about Roger de Busli, who came from Bully-le-Vicompte, now a small town near Neufchatel-en-Brai in Normandy. He died at the end of the eleventh century without a direct heir, though junior branches of the family continued until 1235. He ordered the erection of his castle on Tica's hill, which rose from the edge of the great swamp that separated Yorkshire from Nottinghamshire, about six miles south-east of Conisbrough. On the other side of the swamp, below the 50-feet contour line, he founded Blyth Priory for the Benedictine order. This remained an important ecclesiastical focal point for the honour throughout the Middle Ages. The original Norman nave of the priory church - a remarkable survival from such an early date – rises above the clerestorey and triforium windows to a rib-vaulted roof, and an enormous late-medieval doom painting covers the wall above the former chancel arch; the chancel has long been demolished.[4] So, the castle was built on the Yorkshire side of the county boundary, while the priory lay within Nottinghamshire.

Roger de Busli's honour passed to a kinsman, Roger de Belleme, Earl of Shrewsbury, a brutal man even by the standards of that violent era. His support for the claims to the throne of Robert, Duke of Normandy, against those of King Henry II, led to the loss of his castles at Arundel, Bridgnorth, Shrewsbury and Tickhill and his banishment from England in 1102. The Honour of Tickhill now came under Crown control.

The survival of Crown records in The National Archives enables us to pinpoint 1129–30 as the years when Henry I built the lower part of the curtain wall and gatehouse at Tickhill and 1178–82 as the time when Henry II re-styled the castle in magnificent fashion with a new keep, a stone bridge, higher curtain walls, and new chambers, all in ashlar stone. Meanwhile, Henry II's queen, Eleanor, had founded a chapel within the castle, which she dedicated to St Nicholas.[5] These new buildings were constructed about the same time as the new keep at Conisbrough Castle and the monastic church at Roche Abbey. These were momentous years for the creation of South Yorkshire's finest medieval heritage.

Tickhill's name is first recorded sometime between 1109 and 1119 in the Nostell Priory cartulary, after the Augustinian canons there had been granted all the rights associated with the church. The motte on Tica's hill was raised 75 feet high and about 80 feet in diameter at the top. It must have taken about thirty days to build with forced labour from the local peasants. The inner bailey of the castle was enclosed on the western side of the keep by a massive rampart and a deep ditch, full of water. The only entrance was on the west side, by the millpond and the area known as Lindrick, through which visitors from Blyth could arrive. The east side of the keep was defined by fishponds and open countryside on the edge of the swamp. A generation later, during King John's reign, well over £300 was spent on repairs to the castle and on building a barbican, stable and granary, and making the ditches 30 feet wide.

The Normans laid out a market town alongside the castle in the fashion that spread across the country after the conquest.[6] The market places that were created close to the castles at Doncaster and Sheffield were in settlements that existed before the Normans arrived, but Tickhill was a Norman new town that was created by Roger de Busli. In 1086 Domesday Book recorded that 31 burgesses already lived there. Yet at that time the new name had not yet replaced the old one of Dadesley. Elsewhere in the West Riding, only Pontefract had burgesses, and it too was recorded under its old name of Tanshelf.

Very little is known about the supposed site of the original settlement by Dadsley Well. A halfpenny of Cnut's reign and an Anglo–Scandinavian silver knot ring of the tenth or eleventh century have been found there, together with some post-Conquest coins. The major indicator of the old arrangements is the site of All Hallows church, which served the people of Dadesley before St Mary's church was erected on the north-western edge of the castle's outer bailey. The site on All Hallows Hill was reasonably central for the other outlying settlements in the parish, at Stancil (a deserted medieval village on the site of a Roman villa), Wellingley, Wilsic and Woolthwaite.

A Nostell Priory charter of 1361[7] referred to land 'near the chapel of All Hallows in the field of Tickhill', so by that time it seems that it was still functioning as a place of worship, though it was no longer the parish church. By the seventeenth century, and perhaps long before, no services were held there. A deed of 1664 was concerned with land in 'the North Field of Tickhill at a place called All Hallows Church', and a glebe terrier of 1684 mentioned 'a little close in the north field which hath been a churchyard and known by the name of All Hallows'. A memorandum in the parish chest, dated 1726, noted that St Mary's church had acquired new bells which had been cast from metal from four bells at Tickhill and three old bells taken from All Hallows Church about fifty years earlier.[8] In 1828 Joseph Hunter recorded a tradition of gravestones having been found there and later in the nineteenth century a farmer ploughed up bones and skulls on the site.

Confirmation of the tradition that All Hallows Hill was the site of the former church of Dadesley came from a geophysical survey and small excavation that revealed some of the foundations. *Photo by M. Dolby*

In 1987 these traditions and the outline of the former churchyard, which was suggested by aerial photographs, encouraged Malcolm Dolby and Tom Beastall to organize a geophysical survey of the site. This revealed the foundations of a chancel and a nave, and possibly a tower. A subsequent small excavation uncovered the courses of the parallel walls of the north and south sides of the chancel. The existence of a former church had been proved, but this left the question of why it had been abandoned.

The obvious explanation is that the inhabitants of the new town of Tickhill got fed up of traipsing up the muddy lane to the old church and decided to build a new one on a more convenient site. By then, the town had taken shape, so the church had to be placed on the edge of it, beyond Castle Green, on the far side of the back street, Dadsley Road. On a walk or drive along the main streets of Tickhill the church can be glimpsed only occasionally. It was rebuilt in the fourteenth and fifteenth centuries, but a few clues survive to show that the first church was as long as the present one. The Perpendicular Gothic window in the west wall of the tower had to be squeezed in between two late twelfth-century buttresses, and the remains of a thirteenth-century window can be seen in the north wall of the chancel.

Castle Green may once have been the outer bailey of the castle that was kept deliberately free of buildings. Limited excavations in this area have found no trace of buildings before the fourteenth century. A semi-circular line that encloses Castle Green can be traced along field boundaries to the east and south of the castle, then along Church Lane, St Mary Gate, and the backs of the property boundaries on the south side of Sunderland Street. This line is broken by St Mary's church.

The new town was centred on the Market Place, where Castlegate meets Northgate and Sunderland Street, leading into Eastgate. The original market was larger than the present triangular one. A parliamentary survey of the lordship of Tickhill in 1649 noted, 'The tolls and profits of a weekly market kept on Friday in the sayde towne of Tickhill with the toll booths and houses called the shambles and pirkage [money paid] and stallage there'.[9] This market was in terminal decline when its elegant cross was erected in 1777. The cross would not have been out of place in a gentleman's park.

The shapes of the streets suggest that the town grew from the market place in all directions. Castlegate, which was once dog-legged, now curves towards the cross and Northgate has a double bend to enable it to connect with the old alignment towards Dadesley. Sunderland Street takes its name from the ditch that divided or sundered the town from the castle. In 1975 excavations south-west of the market place located a medieval ditch that was more than two metres deep and over three metres wide and which pre-dated the narrow properties of the burgesses. This ditch was open in the thirteenth century but it silted up naturally later.[10] The parliamentary survey of 1649 noted, 'The Burgar or gate rent payable within a certain streete … called Sunderland …[and] … tolls of waggons, cartes, and all other carriages and drifts passing in or through the way or street called Sunderland'. When a hearth tax was levied in 1672 Sunderland was still regarded as a separate part of Tickhill.[11]

The burgesses who rented plots alongside these streets, and in Westgate, paid rent but were not obliged to perform the services that were expected by the lords of rural manors. Their properties are known to historians as burgage plots and some can still be traced on the ground or followed on early editions of large-scale Ordnance Survey maps, which show farmsteads with open spaces before them facing onto the streets and yards, garths, orchards and paddocks to the rear.

The long, narrow plots that extended back from Northgate as far as St Mary's Road were exceptionally well preserved until recently, when houses

The pattern of long, narrow burgage plots that characterized the Norman new town has been preserved by modern property boundaries, such as these, leading from St Mary's Lane to the Market Place. The photograph was taken in 1974.

were built on some of them. On the east side of Northgate they went as far as a broad public footpath that runs parallel to the road. In Westgate similar plots stretched to Pinfold Lane in the north and to Paper Mill Dyke in the south. The most problematic street is Castlegate, which had narrow burgage plots within the outer bailey. We do not know whether this was an early or a late development. The final form of the medieval town is well preserved, but its development is debatable.

Tickhill was a successful new town, though it never reached the status of Doncaster, which in 1467 acquired a mayor and corporation.[12] When a national tax was levied in 1334 Tickhill ranked second amongst the six towns of South Yorkshire, above Sheffield, Rotherham, Barnsley and Bawtry.[13] The poll tax returns of 1379 name 176 married couples and 109 single persons living in Tickhill, including six shoemakers, five 'barkers' or shepherds, four tailors, three smiths, three websters, two drapers, two spicers, two carpenters, two ostlers, a miller, a mason, a goldsmith, a mercer and a merchant.[14] As in most medieval market towns, the population amounted to only 1,000 to 2,000 inhabitants. Most English people lived in the countryside.

The remains of important medieval buildings demonstrate Tickhill's ranking as a town. An Augustinian friary was founded about 1256 by John Clarel of the adjacent Clarel Hall, who in a long and distinguished career was the warden of the royal chapel of St Nicholas within the castle, clerk to Kings Henry III and Edward I, canon of Southwell, and chaplain to the Pope. The present house on the site, which has a datestone of 1663, retains a lancet window and archways dating from the thirteenth century. In its heyday in the early fourteenth century a prior and between 18 and 24 friars were housed here.[15] Doncaster had two friaries, one for the Franciscans and another for the Carmelites. Friaries were an urban phenomenon and no other town in South Yorkshire had one.

A school was held in the friary and members of some of the leading families in the district were buried there. In his will in 1498 Sir Thomas Fitzwilliam of Aldwark asked to be buried in the church of the Austin Friars of Tickhill near his father, Richard. His tomb, which dates from the 1520s, during his widow Lucy's second widowhood, is one of the earliest examples of Italian Renaissance art in England. It now stands in the parish church and has been restored to its original splendour.[16]

Medieval hospitals, too, were confined to towns. They were religious institutions that cared for the sick and infirm. Most were small institutions and their histories are badly recorded. A hospital dedicated to St Leonard occupied a lonely site on Spital Hill above the extensive marshlands that were crossed by a causey on the way to the inland port of Bawtry, a typical out-of-town position that was suitable for a leper hospital. In 1564 the marsh was estimated at 240 acres and in time of floods it could be crossed only by boat; the causey had to be maintained regularly. The brothers of St Leonard were mentioned in a deed of about 1225 and the lepers of the hospital of St Leonard were recorded in 1236. John Clarel led efforts in the 1290s to improve its endowments and to provide better facilities for its chaplain. No satisfactory explanation can be offered for the removal of the hospital to the northern edge of the market place in 1470. The dedication to St Leonard remained, but the new site was obviously not a proper place for that purpose, so it must have catered for other needs. The timber-framed ground floor of this building is original, but the upper floor was completely rebuilt in mock-medieval style in 1851.

Tickhill also had a Maison Dieu, a group of almshouses, especially for widows, under the care of a priest. Its endowments consisted of about 30 acres of land, two houses and various rent charges. The site to the south of the parish church is commemorated by the name of a group of modern cottages.[17]

Although Tickhill was a town, its arable land was farmed on a three-field system, as in the neighbouring villages, and its communal meadows were divided into strips known as wongs, a name that is preserved in Wong Lane. The township had three water mills and a windmill. The houses in the streets were all timber framed, but little evidence of this former practice survives. A house in Castlegate has an intact timber frame behind its Victorian brick interior, with a crown–post roof similar to those in The Shambles at York, which date from the late fourteenth or fifteenth century. The few substantial halls that dominated the houses and workshops of craftsmen, traders, innkeepers and farmers have left no trace.

The four chantry chapels in the parish church owned between them 164 acres of strips and wongs in the open fields and meadows and various houses, cottages, crofts and orchards in the town streets, with 63 tenants at the time of their dissolution in 1547. One of these chapels belonged to 'the gild of St. Cross'; the chapel of St Helen on the north side of the chancel, which was founded by the Eastfield family and provided with a grammar school.

An ambitious rebuilding of the parish church began in the last quarter of the fourteenth century. John of Gaunt, a son of King Edward III, held the castle from 1373 to 1399 as part of the newly formed Duchy of Lancaster and, as he had claims upon Castile and Leon, the arms of those Spanish provinces appear on the tower. The shields of William Eastfield, the seneschal of Holderness and steward of the Honour of Tickhill who died in 1386, and of John Sandford, esquire, of Sandford Hall on the north side of Sunderland Street are also displayed on the tower exterior. William Eastfield's tomb stands inside the church and his arms also appear near the west door and above the chancel arch. In 1295, his ancestor, Richard de Eastfield, had been one of Tickhill's two MPs. Merchant marks in the nave show that the burgesses also contributed handsomely. For example, in 1390 Richard Raynerson left a bequest of 100s. 'to the works of the church of Tickhill'.[18]

The church underwent enlargement and rebuilding over a long period. It was near completion in 1429 when John Sandford made a bequest of a cart and four horses 'to the mayking of the stepell of Tyckhill'. The nave arcades were remodelled with decorative capitals and ogee arches that were topped with splendid finials. The mark of the former roofline shows how striking ranges of clerestory windows were built above the arches. The aisles were

The tithe owners who were responsible for the chancel did not rebuild the east end of the church in the same splendid style of the nave and tower, but this enabled the parishioners to light their nave with a fine window above the chancel.

reconstructed with larger windows, porches were added to the north and south doors, and a huge west window adorned the tower. The top of the tower was crowned with a parapet and pinnacles in the delicate style of the finest contemporary Yorkshire churches. Tickhill now had one of the most magnificent parish churches in Yorkshire.

As the Augustinian canons of Nostell Priory were the rectors and collected the tithes they were responsible for the maintenance of the chancel. They declined the opportunity to rebuild their part of the church in the same splendid style as the nave, aisles, porch and tower, though they did provide a new east window, rising high and wide above the altar. The canons' refusal to spend more did, however, provide the parishioners with the opportunity to insert a fine new window above the chancel arch, a rarity in this position in parish churches.

The fragmentary remains of stained glass in the windows of the church show that some families continued to prosper in later times. Members of the White family were merchants of the staple of Calais and one of them, William White, a Tickhill-born draper, became Lord Mayor of London in 1489. He remembered the church in his will of 1500 and his merchant's mark appears in a window. Many of the surviving pieces of the glass have been dated by Brian Sprakes to the late-fifteenth or early-sixteenth centuries.[19] But the ambitious plan to vault the inside of the tower was never completed, for Tickhill's fortunes were already on the wane. The great fall in the national population, starting with the Black Death, caused many towns to decay. At the end of Henry VIII's reign John Leland found that:

> The market town of Tikhil is very bare; but the chirch is fair and large … All the buildinges withyn the [castle] area be down, saving an old haulle.[20]

The great age of the castle was over and the townspeople no longer benefited from the trade that it had generated. An inspection in 1564 concluded that the castle walls and the keep were in decay and that the courthouse over the gateway was in disrepair.[21] In 1648 a hall was constructed in the bailey with old masonry from the keep and in the eighteenth century the south curtain wall was partly demolished to let in more light and to improve the view from the hall.

In 1751 Bishop Pococke visited, 'A poor market town, where there are the remains of the old cross, which had a dozen steps up to it'.[22] In 1789 Viscount Torrington found that Tickhill was 'a mean market town'.[23] The Friday market was still held but the fair had withered. Although the occupations that were recorded in the parish register show that Tickhill had a higher concentration of craftsmen than anywhere else in the district and that malting businesses were flourishing, it had been outgrown by the industrial towns, led by Sheffield and Rotherham.

In 1822 Edward Baines's West Riding directory recorded seven inns and a regular stage-coach service, but no market.[24] Seven years later, Joseph Hunter wrote, 'I am informed that the market at Tickhill has been given up for many years; there is no attendance, save that of an old woman with a basket, who takes up her station on a Friday on the steps of the cross as if to retain the prescriptive right'.[25]

Chapter 4

Monasteries and their Granges

Roche Abbey

The beautiful ruins of Roche Abbey, set in the magnesian limestone gorge formed by the Maltby Dike, often draw the response that Cistercian monks certainly knew how to select a lovely place in which to build a monastery. The Cistercians deliberately sought remote sites, such as this one on the boundary between Maltby and Hooton Levitt, but its present appearance has been shaped by events that occurred long after the dissolution of the monasteries. In the 1770s the monastic landscape was transformed by 'Capability' Brown for the fourth Earl of Scarbrough of Sandbeck Park, a former estate of the abbey, by covering up large areas of the ruins, planting trees and constructing terraces, parterres, ponds and waterfalls, then in the 1920s the Office of Works (the predecessor of English Heritage) undid much of Brown's work and the site assumed its present neat appearance.[1]

In its medieval hey-day, Roche Abbey was a busy place in an enclosed world, hidden from external view by a precinct wall that stood perhaps ten feet high; even now its foundations can be traced in part along the crest of the ridges on either side of the valley and down a short stretch to the east. A corn mill, a fulling mill, and tanneries were worked within the precinct, cattle pastures and fish ponds lay just beyond, a grange or home farm was sited in Nor Wood, further up the boundary stream, and all the surrounding woods were managed for their timber and coppiced underwood. The stillness of the modern scene is deceptive.

Cistercian monasteries were dependent on the labour of their lay brothers. Men and boys who worked at the abbey had living quarters in a long range at the west end, next to their own part of the church, the nave which at Roche is still separated from the monks' choir by a few feet of the wall that supported a screen. Other lay brothers were housed at the various granges that were established in the countryside where the abbey had been granted land by the faithful. These granges were often the largest farms in the district and they were commonly distinguished from those of their neighbours by the addition of a chapel.

Most of Roche Abbey's numerous granges had been established by 1186, forty years after the abbey's foundation. In South Yorkshire they were created at Armthorpe, Barnby Dun, Bilham, Bramley, Brancliffe (near Aston), Dunscroft, Lambcote (near Stainton), Marr, Thurnscoe and Todwick. Elsewhere, they included One Ash (in the Peak District) and Thunder Bridge (West Yorkshire, with a flourishing ironworks).[2]

On the moors above Chatsworth, the monks of Roche Abbey had the right to pasture 200 sheep, 60 cattle, 40 hogs, 40 goats, and six saddle horses with their foals. At Styrrup, on the edge of the swamp between Tickhill and Blyth, they had the right to dig peat and sell it as fuel. In the eastern lowlands, William de Warenne, the Norman lord of the fee of Conisbrough, gave them a tenth of the eels that were caught in large numbers in the parishes of Hatfield, Thorne and Fishlake, then in 1345 the monks received the rich gift of the tithes and other dues of Hatfield church, which enabled them to accommodate another thirteen brethren in their monastery.[3]

After the Black Death had reduced the national population dramatically, it became the usual practice of abbeys and priories to lease their granges to local men. Upon the dissolution of the monasteries these tenants were usually offered the chance to buy their properties from the Crown. Thomas Jeffreys's map of Yorkshire, published in 1771–72, marked granges that had once belonged to Roche Abbey at Bilham, Bramley, Brancliffe, Lambcote, Thurnscoe and Todwick, but he neglected to plot the others. All the sites of these granges, except the one at Dunscroft that is now covered with modern bungalows, can still be identified on the ground, though none retains any medieval work. The Cistercians of Roche Abbey have left a permanent imprint on the South Yorkshire landscape.

Other Cistercian Possessions

Distant Cistercian monasteries were also granted lands in South Yorkshire. Rievaulx Abbey had a grange at Falthwaite, near Stainborough, where they kept 200 sheep and mined and forged iron at Stainborough Old Smithies, which are thought to have been in Bagger Wood.[4] Bolton Priory received all the lands of William le Fleming at Wentworth Woodhouse.[5] Kirkstall Abbey had a grange at Bessacarr, where they had common of pasture for 1,000

The possessions of the Cistercian monks of Kirkstead Abbey (Lincolnshire) included a farm at Hordron on the edge of the Langsett Moors. The name means 'store room' and the monks were here by 1208.

sheep and forty mares with their foals and for as many cows and young sheep as they pleased.[6]

Kirkstead Abbey, Lincolnshire, had a grange in Handsworth parish, where Cinder Hill Green at Ballifield seems to have acquired its name from their ironworks, also a grange on the edge of the moors in Langsett township and another on the borders of Kimberworth and Ecclesfield, where a much-altered building known as Kirkstead Abbey Grange retains some medieval work. Here, lay brothers mined and smelted iron from the mid-twelfth century onwards within a 200-acre property that descended to the Blackburn Brook.[7] At the dissolution of the monasteries the forges there were administered from Senoclyff Grange, a name that may have been derived from piles of cinders, in the valley below. A Georgian hall that stands just across the stream from this old monastic site, close to the M1 motorway, preserves the alternative name of Thundercliffe Grange, which was perhaps derived from the sound of these forges.

Monk Bretton Priory

Granges were particularly associated with the Cistercians, but other monastic orders sometimes worked to the same system. The Cluniac, later Benedictine, priory at Monk Bretton had a grange that operated as a home farm whose name is preserved by the modern Grange Industrial Estate, together with other granges at New Laithes (Carlton), Rainborough (Brampton Bierlow) and Newhall (Wath-upon-Dearne).[8]

Adam, son of Swein son of Alric, founded the priory not long before his death in 1159. He gave the monks the manors of Monk Bretton and Carlton, the tithes of the parish of Royston, and corn mills along the River Dearne. Other benefactors donated the tithes of the parishes of Bolton-upon-Dearne and Hickleton and half those of Mexborough, and lands in Abdy, Ardsley, Cubley, Cudworth, Great Houghton, Wentworth and Wrangbrook. A corn mill, a fulling mill, and a tannery were built at the priory and lay brothers may have worked iron mines and forges at Barnsley Smithies, though these are not recorded until after the dissolution of the monasteries.[9]

The geographical range of donations shows that Monk Bretton Priory was thought to serve the part of South Yorkshire that lay within the wapentake of Staincross in the southern half of the Honour of Pontefract. The priory occupied a low and sequestered grassy clearing or 'lound' (perhaps in the Viking sense of 'sacred grove', for this was an unusual place-name in these parts) on the banks of the River Dearne, close to the boundary between the parishes of Royston and Darfield. The priory's original name was St Mary Magdalene of Lund and the district is still known as Lundwood.

The extensive ruins of the priory suggest that it was once a substantial religious house. The 7-acre precinct was surrounded partly by a stone wall and partly by an oak fence and was subdivided into seven enclosures, with a meadow, orchard and fishpond, of which little evidence now remains. The most obvious features are the foundations of the church, most of the monastic quarters, the infirmary, an administrative building, and the gatehouse. Much of the early work was destroyed in a fire in 1386. Upon its dissolution in 1539, most of the priory's buildings were plundered as effectively as were those at Roche.

Other Granges

Distant abbeys that belonged to other monastic orders also established granges in South Yorkshire. Woolley Grange belonged to the priory at Ecclesfield that had been built by the Benedictine monks of the Abbey of St Wandrille in Normandy. Their 600-acre estate stretched as far west as Prior Wood, Grenoside, and the boundary marker known as the Birley Stone, which was recorded in 1161.[10] At Braithwell, the Cluniacs of Lewes Priory, Sussex, built a grange that was known as Moat Hall. In 1379 William Cressy was the 'farmer of the grange' there, but the present ruins are almost certainly the result of rebuilding when John Vincent of Braithwell took a lease of 'Le priorie' in 1427. The footings, low walls and an arched doorway, within a rectangular moated site, provide the best visual evidence of a medieval grange site in South Yorkshire.[11]

Moat Hall, Braithwell, was a grange of the Cluniac priory at Lewes (Surrey). The ruins appear to date from a rebuilding by a tenant in 1427.

The preaching orders, too, farmed their lands by the grange system. The Augustinian priory at Nostell, just beyond the northern border of South Yorkshire, had granges at Barnburgh (Harlington), Swinton (Prior House), Thurnscoe (Howell Grange) and Canonthorpe (between Aston and Beighton). The 1379 poll tax returns record John atte Prious, the lessee at Swinton, and John del Grange at Thurnscoe.[12] The Premonstratensians benefited from substantial gifts of land from the lords of Hallamshire. The canons of Beauchief Abbey acquired Fulwood Grange on the edge of the Pennine moors and those at Welbeck Abbey were given the remote stretch of moorland that descends to Abbey Brook and the River Derwent, adjacent to their grange across the county boundary at Crook Hill.[13]

The lands that were given to the monastic orders or to the Knights Templar and the Knights of St John of Jerusalem were often scattered and the

Abbey Brook takes its name from the Premonstratensian abbey at Welbeck (Nottinghamshire), whose moorland grange was worked as a cattle and sheep farm.

granges tended to be sited in remote places near parish boundaries. Cantley was exceptional in having a substantial part of its parish in the ownership of religious houses. Kirkstall Abbey (with a grange at Bessacarr), Worksop Priory, Hampole Priory, and the hospital of St Mary at Lincoln each had possessions there, and the right to appoint vicars belonged to Wallingwells Priory, just across the Yorkshire border in Nottinghamshire.[14] As we shall see in Chapter 9 the rich peat resources of Inclesmoor, beyond the Cantley parish boundary, were also donated to distant monasteries.

Most of the farmhouses and outbuildings of these medieval granges were probably timber-framed. None survives, but we do have a description in 1649 of 'All that mannor grange, capitall messuage, and scite of the mannor, commonly called or knowne by the name of Barnsly Hall', which had once belonged to Pontefract Priory. It is thought to have stood close to the present Barnsley Town Hall. The survey reads:

Barnsly Hall, being an ancient strong timber house … consisting of a spatious Hall, two parlours, two other nether rooms with a buttery 3 lodgeing Chambers, all which rooms are at the South end of the house from the entry, alsoe a kitchin a parlour a dairy house with 2 chambers over them at the north end of the house from the entry one large barne cont[aining] 7 bayes one stable and severall other outhouses and buildings alsoe one garden one greene hard Corte on the east betweene the house heretofore a bowleing greene con[taining] by estimation 2 roodes; and 2 yards or folds lying together betweene the barne and the streete and all ways passages lights easements commodities and advantages whatsoever to the same belonging and appertaining.

The survey concluded that 'the said capitall messuage with the barne and stable are in good repaire'.[15] The barn survived into modern times and a few of its timbers are on display at the 'Experience Barnsley' museum.

Kirkstead Abbey Grange on Thorpe Common is an enigmatic building that contains some stone features from the twelfth century and a sophisticated fifteenth – or sixteenth-century timber-framed interior, but it was much altered during the restoration in 1900. The monks had iron forges near by.

In Victorian times it became fashionable to name a house The Grange even if the site had no connection with a medieval building, so we must be cautious in taking a name at face value. Nevertheless, it is obvious from the examples quoted above that the religious orders built farmhouses and agricultural buildings in many parts of South Yorkshire. They also owned corn and fulling mills, fishponds and ironworks, many of which have left a mark on the present landscape. Tom Umpleby located eleven water corn mills on the River Dearne and its tributaries that were owned or partly owned by the abbeys and priories at Monk Bretton, Pontefract, Nostell, Hampole, Bolton and Byland.[16] On the banks of the River Sheaf, Yorkshire's southern boundary, the canons of Beauchief Abbey owned a corn mill at Bradway, a fulling mill on the site of the present railway station at Dore, a corn mill that gave its name to the Sheffield suburb, Millhouses, a New Mill for grinding corn further downstream, and a smithy that gave its name to Smithy Wood.[17]

Much of the income that supported religious houses came from grants of parish churches, in other words of the tithes (a tenth of each householder's income, mostly from farming) and other ecclesiastical dues. The income of 35 of the 62 ancient parishes of South Yorkshire was eventually granted to abbeys, priories or colleges, some of which were founded in distant parts of the country or abroad. When monastic houses received these rights, they kept the 'great tithes' amounting to two-thirds of the whole and they appointed a vicar, who received the 'small tithes', to fulfill their role as rector. Their responsibility of maintaining the chancel of the parish church often did not extend to rebuilding in a style that matched the parishioners' nave, aisles, porch and tower. For instance, the chancels at Laughton and Penistone were not refashioned when the parishioners redesigned their naves and towers in the Perpendicular Gothic style in the late Middle Ages. Yet at Ecclesfield, Bradfield or Darton, abbeys and priories did match the efforts of the parishioners in rebuilding their chancels in this new style. Either way, monasteries have left their mark on the principal medieval buildings of many a South Yorkshire parish.

Chapter 5

Timber-Framed Barns

Whiston Long Barn

The Long Barn at Whiston, or the Manorial Barn as it has been known since its restoration in the 1980s, is by far the oldest timber-framed building to survive in the northern half of England. Its basic structure has been dated by dendrochronology to 1233–52. It is well known to architectural historians throughout the country. A visit to the barn, led by Stanley Jones, was a highlight of the programme of the Summer Meeting of the Royal Archaeological Institute in 1980.[1]

The interior of Whiston Barn was in a dilapidated condition in the 1970s, but has now been restored as a village amenity. It is the oldest known timber-framed building in Yorkshire.

By the 1970s it was in a dilapidated condition and there were fears that it would be demolished. One possibility was that it would be removed to an open-air museum in Oxfordshire, but in 1985 Whiston Parish Council bought it and by 1992 it had been re-thatched, re-walled and fully restored for public use.

Stanley Jones, a leading member of the national society known as the Vernacular Architecture Group, recognized early carpentry techniques in the five southern and central bays that suggested a probable date in the thirteenth or fourteenth century. They were similar to those that had been used to construct famous aisled barns in south-east England, notably the Barley and Wheat Barns of the Knights Templar at Cressing Temple, Essex. The arcade posts taper from bottom to top, the same way that trees grow but the reverse of the construction system that was used in Britain later on. Other technical features include the use of passing braces and notched-lap joints instead of the later mortise-and-tenon method. Three bays were added on the northern side in a later phase of building, so that, eventually, the Whiston Long Barn was 47.3 metres long by 10.4 metres broad.

Further investigation revealed that the roof of the earliest bays had been reconstructed much later, perhaps at the time when the barn was extended to the north. Ian Tyers and Cathy Groves, who conducted a dendrochronological analysis of the building, wrote in 2002 that, 'It is perhaps easiest to think of the surviving structure as being composed of two barns one on top of the other'.[2] Sixteen of the twenty timbers that they selected for sampling were dated by comparison with a wide range of oak sequences throughout England and Wales and elsewhere in Europe. Most of these timbers were chosen because they retained at least some of their sapwood. Nine dated timbers from the first phase of construction provided a felling date of 1233–52. It was common medieval practice for the carpenters to use green timbers shortly after the felling. The date for Whiston Barn falls between those of the two barns at Cressing Temple and it is almost identical with that of the barn that was erected for Cistercian monks at Little Coggeshall, close by in Essex.[3]

The dendro date of the three northern bays at Whiston was between 1640 and 1645, a century or so later than expected. It appears that the barn was reconstructed just before the outbreak of the Civil War. Before the 1640s date had been determined, the striking similarities between the barns at Whiston and Little Coggeshall led to a suggestion from Essex that the Whiston Long Barn was a former monastic barn that was remodelled after the dissolution of the monasteries. The possibility was raised that it was looted from Roche Abbey, another Cistercian foundation.

Ian Tyers and Cathy Groves have demolished this idea, not only through their dating but also by their careful observations of the timbers. They made the point that sufficient fresh oak was readily available at the time of the remodelling and so it would not have made a great deal of economic sense to use the hardened ancient posts if they were not already on site. They concluded that the difficulties of transporting such large and heavy timbers some seven or eight miles on post-medieval roads should not be underestimated and that simple casual looting was unlikely. Amongst other technical evidence, they noted that the surviving scarf joints in the arcade plates show no sign of having been taken apart in order to move the timbers.

The dendrochronological analysis provided further surprises. The trees that were used for the earliest parts of the barn were:

> certainly greater than 350 years old at the time they were felled and more likely around 400 years old. The samples uniformly start in the late ninth and early tenth centuries so these trees were alive at the time of Alfred and the period of Danelaw in this area.

At the present time, trees that are 400 years old are extremely rare in the landscape. The Whiston timbers were not used full size, indeed many of the posts are quartered sections. They came mostly from trees that were knotty and twisty and quite slow grown. The contrast with Little Coggeshall Barn is remarkable, for the Essex trees were much younger, smaller and faster grown. Surprisingly, the trees that were used in the 1640s extension at Whiston were also long-lived, some reaching nearly 300 years. This implies that reasonably closed and undisturbed woodland was still flourishing near by.

So, who was responsible for building the earliest part of the Whiston Long Barn in the second quarter of the thirteenth century? A barn this size must have served the manorial estate. The lord of the manor at that time was William de Furnival, the youngest of the three sons of Gerard de Furnival and Maud de Louvetot of Sheffield Castle. Both families took their names from places in Normandy. Gerard, who had previously been lord of Munden Furnival (Hertfordshire), died in Jerusalem on crusade in 1218. His son, William, died without heirs and the manor passed to his nephew,

Thomas de Furnival, who inherited the bulk of the family estates centred on Sheffield Castle and the lordship of Hallamshire.[4]

In Elizabethan times, Thomas Stringer, an agent of the Earl of Shrewsbury, lord of Hallamshire, lived at Whiston Hall and the barn was renovated and extended by his grandson, Francis Stringer, esquire, whom Joseph Hunter described as 'a great lead merchant'. In or about 1821 the Whiston Hall estate was bought by Sir George Sitwell of Renishaw.[5]

Gunthwaite Barn

By contrast, the magnificent barn at Gunthwaite in the northern part of the ancient parish of Penistone was erected in one phase, late in the timber-framed tradition. Samples from four of its principal posts provided a dendro date of between 1560 and 1587, which agrees with the date that was assumed from stylistic evidence.[6] The barn is 163 feet long and 44 feet wide and the floor area covers about 7,100 square feet. An internal wall was built in the

The interior of Gunthwaite Hall Barn as it was about 1900. It is still used for its original purpose. The barn is an aisled structure, eleven bays long, with a king-post roof.

late eighteenth century to provide storage space for two farms, once the Bosville family had left the district to live at Thorpe in the East Riding.

The Bosvilles were originally a Norman knightly family who took their name from Beuzeville-la-Giffarde, not far from Dieppe. They acquired several manors in South Yorkshire from the mid-twelfth century onwards and added Gunthwaite in 1374 when Thomas de Bosville of Ardsley married the heiress, Alice de Gunthwaite. Godfrey Bosville (c.1517–80) was the first of the Bosvilles to live for much of his time at Gunthwaite, but even he described himself in his will as 'of Beighton, esquire'. His wife, Jane, was a sister of the redoubtable Bess of Hardwick.[7] He was also lord of the manor of Oxspring in the parish of Penistone, where he built a hunting lodge, half in timber half in stone. Old photographs show it in a ruined condition shortly before it was demolished in the early twentieth century.[8]

The Bosvilles were the principal family in Penistone parish for about two hundred years. The barn that Godfrey Bosville built at Gunthwaite remains intact, little altered since his day, but his timber-framed house that stood to the south is known only by repute, for it was demolished in the nineteenth century and no drawing of it survives.

The south side of the barn, which once faced the hall, is decorated with large chevron-patterned panels, whereas the north side is plainer with close studding and curved braces. Both sides have local sandstone walls below the bressumer that supports the timbers. The roof has always been stone-slated. Loaded carts once passed through harr-hung doors, whereby an iron-shod lower projection in the stone threshold and an upper projection in an oak bracket allowed the door to swing open.

Inside, the barn is divided into eleven bays by ten impressive timber trusses standing on stone stylobates or padstones. The principal posts throughout the barn are identical in style with deep, curved arch-braces to both the arcade-plates and the tie-beams. Each post is fourteen inches wide and nine inches thick. An exceptionally large number of dowels were used in the securing of the mortise-and-tenon joints. The whole barn is fully aisled and the roof is supported by king posts that reach up from the tie-beams. King-post roofs were the favoured style in the better quality houses and barns on the south-eastern edges of the Pennines in the late fifteenth and sixteenth centuries. Elsewhere in Penistone parish, however, high quality aisled barns at Shore Hall (now demolished) and Dean Head were constructed with common rafter roofs.[9]

Cruck Barns

The cruck frame was by far the most common method of constructing farmhouses, cottages and barns along the edges of the Pennines and on the coal-measure sandstones further east. Yet the surviving evidence for the use of crucks on the magnesian limestone belt and the eastern lowlands consists of just one blade in a shop at Braithwell. Cruck frames are rarely found in eastern or south-eastern England, but they are common in the Midlands and the West, in much of Wales, in many parts of northern England and to a lesser extent in Scotland. This distribution pattern remains a puzzle.[10]

Dendro tests on hundreds of buildings up and down the country have shown that surviving cruck buildings range widely in date from the thirteenth to the seventeenth centuries, with a few later ones. Nearly all the Yorkshire crucks that have been examined by this method date from the second half of the fifteenth to the early seventeenth century and most of them are from the second half of this period. Documentary evidence, however, tells us that this method of construction was in use in Yorkshire much earlier. For example, in 1352 'Margery of the mill' at Holmfirth was fined by the jury of the Wakefield manor court for felling trees and selling six 'crokkes'. [11]

About 120 cruck-framed buildings survive, at least in part, in south-west Yorkshire.[12] Fewer than a quarter of these buildings are found in houses or cottages, and very few barns and outbuildings contain evidence in the form of fireplaces or smoke-blackened beams to suggest that they were once dwellings. Most of the surviving cruck frames are found in small buildings and they have no architectural details, such as mouldings or decorative bosses, to distinguish them. Their sturdy timbers are often rough and some still have bark upon them.

The carpenter's first task was to find suitable trees with trunks and curving branches of the right length in the local woods and hedgerows. A sale of the manor of Barnburgh in 1692, for instance, noted that the 37-acre Loscoe wood was 'full of large Oake Timber' and that 'Much very fine Timber' could be obtained 'in all the Hedge Rowes'.[13] The carpenters were often able to create a pair of cruck blades by splitting the timbers lengthways.

The cruck blades were fastened at mid-level by a tie-beam and higher up by a collar beam, both of which were slotted, or 'halved', into them and secured by pegs. The tie-beam extended beyond the cruck blades in order to support horizontal timbers known as wall-plates, which stretched as far as the next pair of blades. South Yorkshire carpenters used nine different ways to fasten the blades together at the apex so as to support a ridge-piece between two pairs of crucks. Occasionally, they used two methods in the same building because the blades did not reach exactly the same height. Halfway down the roof slope between the ridge-piece and the wall-plates other horizontal timbers, known as purlins, were fixed to the outer part of the blades in order to carry the rafters, which in turn took the weight of the roof covering. As the wattle-and-daub walls that descended from the wall-plates did not shore up the roof, they were easily replaced by stone walls in later times. When this happened, the wall-plates became redundant and so they were sometimes removed.

The space between each pair of cruck blades formed a bay. These bays usually had roughly the same measurements, but they sometimes varied in length, even within the same house or barn. Cruck-framed buildings were commonly two or three bays long, but they could easily be extended. The longest cruck-framed building in South Yorkshire is the six-bay former barn at Green Farm, on the hills above Stocksbridge, which has been converted into a house in modern times. The names of William and Sara Couldwell and the date 1688 are carved into the walls in an earlier modernization of the timber-framed barn.

The former barn at Green Farm, near Stocksbridge, is six bays long. The stone walls and roof date from 1688. In modern times it has been converted into domestic accommodation.

Carpenters' assembly marks show that cruck frames were designed in the workshop or in the wood where the trees were felled. Holes were drilled near the base of the blades, so that poles could be thrust through them. Strong men using ropes could then lift the timbers on to stone footings, which prevented rotting from rising damp, provided extra height, and sometimes adjusted the level of a building on a slope.

Sometimes, when a farmhouse was built in a superior style of carpentry, cruck frames were thought to be adequate for the outbuildings. This is well

When this cruck-framed barn at The Nab (otherwise Hawksworth's Cote) was demolished in the early twentieth century upon the construction of Midhope reservoir, the local historian Joseph Kenworthy arranged for photographs to be taken while the walls were being dismantled, revealing the timber-framed interior.

illustrated at Swaithe Hall, near Worsbrough, where the box-frame hall was roofed with a king-post structure, which has been dendro dated to sometime after 1522, but the barn was built with crucks.[14]

Cruck-framed barns are very common on the edge of the Pennine moors, but they are not immediately recognizable because they are now hidden from external view by later stone walls and stone-slated roofs. The timber-framed tradition in all parts of England gradually came to an end during the course of the seventeenth century. When Celia Fiennes journeyed from Hemsworth to Rotherham in 1697 she remarked on the number of fine houses newly built of freestone.[15] In many cases, however, the impression gained from outside is misleading. When we go into an old barn we often find that at least part of the timber frame is preserved within the later stone walls and stone-slated roofs. Those that have been dendro dated include the barns at Hall Broom Farm, Dungworth (1495–6), Ughill Manor (1504), Hallfield House (c.1505), Manor Farm, Upper Midhope (1551), Well Bank Farm, Upper Midhope (c.1565), Raynor House (1593), and Well House Farm, Stannington (1591–1600).[16] They are sturdy survivors from the late-medieval and Tudor era.

Chapter 6

Pennine Farms

Belle Clive and Langsett

It is rarely possible to date the beginnings of South Yorkshire's medieval farms accurately. Domesday Book names some of the places that existed at the time of the Norman Conquest, but no other local documents survive before the late-twelfth or thirteenth century, by which time some farms may already have been old. Belle Clive, for instance, first appears in a document that can be dated between 1208 and 1211,[1] but the original farm there may have been created decades or even centuries before. This striking site, high on the hillside overlooking the valley of the Little Don, was 'Billa's cliff'. It did not assume its present name of Belle Clive until the first edition of the six-inch Ordnance Survey map of 1854, though some of the medieval forms of the name are close to that. The local pronunciation is Bilcliff or Billcley,

This photograph of Upper and Lower Belle Clive Farms was taken about 1900 by the local photographer, Joshua Biltcliffe, whose surname was derived from them in the thirteenth century.

and the farmstead is the source of the local surnames Bilcliff, Biltcliffe and Bintcliffe.

Thirteenth-century documents in the Savile of Rufford collection at Nottinghamshire Archives that cannot be dated precisely show how the surname developed. A grant by Simon of Hunshelf to Thomas of Billecliva, his brother, of land in Billecliva was followed by another grant by William, the son of Simon of Hunshelf, to Thomas of Billeclive, of all the land that had been given by Simon, his father, and which was now occupied by Ralph of Billeclive and Robert, his brother, who were presumably the sons of Thomas.[2]

The farm that is now called Lower Belle Clive is perched on the top of the cliff and so it probably occupies the original site, but Upper Belle Clive Farm may also date from the thirteenth century. Two further deeds show that Thomas of Billeclive rented half his property to Adam, the son of Robert of Ecclehules (nearby Ecklands), and that, later, he agreed that Richard, the son of Osbert, his nephew, should rent an acre of building land near his house and twelve acres of land.[3] A generation later, when Henry, the son of Adam of Billecleve, granted half his land to Robert of Holand, the property was described as being at 'Langkeside in Billecleve'.[4] The second of these two deeds named Henry as the son of Adam of Smalschahe (Smallshaw), so at the time Billcliff was not securely established as a hereditary surname.

'Langkeside', or Langsett as it became known, was one of the eight townships of Penistone parish. The name is now attached to a small settlement by the reservoir that was completed in 1904 at the edge of the moors, but it was originally applied to the whole of the 'long side' of the great ridge that rises up from the northern banks of the Little Don. An alternative name for this township was Penisale, a hybrid name from the Celtic word *pen*, denoting a dramatic headland, and the Old English word *halgh*, meaning a nook of land on the edge of an estate; the earliest references date from 1190–1208.[5] Penistone, the settlement that stood on the other side of the great ridge that dominates the skyline from Hartcliff to Green Moor, was the centre of this estate. In the late twelfth-century William, the son of John, lord of 'Peningeston', granted land to Kirkstead Abbey, a Cistercian monastery in Lincolnshire, together with his 'right in the moor next to their grange of Peningeshalg'.[6] It is not known where this grange stood, though the name Sheephouse Farm is suggestive. When the abbey was dissolved in the 1530s it was said to have possessions in 'Penynghall', Midhope and Langsett.[7]

To the east of Belle Clive, the farm at Alderman's Head stands strikingly on a promontory on the 'long side' below the ridge. Both the site and the mysterious name suggest an ancient establishment, yet the earliest surviving reference to the place-name is from 1581.[8] The names of other medieval farmsteads in Langsett township are more readily explained: Hartcliff (deer), Brockholes (badger setts), Swinden (swine), Brookhouse (by the stream), and, less obviously, Hordron (a store house).

On the very edge of the moors, at the highest point of settlement in the Little Don Valley, Hordron was one of seven farms that were either submerged under Langsett Reservoir when it was constructed about a hundred years ago or demolished because of fears that they would contaminate the water supply. The ruined farmhouse is nineteenth century in style and the ornate sheep dip in the valley below is Victorian, for it was not shown on the first edition of the six-inch Ordnance Survey map in 1854. Yet Hordron was mentioned in the same document as Bilcliff in 1208. It was an outlying possession of the grange that had been established a mile or two away by the Cistercian monks of Kirkstead Abbey. Hordron, too, became a local surname, though it no longer survives.

Thurlstone township

These old farms in the upper reaches of the Little Don Valley have much in common with those on the other side of the great ridge that separated the moorland townships of Langsett and Thurlstone. The lord of Thurlstone had a vaccary, or cattle-rearing farm, at Windleden, the 'windswept hill and valley' high above Dunford Bridge. At 1,200 feet above sea level, it is the highest occupied site in the parish of Penistone. The present building dates from the nineteenth century, but a predecessor was recorded in an undated deed from the early fourteenth century and another deed of 1484 granted a lease of 'a certain vaccary and certain cattle there'.[9]

In the centuries before accurate maps were drawn, stone crosses were often used as boundary markers. Catshaw Cross takes its name from a boundary stone that stands by Lee Lane, and the name Fullshaw Cross commemorates a lost marker less than a mile away to the west. Narrow strips of woodland known as shaws were often used as boundary markers in the foothills of the Pennines. In the 1379 poll tax returns for Bradfield, Earnshaw Ridge was recorded as Hernchagh ('the eagle wood') and Shaw House was mentioned as Schagh; both places gave rise to local surnames. A few shaws were also found in the hilly and more exposed parts of the Holmfirth district, at Bradshaw, Deershaw, Hepshaw, Millshaw and Shaw Bank. Langsett township has another Bradshaw and a Lady Shaw, and Thurlstone township not only has Catshaw and Fullshaw but Smallshaw, Reddishaw and another Shaw Bank.

Most of these strips of woodland gave their names to medieval farmsteads.[10] Smallshaw is of particular interest, for it was often referred to as a manor. In 1598 the manor of Smallshawe contained ten farmsteads ('messuages'), four cottages, fourteen gardens, two water corn mills (perhaps at Bullhouse and Thurlstone) and a fulling mill (Millhouse Green), 400 acres of land, sixty acres of meadow, forty acres of pasture, thirty acres of moor, and twenty acres of furze.[11] The present farmstead that nestles securely under the ridge at Smallshaw bears a datestone, which shows that it was rebuilt in 1664.

Looking down the Upper Don Valley from Windleden we see the hamlet of Carlecotes, 1,100 feet above sea level, at the limit of cultivation. Carlecotes takes its name from 'the churls' cottages'. In districts settled by the Vikings the Old English ceorl, meaning 'free peasant', was replaced by Old Norse karl. Although this word continued in use after the Norman Conquest, it is

This view from the lord of Thurlstone's cattle-rearing farm at Windleden looks down the valley to the hamlet of Carlecotes, encircled by the moors. The pattern of settlement was created in the Middle Ages.

likely that Carlecotes was settled in the Anglo-Scandinavian period before 1066, for the numerous Charltons and Carltons up and down the country and the comparable place-name Charlecote (Warwickshire) were all recorded in Domesday Book. So here we have a group of peasant farmers who lived in relative freedom.

The earliest evidence for settlement in this unpromising terrain comes from personal names in thirteenth- and fourteenth-century deeds and the court rolls of the neighbouring manor of Wakefield, where Carlecotes farmers were sometimes fined for allowing their livestock to stray across the moorland boundary, though this may have been a method whereby farmers who lived beyond the manor paid for grazing at an agreed rate.[12] The farmers of the hamlet shared all the land that was fit for growing crops within strips or doles in the communal townfields. As late as 1738 a deed mentioned '3 doles of land in the townfields of Carlcoates'.[13]

One of the farms in Carlecotes, known now as Eltock and formerly as Elcock House, is first mentioned in a deed of 1585,[14] but we can identify the personal name that was applied to it much earlier. Farms such as Bilcliff and Hordron produced surnames, but in some cases it was the other way round: farms took their names from the farmers; the addition of 'house' is often a tell-tale sign. The Wakefield manor court rolls for 1297 mention a Richard son of Elcock, who appeared as a witness for a Carlecotes man. Ten years later, Richard son of Elcock gave similar support to 'Litel Dobbe' of Carlecotes, and in 1315 Richard, son of Richard son of Elcock, was named in the rolls. Finally, in 1414 William Elcock of Thurlstone (the township in which the hamlet of Carlecotes was situated) appeared as a witness in a case involving Carlecotes.[15] By then, the personal name (a diminutive of Elias or Ellis) had become a hereditary surname. We cannot put a precise date on the creation of Elcock Farm but it seems likely to have been in the period of expansion and population growth before the Black Death of 1348–50. Numerous deeds from the seventeenth and eighteenth centuries refer to 'Elcockhouse in Carlecotes' and to Elcockfields and Elcock Intake.

A similar example a little further east is Illions Farm. The English Place-Name Society's earliest record is from 1565, but the farm had been in existence for well over two centuries before then. In 1359 Brian of Thornhill, knight, the lord of the manor of Thurlstone, granted to Robert Illian and Alice, his wife, 'a messuage next to Smalsagh', for life.[16] It is unlikely that a new farm was created in the decade after the disaster of the Black Death, so Robert may have been inheriting what was already his family's property. In an undated charter from the beginning of the fourteenth century Baldwin del Hill of Thurlstone was granted a plot of land that lay 'by land of John Ylian' at Smallshaw.[17] Unlikely as it may seem, this rare surname was derived from a Breton personal name.

In studying the farming systems on the edges of the Pennines it is important to realize that the township rather than the parish was the unit that mattered and that townships were sometimes divided into hamlets, such as Carlecotes. Today, we use hamlet to mean a small group of buildings, but originally it referred to a farming unit that might include a cluster of dwellings, some isolated farms, communal townfields, and common pastures and wastes. Ecklands hamlet stretched from the River Don to the moors three quarters-of-a-mile to the south, where it reached a height of just over 1,000 feet above sea level. A deed of 1340 refers to the townfields of Ecklands.[18] Field Lane, which acted as the back lane immediately east of the farms, is still in use. A map of 1813 depicts the townfields of Ecklands divided into eight blocks of former strips.[19]

Pennine townfields were very much smaller than the vast open fields of Midland England and we have only meagre information about them, for most of them were enclosed well before the period of parliamentary enclosure. However, we know that Thurlstone's townfields survived until 1696–99, when they were enclosed by the agreement of the 26 farmers who owned strips within them.[20] The narrow, curving pattern of these strips is preserved by many of the walls within the former West Field, though not in the East Field, which was enclosed at the same time.

As the medieval population expanded in the twelfth and thirteenth centuries new land was cleared from the wastes beyond the townfields with the willing co-operation of the lord of the manor who benefited from the extra rents. In much of the West Riding these clearings can be identified by names ending in –royd, a localized pronunciation of the more widespread Old English rod. In West Riding dialect the letter 'o' is often pronounced 'oy'.

Royd was used to describe a clearing that was newly cleared of trees. On 1 April 1307 an inquisition jury in the manor of Wakefield explained that 'it is called rodeland because it was cleared from growing wood'.[21] The hard labour that was involved meant that these clearances were often small, frequently less than an acre in size; most of them were used for grazing livestock. In the Calder Valley, west of Halifax, a number of royds gave rise to distinctive surnames such as Ackroyd, Boothroyd or Murgatroyd, for they were from

The present Royd Farm in the township of Thurlstone was built in the seventeenth century on the site of a medieval farm that took its name from a woodland clearing.

the sites of new farmsteads. George Redmonds has identified forty royds in the township of Almondbury, a few miles north of Thurlstone.[22] Almost half of them had a personal name as the first element. Some of these were Old English or Old Norse in character, but many more were Middle English names dating from about 1175 to 1350.

Royd was not used as a term for new clearances after the Black Death, nor was hey used to describe a newly hedged enclosure or shaw for a new strip of woodland, so even if we do not have medieval documentary evidence we can argue that such names arose in the Middle Ages. When large-scale clearing was resumed in Elizabeth I's reign the newly won fields were called by other old words – intacks, stubbings and ryddings. Thurlstone township has numerous royds, such as Royd Farm, on the southern slope of the escarpment between Thurlstone and Smallshaw, which was recorded in a deed of about 1300.[23] Yet few royds are found south of the Little Don, which formed the boundary of Penistone parish.

Midhope

In medieval times Penistone parish lay at the south-western edge of the great Honour of Pontefract, but the moorland farms on the southern side of the Little Don were within the Lordship of Hallamshire, the whole of which was administered from Sheffield Castle and which was originally contained within the huge parish of Ecclesfield, with chapels-of-ease at Bradfield and Sheffield. In the Middle Ages the several sub-manors of Hallamshire included those of Midhope and Bolsterstone.

Midhope acquired its name from its position mid-way up the *hop*, or enclosed valley of the Little Don, and its lords took their surname from the settlement. The earliest reference to the family is to John of Midhope in 1227. In 1243 this John was described as the seneschal (the leading officer) of Hallamshire. Nine years later, his son, Elias of Midhope, also acquired the manor of Langsett (or Penisale), so he was now the lord of both sides of the valley and the surrounding moors.[24] In 1290 Elias obtained charters to hunt throughout his manors and to establish a Tuesday market and three-day annual fair somewhere within Penisale. These charters were renewed in 1307, but the market and fair did not last long.[25]

When John of Midhope died between 1327 and 1337 the estate passed to his widow's brother, Thomas, a clerk or clergyman who lived at Barnby Hall near Cawthorne.[26] Surviving fragments of his hall at Midhope include the wooden frame of a window in a building that is now a barn. Hall Farm was once known as the Court House, for this is where the meetings of the manor court were held. The chapel-of-ease of St James, which Thomas built near by, was restored and re-furnished in 1705, but the basic structure remains medieval.

The boundaries between the manors in this wild moorland district followed natural features wherever possible, but elsewhere they were marked by stone crosses. Disputes inevitably arose and so, from time to time, a lord or his steward would lead a group of his tenants on a perambulation of the bounds. A record of such a journey around Midhope and Langsett that was made in 1695[27] describes the route along the county boundary southwards from:

> Salter Brook, to the Great Small Clough Brook; there dividing between the Lordship of Midhop and Langsett, and the Lordship of Longdendale and Tinsel [Tintwistle], being the bound betwixt

Yorkshire and Cheshire, the W[est] side of the said clough being within the Lordship of Glossopdale in the C[ounty] of Derby; then up the said clough to the Swaine Greave Head, thence to Great Howden Head, along Howden Head to the Horestone, and by Steiner Clough Head, and so along to the Craw Stone Edge, and Bullstones, and Margery Pike or Nabb, and from thence to the Black Dick Head.

This tallies with the memory of John Hatfield of Bullhouse, who in 1753 recalled that:

Above 50 years since he was present at the riding of the boundaries by Justice Bosville; [Godfrey Bosville, the lord of the manor who restored Midhope chapel] at which riding were present Richard Greaves, above 80 years old at that time, of Tin Wood, near Lady Bower in Derbyshire, and Humphry Bray, who had been a soldier in Oliver Cromwell's army; these chiefly directed where they were to go, having rode them formerly.

The party set off at Blakeroyds, at the north-eastern edge of Langsett township, where they laid their hands on the wall, and headed along the ridge to Sandy Ford and the boundary markers known as the Greyhound Stone and the Standing Stone. From Hartcliff, they rode along the northern side of the highway to South Nabb and Saltersbrook, where they followed the route described above. Having climbed the Great Small Clough up to the top of Swaines Greave, they proceeded down the edge of Featherbed Moss, to the south end of the place then called the Black Dyke, or Cut Gate, until they came to the Candlerush Rig, above Candlerush Spring, so-called because the rushes here were gathered to make candles. They then ascended Earnshaw Rig and descended the side of Ewden pasture to Wolf's Hill, before crossing Barnside Moor to the Intacks and following Langley Brook to the Little Don. Wolf's Hill is the only one of these names that is no longer in use and cannot be identified with certainty.

The lordship of Midhope contained several isolated farms and the two hamlets of Over and Nether Midhope. The upper hamlet consisted of a few farmsteads on a small ridge on either side of the lane that winds its way down to the lower hamlet, whose alternate name was Midhopestones, after the stepping stones that took the ancient highway known as the Strines over the Little Don before its steep climb up the *pen* to Judd Field Farm. The present main road along the Little Don Valley was constructed in 1805 as the Wadsley-Langsett turnpike, connecting Sheffield to the Woodhead Pass.

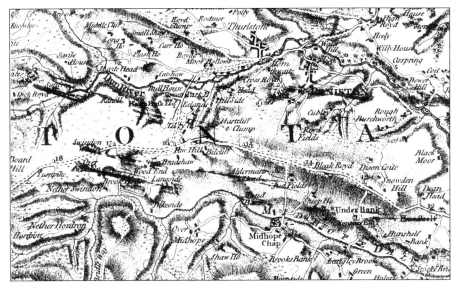

This section of Thomas Jeffreys's map of Yorkshire (1772) shows some of the farms mentioned above and the extensive moors around Midhope (marked by hatched lines in contrast to the unmarked areas of cultivation) on the eve of parliamentary enclosure.

Midhopestones contained the hall, chapel, farms, inns, blacksmith's shop, corn mill and a pottery at Nether Mill Green, which was founded in 1720 by George Walker of Hunshelf Hall and Robert Blackburn of Alderman's Head, the owner of the Bolsterstone Glass House. William Gough, the potter, specialized in decorated slipware and earthenware pots, bottles, jugs, pitchers, teapots, vases, etc., and he built thirteen houses for his workers in Pot House Fold, alongside his ovens, drying sheds and store houses.[28] Although Over and Nether Midhope stand amidst three reservoirs that were constructed in the late nineteenth and early twentieth centuries, the residents had no piped water until the mid-1930s.

Like other hamlets along the Pennine fringes, such as Carlecotes and Ecklands, Midhope had townfields that were divided into strips for the tenants to grow oats. In 1674 these were enclosed by the agreement of the farmers.[29] Most of the lordship, however, was characterized by the 3,302 acres of extensive commons and moorland wastes that were of little use except as rough grazing for sheep and a source of peat for winter fuel. When they were partitioned under the terms of the 1823 enclosure award, the lord of the manor, Godfrey Bosville received 2,080 acres of the bleakest moors and three other landowners shared 339 acres. When Langsett, which had long since become a separate lordship again, was enclosed between 1811 and 1814, the absentee lord of the manor, William Payne, received 2,547 of the 3,057 acres of the commons and wastes that stretched over Boardhill to Saltersbrook.[30]

Parliamentary enclosure led to the creation of stone-walled, rectangular fields on the edges of the moors and the erection of new farmsteads, including the whimsically named North America, the furthest point west, but the bleakest wastes were soon converted into grouse-shooting moors. Their present appearance is due to their management for this purpose ever since. Had the interest in grouse shooting not taken hold, large stretches of these moors would probably now by covered with conifers. Instead, they and other grouse moors form a landscape that is unique to Britain.

Midhope Moors were bounded to the south-east by the famous grouse moor of the Rimington-Wilsons at Broomhead to the west by the Duke of Norfolk's Howden Moors, and to the north-west by Sir Thomas Pilkington's Boardhill Moors. On 9 May 1831 The Right Honourable Godfrey Bosville, Baron Macdonald, Lord of the Manor of Midhope, appointed Benjamin Mate of Langsett, farmer, to be a gamekeeper, to kill grouse, hares, pheasants, partridges or any other game, and to:

> take and seize all such guns, bows, setting dogs, lurchers, or other dogs, Ferrets, Tramels, lowbels, hays or other nets, haupipes, snares or other engines used by others.[31]

Some of the shooting rights on the local grouse moors were leased to middle-class clubs such as the fifteen members of the Bradfield Game Association, whose treasurer, Mr Elmhirst of Round Green, had sole charge of management and the prosecution of poachers.[32] In the 1840s Midhope Moors were leased by the Bosvilles to a similar group of seventeen members, led by a corn miller and then by his nephew, John Ness Dransfield, a solicitor and the local historian of the Penistone district. Dransfield wrote of the final day's sport on 6 December, followed by dinner at the Club Inn, Midhopestones:[33]

> One of the most enjoyable days we had for many years on Midhope Moors was one old sportsmen christened the 'Duffers' Day'. I invited annually a number of friends who were not regular shooters and had not otherwise the opportunity of showing their skill on the moors to a day's driving.

He also observed that in the 1830s his uncle walked eight miles from his home to Midhope Moors, shot all day with a twelve-inch bore muzzle loader weighing twelve pounds, then walked home at night. It was, Dransfield observed, rather different from sitting in a grouse butt all day. Whereas in the past birds had been shot as they flew away, now they were driven towards the butts by beaters. This new method of shooting was made possible by successive improvements in gun manufacture, particularly the invention of the breech-loading shotgun. Several thousands of these were in use by the early 1860s. It was then that the management of the moors, particularly the burning of sections on a rotation basis, began in earnest in order to provide enough birds to shoot. By the 1880s the 'bags' shot each day were enormous. Other improvements included the digging of drains in the wettest parts of the moors to encourage heather at the expense of cotton-grass, bog-moss and purple moor grass; the digging of ditches to prevent the spread of fire; the construction of pony and cart tracks; and the erection of single-storeyed stone cabins for shelter at lunchtime. Midhope Moors were used for army manoeuvres and target practice during the Second World War, but reverted to grouse shooting afterwards. Their careful management for this sport has had a major impact on the vegetation and has preserved much of the archaeological evidence for former activities.[34]

Chapter 7

Tankersley Park

Medieval England had nearly 2,000 deer parks at one time or the other. Some large ones that are commemorated by minor place-names such as Conisbrough Parks and Park Hill, Sheffield, were associated with great castles, but most of the smaller parks were created by lesser lords during the thirteenth and fourteenth centuries. As deer were the property of the Crown, lords who did not have hunting rights that were based upon immemorial custom had to pay for a royal charter to proceed. The normal method in the North was for a grant of free warren to be enrolled in the charter or patent rolls. This gave a lord a general right to hunt in his manor, part of which was then made into a park.

Many of these parks went out of use by the end of the Middle Ages, but eight of the largest were marked on Christopher Saxton's map of the West Riding in 1577, at Aston, Brierley, Conisbrough, Kiveton, Sheffield, Tankersley, Thrybergh and Wortley. Tankersley Park is one of the most complete and interesting of these parks to survive in the present landscape, though deer no longer roam within its bounds. Its origin can be dated fairly precisely, for the charter rolls of King Edward I record a royal grant of free warren in 1303–4 to Hugh of Elland in his manors of Elland and Tankersley. His family had succeeded the earlier lords who had taken their name from Tankersley.[1]

Driving north up the M1 motorway, we see Tankersley church standing alone on the skyline, just above the golf course that occupies much of the former park. A church was recorded here in Domesday Book and the present building retains some Norman architecture, though it is mainly a late-medieval structure that was 'improved' in Victorian times. The motorway takes us towards a welcome stretch of greenery in the South Yorkshire countryside, which has been preserved from the spread of the coalfield largely because of the self-interest of the major landowners. Yet, as we shall see, part of the interest in exploring Tankersley Park comes from the legacy of industrial activity once the deer had been removed.

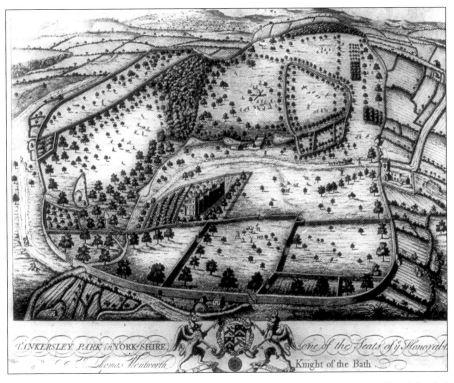

This engraving of the late 1720s shows Tankersley Park enclosed by a strong wall and divided into separate compartments. The stream through the centre was dammed to provide fish ponds. The Elizabethan house was the successor to a medieval hunting lodge. The parish church stands just beyond the park wall.

The management of a deer park was the responsibility of the keeper or 'palliser', a term that has produced a distinctive Yorkshire and Durham surname. The deer in the medieval parks were native red and roe deer, and fallow deer that were probably introduced by the Normans. They needed a varied environment of open grassland, wood and coppice. Venison was not produced for the market but was a highly valued gift in aristocratic circles. Only the larger parks were used for hunting on a regular basis; in the smaller ones the keeper culled the deer as demand arose. For most of the year, parks were grazed not only by deer but also by cattle, horses and pigs, and some sections were devoted to the production of timber and coppiced wood. In winter, the deer were fed on hay and by browsing the woods, especially the leaves and bark of the holly trees that had been purposely planted there. In the late sixteenth and seventeenth centuries, when hunting deer declined as a sport, parks such as the one at Ecclesall were converted into coppice woods whose products attracted high prices from ironmasters and lead smelters.

Medieval deer parks were enclosed by a deep ditch and by an oak palisade, or a quickset hedge, fence or stone wall on the top of a high earthen bank. These barriers were costly and troublesome to maintain. Special leaps were contrived to allow wild deer to enter the parks but it was made impossible for the animals to escape. Parks were also provided with fishponds. An eighteenth-century engraving that is on display in Tankersley church and a map drawn by William Fairbank in 1772 show that the park also had paddocks, coppices, and fish ponds, and that the whole area was enclosed within a stone wall. A lease of 1653 refers to 'the wall and outmost fence of the said Parke'.[2]

The boundaries of Tankersley Park can be followed for 4½ miles along footpaths and by the side of hedges and walls, with the aid of such place-names as Park Side, which marks the boundary with Hoyland township, and Park Gate at the entrance to the golf course; the site of the nearby deer sheds is still remembered. The area to the south retains the name of the Warren and it is only in modern times that the Tankersley side of Warren Lane has been built upon; the older houses are all along the other side of the lane within the ancient parish of Ecclesfield. Warrens were originally those parts of a deer park that were set aside for breeding, and it was not until the fifteenth century that the name became associated with rabbits. As we do not have early references to this name it is not clear which type of warren was the source of the name.

The creation of the park seems to have stifled the development of the village, though the parish of Tankersley was never very populous. The church stands in a lonely position on the horizon at the edge of the park and only a few farmsteads remain at Upper Tankersley. The early eighteenth-century engraving shows that the village had already dwindled to its present size, and though ridge-and-furrow patterns and names such as Twelve Lands and Town Fields speak of former open-fields, these arable lands covered only a small area. Unfortunately for the historian, Pilley was always included with Tankersley in the medieval taxation returns, so it is impossible to say whether or not small farmers were driven away, as they were in the neighbouring lordship of Wortley, when Sir Thomas Wortley enclosed his park in the reign of Henry VIII.

It is worth considering whether the park altered the landscape in another way by diverting the old highway from Barnsley to Sheffield. The eastern boundary of the park almost coincided with that of the manor and park, and the road, instead of following the most direct course, loops around the park along this boundary. Examples could be cited from other parts of England to show that it was a common practice to divert a road upon the creation of a park, and in more modern times, in 1838, the same road from Barnsley to Sheffield was made to by-pass Worsbrough Park on its climb up the hill to Birdwell instead of following its ancient course through Worsbrough village.

The eighteenth-century engraving shows that a less important road climbed up Church Lane and then passed through the middle of the park along the present rough track that zig-zags around Tankersley Hall and along Black Lane to Harley Road and Wentworth. At that time, the present road that takes two sharp bends from Church Lane around the moated site and on towards Hoyland Common was not there. Most of the three or four thousand moated sites in England were constructed between 1150 and 1400,

The moat around the Old Rectory and Glebe Farm at Tankersley probably once enclosed the medieval manor house. The later road had to take two right-angled bends around it. A wall now hides it from view.

especially during the late thirteenth and fourteenth centuries, the peak period also for the creation of deer parks.[3]

It was not until the sixteenth century that it became fashionable to build country houses inside parks away from the villages. However, at Tankersley the ruins of the Elizabethan Old Hall - or Lodge as it was called in 1653 - incorporate a late medieval hunting lodge. The same movement into the park can be observed at Sheffield, where the Earls of Shrewsbury reconstructed a late-medieval Manor Lodge to replace the castle as their chief residence. The withdrawal from Tankersley village left the old moated site available for the rector and his glebe farm and it was one of these rectors, Richard Goodwin, who built the pigeon-house at the entrance to the site in 1735.

Only one rectangular block of the Old Hall survives, albeit in an advanced state of decay. The early eighteenth-century engraving shows it to have been a long structure with several projecting tower-like bays on the north front. In the fourteenth century Tankersley had passed to the Savile family, but in the reign of Queen Elizabeth George Talbot, the sixth Earl of Shrewsbury, held the wardship of the owner and he seems to have been responsible for the remodelling of the hunting lodge. A letter addressed to the earl in 1585 was sent from 'Your house at Tankersley', while another letter written by his son, Gilbert, the seventh Earl of Shrewsbury, in 1609, was headed more specifically as 'At Tankersley in bedd this Thursday'.[4] The continued use of the deer park is made evident by a letter from William Dickenson, bailiff of Hallamshire, to the sixth Earl in 1580, for it mentions 'A fine buck killed at Tankersley, which left not his make in all that parke'.[5]

An earlier documentary reference is found in a law suit of 1527 when Henry Savile was said to have been 'hunting at dere wythe houndes in hys parke of Tankersley'.[6] At the same time, Henry was involved in a bitter struggle with his neighbour, Sir Thomas Wortley, who had enclosed a deer park, which later came to be known as the Old Park, next to his manor house in Wortley. Savile claimed that the grant of free warren in 1303–4 meant that no-one could hunt in Tankersley lordship without his permission.

Wortley was a separate lordship within Tankersley parish, so the legal right was on the side of the Wortleys, but friction may have been caused by the inclusion of part of the township of Pilley in Wortley Park. It was certainly exacerbated by the rival personalties of the two lords. Henry Savile and his party frequently chased and killed deer in Wortley Park during the 1520s. They destroyed pales and rails and threatened William Patryche, the Wortley park-keeper, on two occasions in 1525 and 1526. In 1527 Henry

Savile and some of his men were charged in the Court of Star Chamber with breaking into Wortley Park at night time to hunt deer, armed with bows, arrows, bills, swords and bucklers, and accompanied with a pack of hounds. It was said that on one occasion they broke into the alehouse in Wortley and emptied barrels of ale in the street. Tempers ran high, and when Savile's party made a fresh invasion in 1527 they were assaulted by Patryche and forty men armed with bows and arrows. The following night Patryche assembled 200 men from a wide area and threatened Savile further.[7]

These measures seem to have had some effect, but after Savile's death, Robert Gargrave, esquire, took a lease of Tankersley and made fresh claims to have sole hunting rights in the disputed area. The Quarter Sessions recorded Patryche's statement that during February 1530:

> in the walking of his pale within the said parke, [he] perceyed and founde where a male dere had been killed within the same parke, and a crossbowe arrow and a knyff lying in the same place, where the faule of the same dere was, and also found within the seid parke other [two] male dere strekyn with arowes.

Patryche fetched his bloodhound and followed the trail through the broken fence to Tankersley, where he was immediately assaulted and his hound taken from him. The judgement of the court is not recorded, but the lords of Tankersley made no fresh claim on the hunting rights in Wortley Park.

In the 1630s Sir Thomas Wentworth, the first Earl of Strafford, became the owner of the manor of Tankersley and appointed his cousin, a member of the Rockley family, as master of the game in his park, with orders to keep the mansion house in repair, to preserve the woods, and to maintain the park and ponds. Soon afterwards, Wentworth was arrested – though not as legend would have it while he was seated under his favourite oak tree in Tankersley Park – and subsequently executed by order of Parliament. During the Civil War the Earl (later Duke) of Newcastle led 'a considerable party' of Royalist troops into South Yorkshire, and his duchess's memoirs recall that:

> they met about 2,000 of the enemy's forces, taken out of their several garrisons in those parts to execute some design upon a moor called Tankersley Moor, and there fought them, and routed them; many were slain, and some taken prisoners.

Unfortunately, there is just one other contemporary reference to the event and only a few cannon balls and bullets have been found to lend credence to the duchess's account.[8]

The Old Hall and the park survived the war and on 1 March 1653 a lease was taken by Sir Richard Fanshawe, esquire, of Ware (Hertfordshire), an old friend of the Wentworths and a member of a family from Dronfield parish in north Derbyshire that had long held, in succession, the office of the Queen's Remembrancer. Later references to the 'new park' and 'the present park' at Tankersley are explained by the clues in the lease which said that several closes which had been 'formerly used as parte of the [park], but then divided and severed from the deere' were to be restored to their former state. The stock of deer was increased to 280, holly and hay were to be used as winter fodder, and many oaks and yews were available for timber. Tankersley was undoubtedly a fine country seat and Lady Ann Fanshawe wrote in her memoirs:

> We lived an innocent country life, minding only the country sports and the country affairs … The house at Tankersley and park are both very pleasant and we lived there with great content.

Deer were kept at Tankersley for another two hundred years. In 1662 a local man was charged with 'coursing, hunting and killing of deare in Tankersley Park',[9] and when Daniel Defoe visited Yorkshire in the 1720s he was greatly impressed by their size:

> From Rotherham we turned north-west to Wentworth on purpose to see the old seat of Tankersley, and its park, where I saw the largest red deer that, I believe, are in this part of Europe: One of the hinds, I think, was larger than my horse.[10]

In the eighteenth century deer were often kept to adorn landscaped parks.

The natural beauty of the landscape was improved by the Marquis of Rockingham a generation or so later, when it became the national fashion to plant trees, create artificial lakes and erect follies. His account books for 1753 note 'A Plantation of Scotch Firs on the Side of the Hill in Tankersley Park next the Newbiggen Side',[11] and the map drawn for him in 1772 by William Fairbank marks a 'Rotunda or Deer House' in the middle of the park and also the 'Marchioness's Summer House' that Arthur Young had so much praised three years previously. This was a psuedo-Grecian structure, known in later times as 'Lady's Folly Tower', from where the Marchioness regularly admired the view. It was demolished in 1960, but a plaque marks the place where it stood on the top of the escarpment, near the third green on the present golf course.

Tankersley had been successfully converted from a medieval deer park to the more refined requirements of the eighteenth century. But its misfortune was that it was overshadowed by the magnificent house and landscaped grounds at Wentworth Woodhouse, the chief seat of the Marquises of Rockingham and their successors, the

Thomas Jeffreys's map of Yorkshire (1772) shows Tankersley Park under the ownership of the Marquis of Rockingham at Wentworth Woodhouse.

Earls Fitzwilliam. Though these noble lords occasionally visited the park at Tankersley, they did not live in the Old Hall, which was thus allowed to fall into decay. When Dr Richard Pococke travelled through the district in 1750–51 he wrote, 'I passed by Tankersley park, where there is an old ruined mansion house. Here the Marquis of Rockingham has red deer, and it is a very fine park'.[12]

Arthur Clayton showed how the Old Hall was dismantled and the destruction of the park begun with the erection of the two cottages that stand 300 yards inside the old park boundary by Hood Hill Plantation.[13] At the end of a rental of 1723 a note was added in different handwriting to record, 'Mr. Simpson a new farm out of the Park, and several other parts of the Park'. A series of household vouchers for 1732 shows that forty acres of land at the east side of the park had been measured and enclosed with quickset hedges. Sampson's farm buildings were (at least partly) constructed with stones from the Old Hall in the late 1720s and early 1730s. One of the cottages has a 1729 datestone, and a Wentworth voucher refers to work that was done in Tankersley Park from 21 August to 29 September 1732, 'helping to fill Stones for Sampson's Barne, Shifting the ston's att the old hall, helping down with the old Timber', etc. Another voucher dated 7 October 1732 mentions further work in pulling down part of the Old Hall and the process of demolition continued until only one wing of the hall was left standing.

Even while the park was being improved by landscaping its future was made doubtful by agricultural and industrial developments. The second Marquis of Rockingham was a keen experimenter. His memorandum book records that in 1753 a few acres of the park had been pared and drained and then sown – by means of a Jethro Tull seed drill – with turnips, sainfoin, and

This aerial view shows the rows of bell pits that were sunk to mine ironstone within Tankersley Park during the late eighteenth century. *Photo: Directory of Aerial Photography, University of Cambridge*

rye grass, and his account books for the 1760s contain numerous entries about improving parts of the park in this way. Yet it was his industrial enterprises that brought about the park's disintegration. These had already been foreshadowed in the seventeenth century when a deed that authorized the exchange of lands in 1639 in order to straighten the park wall referred to 'Coalpitt Close',[14] and when the 1653 lease expressly left the lord the right 'to sett one or more Iron Mills att his lordshipp's pleasure within the said new Parke'.[15] That option was never taken, but ironstone mining began during the next century.

The 1772 map marks 'Many New Ironstone Pits' along the southern boundary of the park, and the Warren was said to be 'full of Old Pits'. The slag heaps of the shallow bell pits used by the ironstone miners now form natural obstacles on the fairways of the golf course, and have given their name to Bell Pit Wood behind the Old Hall. More extensive mining of the Tankersley seam, as it became known along its entire course through South Yorkshire, began in the 1790s by John Darwin & Co., and much later, in the 1860s, the Tankersley Park Colliery started to work the seams of coal. A railway and a tram road were constructed across the park to connect the pits with the Thorncliffe and Elsecar Railway, and the remaining deer were finally moved from the park to Wentworth Woodhouse, two miles to the east.

With the closing of the colliery in 1927 the park began to recover much of its former character. The industrial monuments have mellowed with time and now add to the interest of the landscape; some are hidden within plantations. As early as 1907 the Newton Chambers Company at Thorncliffe had taken over the western part of the park and converted it into a nine-hole golf course. This was extended into a full-sized course after the Second World War, and so the old park now forms a welcome oasis among the neighbouring industrial villages. Even the M1 motorway has not destroyed its character and there are plenty of reasons to be grateful that a medieval deer park was created here seven hundred years ago.

Chapter 8

Wombwell Ings and Old Moor[1]

Ings

In the North of England and parts of the East Midlands low-lying meadows that were liable to flood and which were managed by a system of embankments, dikes and channels were known as ings, a word that was a dialect form of a Viking place-name element -*eng* which meant 'pasture, grassland'. The present 1:25,000 scale Ordnance Survey Explorer map 279 marks a series of fourteen ings in the lower reaches of the River Don, stretching from Bentley to Fishlake. Explorer map 278 is equally informative about the Dearne Valley, naming ings in the flood-plains of the townships of Wombwell, Darfield, Billingley, Bolton, Little Houghton, Mexborough and Denaby. The Wombwell Ings cover an especially extensive area of flood-plain that stretches above and below the confluence of the Rivers Dove and Dearne for almost 500 metres at its widest point.

It is clear from documentary records that these ings were farmed in common and managed as meadow. They were not grazed between late spring and the time when they were mown to provide a summer hay crop. Throughout medieval England, meadows were valued three or four times more than arable land, for hay was the main winter fodder for plough animals and livestock, with the corn fields also providing precious summer grazing after mowing. The fertility of these ings and their ability to produce annual crops of hay was maintained by the winter flooding of the rivers and the deposition of fine sediment, an essential source of nutrients when so much of the dung of the township stock went to fertilize the arable crops of the open fields. The amount of productive meadow in Wombwell explains why Joseph Hunter, South Yorkshire's leading antiquary, described the township in 1831 as 'an extent of agricultural ground remarkably rich and fertile'.[2]

The stoneless, alluvial gley soils of the Wombwell Ings were potentially the most fertile in the local landscape, but they were difficult to cultivate without control of the river flood waters and drainage of the high ground

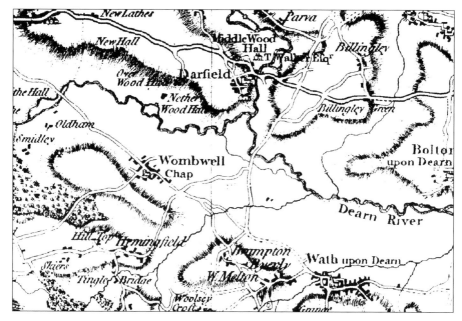

This detail from Thomas Jeffreys's map of Yorkshire (1772) shows the River Dove flowing into the River Dearne and separating Wombwell from Darfield in the low-lying area known as the Ings.

water-table. In early times occasional flooding of the Dearne and Dove rivers hindered communications across the valley bottom. In 1547, for example, it was stated that 'there is a water betwyn [Darfield] church and the chapel [in Wombwell], that th' inhabitantes there can by no means come to the sayd church at divers tymes'.[3]

The apparent peculiarity of a group of fields on the southern edge of the ings with the names Wombwell Top, Chirl Hill, Overhill, Broom Hill, Hard Hills and State Hills, most of them rising only a few feet above the flood-plain, may be explained by their having stood proud when the rest of the fields around were under water. Chirl Hill was land that once belonged to the churls, or free peasants; Overhill was where oats (haver) was grown; and State Hill was where draught horses (stots) grazed.

Old Surveys and Maps of the Wombwell Ings

Our major sources of information about the medieval farming system in Wombwell are two Tudor surveys, one made for Roger Wombwell, lord of the manor, in 1516[4] and the other made shortly afterwards for Healaugh Priory, which owned a small estate that was scattered throughout the township.[5] Roger Wombwell's survey is an invaluable resource for historians for it is the most detailed account that we have of any place in South Yorkshire in the late Middle Ages. Then, during the seventeenth and eighteenth centuries, Trinity College, Cambridge, owner of glebe land and a half share of the tithes of the people of Wombwell since the dissolution of the monasteries, also surveyed and mapped its properties in the township.[6] Many of the field names that were recorded in these surveys can be identified in the 1840 tithe award, whose accompanying map depicts the landscape just before the major changes that were brought about by railways and coal mining. Some of these names are still in use today.

The regularity of the pattern of farmsteads, tofts and crofts on both sides of the street that is depicted on the tithe award map[7] suggests that Wombwell was a planned medieval village. This suggestion is borne out by the 1516 survey, which notes that 28 of the properties, consisting of houses, barns, gardens and crofts, covered exactly one acre each. As the open fields began immediately north-west, south, and south-east of these properties, it is likely that they were laid out at the same (unknown) time as the village. The residential expansion of Wombwell to the south of the street which occurred with the advent of deep mining in the township after 1840 matches the extent of the former open fields almost exactly. Much could be said about them and about Wombwell Wood and the adjacent farms. They were all essential to the working of the local farming economy, but here we shall concentrate on the distinctive landscape of the low-lying lands by the Dearne and the Dove.

The two Tudor surveys show that the flood-plain land in Wombwell was arranged into blocks of land known as furlongs, each of which was divided into strips or doles (as strips of meadow were customarily called), in the same manner as the common arable fields. The tofts and crofts on the northern side of the village descended quickly to the flood-plain. Between the village tofts and Woodhall Park lay 'a meadow called Fuldewe', a name that was derived from 'a dirty, damp place'.[8] The tithe award of 1840 mapped Great and Little Full Dews, which covered 24 acres. To the east, closes stretched alongside Well Lane, a causeway, and Cuckstool Bridge on the way to the marsh and to the ings by the River Dove. The eastern boundary of the Well Lane closes curved along the line of the Crooked Syke, a natural drainage channel that wound its way northwards from the acid soils of Sour Lane Close near Wombwell Hall. The 1516 survey mentioned Well Lane, a furlong called Causey Lees, and the Crooked Syke. The Trinity College survey in 1620 noted that in the marsh the college held a rood (a quarter of an acre) of arable land and meadow abutting on the Crooked Syke on the south and the River Dove on the north. The canons of Healaugh also held half an acre in the marsh, consisting of arable and meadow by the Dove.

Another example of how the meadow furlongs were divided into strips or doles is provided by Haverhill, where Healaugh Priory's possessions averaged half an acre each. The lane rose to 81 feet above sea level at Broomhill furlong, where the canons had several strips or doles that varied in size from a rood to an acre, and Roger Wombwell owned nineteen strips covering eleven acres. All the other furlongs in this lowland area were divided in a similar manner. The furlong was the recognized unit within the township wherever land was farmed in common.

So, these sixteenth- and seventeenth-century surveys reveal that farming was organized communally in Wombwell and that these valuable meadows were shared between the farmers in small, scattered doles. Heaulaugh Priory's properties included six separate doles of meadow in the ings by the Dearne and Dove, ranging in size from three roods – a rood being a quarter of an acre - down to one as small as fourteen feet long. In 1516 Roger Wombwell had doles scattered throughout the various ings of his lordship. In Dove Ing furlong, for instance, he owned 52 doles, amounting to about eighteen acres; half the doles measured just one rood. In Dearne Ing he had a further 48 doles, amounting to 24½ acres and a few swaithes and small doles that were just fourteen feet wide.

The 1620 survey shows that Trinity College also had scattered properties in the ings, including seven acres of meadow in Deans Ing lying in seven separate doles south of the River Dearne. In 1690 a Darfield parish glebe terrier noted that each year these seven doles were exchanged with the parson's equal share of the glebe in Deans Ing, a hint perhaps that, as was customary on many other manors, the doles in the common meadows were once reallocated to the tenants on an annual basis so as to ensure fairness in the distribution of ground of varying productivity.

Meadow management and the Bulling Dike

The meadows of flood-plains need moist, fertile soils which are free-draining. Though in traditional systems such meadows could be inundated by river water for some weeks in winter, prompt removal of the surface water after the recession of the flood and good aeration of the alluvium during the growing season was essential. Ensuring this often involved the construction of drains and banks to manage the river waters. Alternatively, in 'water meadows' in the stricter sense, the land could be kept largely flood-free except where it was 'floated', either downwards, whereby river water was conducted along systems of channels through the meadows, or upwards, by blocking the flow of streams with dams and sluices. An inundation in spring ensured an early bite for grazing stock and substantial herbage in a summer hay crop.

The floating of meadows has usually been considered an Elizabethan innovation, but recent studies have noted much earlier examples.[9] The difficulty in studying the ings at Wombwell (with the loss of manorial records) is in knowing just what form of management was used and when. Some of the changes that were made to the system in later centuries can be identified, however.

Something of the way that the farmland of the Dearne Valley flood-plain was managed in the early modern period is indicated by the fining of

This aerial view of Wombwell Ings shows the Bulling Dike (centre) and the straightened course of the River Dove (beyond the modern ponds) as they approach their confluence with the River Dearne (bottom). The straight channels within the Ings correspond to the property divisions shown on 1795 and 1840 maps and may be older. Modern embanking has obliterated their former links with the dike and rivers. *Photo: English Nature, courtesy of Jeff Lunn*

farmers in the manor court of neighbouring Wath-upon-Dearne in 1617 'for not making up the bank of the brook end whereby the water runneth out of its right course to the mores and medowes beneath them', and by a seventeenth-century list of persons responsible for maintaining the dikes.[10] That some method of floating the Dearne Valley ings was in use in the early modern period is suggested by a reference to 'the floyt yate' (a West Riding dialect pronunciation of float gate) and 'a place called the Floyte' in a seventeenth-century Thurnscoe glebe terrier.[11] The Wombwell taxpayers in 1379 included Richard Diker, the only person with this surname in the Dearne Valley.[12] Was he the man in charge of the dike system or perhaps the descendant of the man who constructed it? At the very least, his name is evidence of man-made ditches on a considerable scale at this early date.

In Wombwell, the dike that was dug along the southern edge of the flood-plain of the River Dove to its confluence with the Dearne two miles downstream is known as Bulling Dike. The name was first recorded on a 1795 map and it perhaps came from a meadow that was grazed by the town bull after the hay was cut, for such field names are found in other parts of the country. The survey made for Trinity College in 1620 recorded a rood of land bordering upon 'bulling' and the River Dearne.

The lower course of the Bulling Dike flowing towards the River Dearne.

The Bulling Dike can still be followed through the flood-plain and into the River Dearne, but the upper part of its course is uncertain. Although the Tudor surveys do not name Bulling Dike, they use the name 'Butdykes' for what seems to be a section of it before it met the natural Crooked Syke, which was spring fed and wound its way to the Fleet Dyke near Broomhill and the 'gospytt dyke', which in 1516 led into the Ox Pasture and the Wet Moor. Gorse Pits Bridge is marked on the first edition six-inch Ordnance Survey map as the alternative name for the smaller of the two Marl Bridges – the northern one over the Dearne and the southern one over the Bulling Dike – which were rebuilt in stone in 1641.[13] We are left with the impression that the Bulling Dike was modified from time to time over the centuries.

Comparison of the various maps that are available also shows later changes to the management of the river waters. Some time between 1772 and 1795, the course of the Dove between Woodhall and the confluence with the Dearne was straightened and between 1795 and 1840 so was the stretch between Aldham Mill and Woodhall. We have no detailed records to show precisely when these changes came about but this period coincided with, first, the construction of the Dearne & Dove Canal through the flood-plain and, second, running parallel to it, the opening in 1840 of the Barnsley to Doncaster railway. Thereafter, the upper course of the Bulling Dike became obscured.

The Bulling Dike, under its various guises, clearly served to carry away the water from the springs below the sandstone brow, but it may also have been used to float the ings. Were the long, straight channels, some of which can still be seen running across Wombwell Ings from the Bulling Dike to the Dove, merely land divisions dating from the eighteenth century or were they originally part of a floating system? It is unfortunate that no estate or manorial records survive to enlighten us on this point.

The Old Moor

Another distinctive feature of the Dearne flood-plain is the occurrence among the field names of the element 'moor', as in Old Moor and Wet Moor in Wombwell and Great Moor, Well Moor and Wet Moor in neighbouring Wath. The meaning of the Old English word mor is complex[14] but implications of wetness or barrenness are certainly earlier than the modern notion of moor as heathy upland, and it may be that, at first, the term meant 'low-lying marshy place'.

On the generally very fertile Dearne flood-plain 'moor' may have been used to distinguish ground that was less productive for agriculture. Perhaps that was because the drainage of the flood-plain was here, for some reason, not so manageable, so the land could not be treated as meadow. Another possibility is that there was local accumulation of peat on the alluvium that was cut for fuel, though in the absence of manorial records we cannot say whether the Wombwell tenants had common rights of turbary. Interestingly, the term 'carr', signifying wet woodland, hardly figures in the place-names of Wombwell; it survives on the 1840 tithe map only in Fen Carr Close and Near Carr Close, two fields adjacent to the tiny Willow Holt towards the head of a side stream of Knoll Beck. Such a landscape element seems to have disappeared early from the valuable farmland of the flood-plain.

East of the old road from Rotherham to Pontefract which crossed the flood-plain at one of its narrowest points for several miles both upstream and down, enclosures that were known variously in the late eighteenth century as the hills, ings and moors of the Old Moor estate were also originally

The RSPB have converted the watery landscape of the Old Moor into a Visitor Centre with numerous hides for birdwatchers. This photograph was taken from one of them.

divided into furlongs. Both of the Tudor surveys refer to Old Moor in its unenclosed state. The 1516 survey noted 'Derne bank', which stopped the river overflowing into the ings, including the Lower Wet Moor or Deans Ing, which took its name from the Deyne family who were recorded in the Wombwell poll tax returns of 1379. The Trinity College survey in 1620 included 'half an acre in one land lyinge in the old moore' and another rood nearby. It also mentions the adjoining 'Common Pasture' or 'Ox Pasture', which was divided into properties as small as a quarter of an acre.

The Wet Moor formed the eastern extremity of Wombwell township, where the Knoll Beck flows into the River Dearne as it enters the township of Wath. In 1697 the Wath manor court ordered: 'That no person shall put any Beasts or horses into Weetmoor after the second day of February next' (Candlemas).[15] In 1776 the township of Wombwell's share of this Wet Moor measured 64¼ acres.[16] In 1516 Roger Wombwell owned about 29 acres there, scattered in 51 properties, including eighteen that measured a rood, seven half an acre, and thirteen a full acre. The lower lands were used for pasture, but the north-westerly half of the furlong consisted of arable lands.

Later Changes

In 1516 Roger Wombwell owned about 1,120 acres in Wombwell, but by 1764 the family's estate had more than doubled to 2,400 acres.[17] The steady accumulation had started with the acquisition of former monastic lands and had continued with the purchase of small freeholders' estates whenever they came on the market. The Wombwells were also the lessees of the half share of the glebe land that belonged to Trinity College. The enclosure of the common arable fields and the common ings was a gradual process, made possible by the overwhelming ownership of the lords of the manor, but achieved only piecemeal because of the presence of Trinity College. In 1743 the lord's and the college's properties in Deans Ing were so intermingled that the rector and leading parishioners were unable to distinguish them, but in the following year the college accepted a proposal that they should have instead four adjoining closes in the Ings, amounting to 35 acres. During the late eighteenth century, the flood-plain economy and landscape were altered upon the selling of land in lots and by the changes to the watercourses mentioned above. Wombwell Ings were no longer farmed communally and some of the new closes were converted to arable.

By the time of a survey in 1757,[18] the moors, ings and common pastures to the east of the Rotherham-Pontefract road had been enclosed within a new 256-acre property known as Old Moor Farm, though some of the field boundaries were subsequently altered up to 1776, when the Marquis of Rockingham of nearby Wentworth Woodhouse was the owner. It remained a working farm into modern times before it became the present nature reserve. The 1840 tithe award shows that some particularly substantial blocks of fields on Wombwell Ings and at Old Moor had been converted to arable cultivation. This must mean that, by that time, natural flooding had been prevented by embanking and drainage and that any system of floating was defunct enough to allow ploughing. Turning this most fertile land in the township to arable crop production would have been an appealing prospect if the flooding could have been controlled.

Between 1840 and c.1870 three collieries were opened in the township – Lundhill in 1855, Darfield Main in 1860 and Mitchell Main in 1870. An extensive network of railways was constructed to serve the collieries and the population more than doubled from 1,627 persons in 1851 to 3,738 in 1861. By 1942 the farmland had been reduced by about a third.[19] Since the collapse of the coal industry in the 1980s the landscape of Wombwell has undergone further dramatic change. The collieries have been obliterated, their spoil heaps levelled and their network of railways abandoned. Much former agricultural land has also been given over to the kind of mixture of light industry, distribution depots, retail parks and housing that is indistinguishable from regeneration projects elsewhere. Yet the Ings and Old Moor Farm remain welcome open spaces that can be explored by naturalists and landscape historians alike.

Chapter 9

The Transformation of Inclesmoor

Inclesmoor was the ancient name of the great marshy moorland in the eastern lowlands that stretched from Thorne in the south to Snaith in the north. The most likely explanation of the name is that it was derived from an Old Norse personal name, Enkil, but who such a person might have been we do not know. The place-name is first recorded about 1200. It was still in use as Inkle Moors in the Thorne tithe award of 1841, but it is hardly known today.[1]

In the Middle Ages some of the largest monasteries in Yorkshire benefited from generous grants by wealthy barons of rights to fish the extensive meres of these eastern wetlands of South Yorkshire, to dig 'turves' in the huge peat moors for sale as fuel far and wide, and to graze cattle on the extensive pastures. Kirkstall Abbey became the principal landowner in Bessacarr and in the early fourteenth century the Earl of Lincoln granted generous 'turbary' rights in the vast waste of Inclesmoor to the Abbey of St Mary's, York, one of the leading Benedictine foundations in the country.[2] The earl made further grants to other religious houses and distant institutions, all of which made great advances into the moor by digging peat for domestic and industrial fires on a huge scale. Enormous loads of 20,000 to 40,000 turves were transported by carts and boats from Inclesmoor to the towns of Doncaster, Hull, Selby, York, Wakefield, Leeds, Gainsborough and Lincoln. Inevitably, this reduced the level of the land and led to serious flooding. Similar monastic and lay activity in medieval East Anglia on an even greater scale produced a series of deep pits that became flooded and which now form the distinctive landscape of the Norfolk Broads.

Property rights on Inclesmoor had never been well defined and so the increased scale of digging meant that boundary disputes became common. In the winter of 1406–7 contention between the Duchy of Lancaster and St Mary's Abbey, York, over turbary and pasture rights led to the production of a map of Inclesmoor to help resolve the dispute.[3] This is kept in The National Archives and it has the distinction of being the oldest surviving

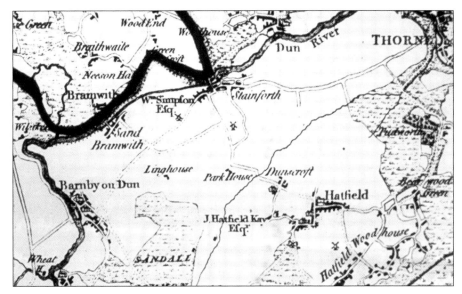

This detail of Thomas Jeffreys's map of Yorkshire (1772) shows the lowland district south of the River Don, with extensive commons before the era of parliamentary enclosure.

map of an English local district. It dates from more than two centuries before Vermuyden's drainage scheme and shows the wetlands bounded by the rivers Aire, Ouse, Humber and Trent, Don and Torne. Most of Inclesmoor lay in Yorkshire, but a part extended into Lincolnshire towards Crowle. The map depicted a vast tract of moorland, meres, pastures, a park, trees and plants, surrounded by market towns and villages that were connected by roads and bridges. Churches dominated the settlements and Thorne was shown with a stone tower on top of the Norman castle motte known as Peel Hill. The houses of the peasants were timber-framed and one building at Hatfield appears to have been supported at ground floor level by a base cruck frame.

When John Leland, the king's topographer, headed for Thorne about 1540, he saw a great mere, a mile or so wide, that was full of fish and wildfowl.[4] Fishing, fowling and the digging of peat were valuable by-employments for the farmers of this fenland district and generous common rights of pasturage were essential to their survival. But much of this district lay within Hatfield Chase, a huge hunting area that had belonged to the lords of Conisbrough castle until 1347, when it became a Crown property. A survey of 1607 concluded that red and fallow deer had become 'so unruly that they almost ruined the country'.[5]

An extravagant day's hunting, which was organized in 1609 for the eldest son of King James I was recorded later in the century by the diarist and historian, Abraham de la Pryme.[6] The party set off at Tudworth, where 'they all embarked themselves in almost 100 boats that were provided there ready, and having frightened some 500 deer out of the woods grounds and closes adjoining' they pursued them through the water to Thorne Mere 'and there up to their necks in water their horned heads raised seemed to present a little wood'. Several deer had their throats cut, while others were dragged by strong ropes around their heads and slaughtered on land.

In the late 1620s an ambitious drainage scheme was attempted on Hatfield Chase under the leadership of Cornelius Vermuyden, whose Dutch and Flemish company was offered a third of the reclaimed lands in this royal manor and the opportunity to purchase the Crown's share; the remaining third was divided among the local farmers in compensation for their loss of common rights. The meandering southern branch of the River Don was blocked so that the whole river flowed along the straight channel that had been cut from the northern course at some unknown date much earlier, perhaps as far back as Roman times. But this diversion resulted in the flooding of lands in Fishlake and Sykehouse that had not previously been at risk. In 1630 Richard Bridges of Sykehouse wrote as 'a woeful spectator of the lamentable destruction of my native soil and country'.[7] The foreign engineers were attacked by angry local farmers and some of them were killed before the problem was solved.

Vermuyden's scheme caused the decay of Tudworth on the former southern branch of the Don, but it helped Thorne to flourish as an inland port and small town after it had acquired the right to hold weekly markets and annual fairs in 1659, and it benefited the Dutch and Flemish settlers who improved much of the new land of the Hatfield Levels by the practice known as warping, whereby silt was deposited from controlled flooding. Meanwhile, many of the native farmers continued to farm in their accustomed manner. They grew oats, some winter corn, and rapeseed, and some were encouraged by the mild climate to cultivate hops for the market at Doncaster, but the district was noted principally for rearing and fattening cattle, together with some dairying and horse breeding. For instance, in 1697 Thomas Hoyland of Thorne, yeoman, had 32 beasts and five calves, a bull and five milk cows at the time of his death.[8] The wettest tracts of the moors remained out of bounds, for they could not be drained effectively until steam engines were used in the nineteenth century.

This map, based on the first edition of the six-inch Ordnance Survey of the mid-1850s, shows the market town and inland port of Thorne on the northern bank of the River Don, with long, narrow fields across former moors, and extensive wastes beyond.

The digging and transporting of 'turves' remained a regular employment for Thorne farmers long after Vermuyden's drainage scheme was completed. Probate inventories attached to Thorne wills regularly noted the value of 'turves on the moors'. In 1719, for instance, John Watson, a Thorne boatman, had 'Turf on the More £6, a little boat £5' and in 1726 Robert Ambler, another Thorne boatman, had 'Turfs on the Moors' worth £1. That same year, the inventory of William Middlebrooke, sailor ('mariner' in his will) recorded a substantial farm and 'Turves paid for Deliver'd & undelivered £10'. His part in 'Loppingtons Keel' was valued at £2.10s.0d. and his 'share Right and title of in and to the good Keel or Vessell called the Prosperous' was mentioned in his will. Most of the local farmers and boatmen operated at a modest level. In 1727, for example, Thomas Sutton of Thorne had '2 Cows an old boat & riggin £8.10s.0d., 2 small heiffers £2, Turves on the Moores £2.10s.0d.', and in 1739 Samuel Watson, a Thorne boatman, owned 'A Catch or Vessel' valued at £2.[9]

The reason why so many Thorne inventories recorded 'wood and turves' together is apparent from Dr Richard Pococke's record of his visit there in 1750:

I took a guide [from Hatfield], and went three miles to Thorn, riding a mile over a marsh through water, the floods here and in all parts being greater than have been known for many years. Thorn is a populous market town, and subsists by the water trade, by farming, and by the wood which they raise out of the moors; the oak they all call black-oak, and the firs moor-wood, they find it from two to three feet under ground; the deeper it is the better; that found near the clay or surface is rotten and good for nothing. At about the depth of 3 feet they meet with a white sand when they dig for peat and for this wood, and so throwing in the surface on the sand they plough it, and it makes very good land.[10]

Joseph Hunter knew these lowlands as they were before the Victorian drainage schemes. In 1828 he wrote that a remarkable feature of Hatfield Chase 'was, and still is, that very large tracts were covered with a thick crust of turf. Many thousand acres were in this state. Thorne-waste and Hatfield-turf-moor were entirely covered with it, and were once more extensive than at present, having supplied for many ages a great part of Yorkshire with much of its fuel'. He went on to say:

The turf consists of a congeries of the roots and fibres of about forty different species of plants, mixed with earthy matter. In some places it is several yards in depth, in others only a few inches. … In ordinary times the turf in its natural state was so soft that it was impossible to tread on it. A pole might with ease be thrust into it to the depth of several feet. … Firs have been found thirty yards in length, and oaks twenty, thirty, and thirty-five yards. … Trees of other species are found, as the ash, birch, yew and willow. But the fir is the most abundant. Large quantities of fir cones and hazel nuts are discovered.[11]

He also noted that the turf moors 'are covered with such plants as the heath, ling, and fern. The *myrica gale* is found in abundance, and a grass with a beautiful white tuft, called here the Cotton Grass.'

Modern Drainage and Peat Workings

Soon after Hunter wrote this account, an Act was passed to provide for the drainage of lands alongside the lower reaches of the Don from Doncaster and

Bentley to Fishlake and Stainforth. The award was signed in 1839 and Makin Durham, a Thorne engineer, was put in charge. Durham was also responsible for drainage works in Hatfield Levels and Thorne Moors and he became known as 'the second Vermuyden'. His work on Thorne Moors up to his death in 1882 was invaluable in restoring the fortunes of the Thorne peat-cutting industry at a time of increased demand for bedding for the growing number of horses. In 1900 Britain had an estimated 3½ million horses, of which 2 million were directly employed in agriculture; the rest were put to work on public transport in the populous towns and cities. The other uses to which peat from these wetlands was put included the production of paraffin, creosote, tar, methyl-alcohol, etc. and as an ingredient in cattle food. A Paraffin Mill, with four presses, remained in use on Thorne Moors until 1922.[12]

Meanwhile, the opening of the Stainforth & Keadby canal in 1802 had linked the Don and the Trent via Thorne for craft up to 200 tons. In 1874 John Murray described Thorne as:

> an active market town, carrying on considerable trade in corn, coal, and timber… the Quay called the Waterside [is] resorted to by sailing-vessels, and when the tide permits, by steamers from Hull.[13]

The peat that was dug on these moors in the nineteenth and early twentieth centuries was exported to most parts of England, except the South West, and to parts of Scotland, and sales were particularly strong in industrial

A photograph taken in 1969 of the peat moors near Hatfield and Thorne.

Peat being worked on the Hatfield and Thorne Moors in 1969.

Yorkshire, Lancashire and Cheshire. The modern workings on Thorne Moors began in 1894. Two years later, The British Peat Moss Litter Company was established by the amalgamation of four companies that operated between the Don and the Trent. Peat was exported via branch lines, which connected with the railways that bordered the moors, and by the continued use of canals. The BPMLC had a strong Dutch component and by 1900 Moorends had a small colony of about 100 Dutch immigrants who were employed in peat cutting. Dutchmen continued to arrive up to the outbreak of the First World War, but afterwards demand for peat declined sharply when motor transport began to replace the horse.[14]

The chequerboard appearance of cuttings and baulks from this period can still be seen, but from the 1960s to the 1990s, when the chief market for the peat on these lowland moors was for gardening compost, peat was extracted on an unprecedented scale by industrial strip milling. At the same time, however, a vigorous and ultimately successful public campaign was launched to protect this rare environment. The commercial milling of peat on Thorne and Hatfield Moors was stopped in 2001.

The Humberhead Peatlands National Nature Reserve

The 3,318 hectares (8,201 acres) of the Hatfield, Thorne, Goole and Crowle Moors are now known as the Humberhead Peatlands National Nature

Reserve.[15] They form the largest complex of lowland raised bog in Britain (31 per cent of the whole) and in 2004 they were designated a Site of Special Scientific Interest under the management of English Nature (now Natural England). They have special protection under the European Birds Directive and the European Habitats Directive, and they qualify as Wetlands of International Importance under the terms of the Ramsar Convention. A long-term project aims to restore abandoned workings to their former boggy condition, by the damming of some of the old peat drains and the formation of water-retaining compartments, in order to attract wildlife. People are encouraged to visit these wetlands by a network of waymarked walks, viewing platforms and hides, and a regular programme of guided walks, events and open days.

Chapter 10

The Old Halls of Worsbrough

In 1577 William Harrison wrote in his *Description of England* that 'the greatest part of our building in the cities and good towns … consisteth only of timber'. The same was true of the English countryside. Only when oak became scarce and many ancient woods were converted to the production of coppice underwood for fuel for the ironmasters and lead smelters did men turn instead to stone or brick. Two houses near the boundaries of the township and chapelry of Worsbrough – Houndhill and Swaithe Hall – illustrate this period of change by having an early part constructed of timber and newer wings built of stone.

Houndhill

Houndhill was – and in 1932 became again – the home of the Elmhirst family. The local origins of this family go back several centuries, for the surname was formed from 'the small elm wood on the hill' that is now known as Bank Top. The surname first appeared in surviving written records in 1340–42, when Robert of Elmhirst was recorded as a peasant farmer in the manor courts of Rockley and Worsbrough. His son, Richard, survived the Black Death of 1348–50 and in 1363 he was able to take a modest advantage of the changed circumstances to buy land at a moderate cost. When a poll tax was levied in 1379, however, the Elmhirsts were taxed only at the basic rate of 4d. and in 1409 John Elmhirst was still a manorial tenant at Elmhirst.[1]

His descendants improved the family's standing in a modest way, but it was not until the mid sixteenth century that they began to prosper as substantial yeomen, when Roger Elmhirst of Houndhill and Elmhirst (c.1520–94) took to sheep farming on a large scale. The ruins of his weaving mill, where the entire process of cloth-making and dyeing took place, can still be seen at Houndhill. In 1575 he bought the neighbouring Kendal Green House and its five fields; the name seems to have been associated with the distinctive green cloth that was made at Kendal in Westmorland. When he made his will in 1594, Roger described himself as a yeoman.

His son, Robert Elmhirst (1559–1618), who was described as a yeoman-clothier making 'Northern cloths' in 1615, built the timber-framed east wing of the present house at Houndhill. This wing now carries the date 1566 and the initials RE, but in Victorian times the inscription read 1606. Stanley Jones has argued that the presence of a large central chimney stack (an original feature of the wing) supports the later date and that the pattern of the timbers in the gable and the use of a cove at the gable ends remained fashionable into the seventeenth century, as at Oulton, near Wakefield (1611), and the demolished Gawber Hall, near Barnsley (1619). The ground floor of this timber-framed east wing provided a parlour and a kitchen.[2]

Robert's son, Richard (1597–1654), was the first of the family to be described as a gentleman. His fortunes rose when he worked for Sir Thomas Wentworth of Wentworth Woodhouse, the first Earl of Strafford. When Sir Thomas was appointed President of the Council of the North in 1629, Richard bought a town house and two cottages in York. He had become a rich man with a landed estate of 464 acres, centred on the 73 acres of Houndhill. In 1638 he wrote with satisfaction:

Our Family as I conceive assumed their surname from a messuage in Worsborough-dale in the County of Yorke, which now ys and for many Ages hath beene, our peculiar Inheritance, and doth not appeare by any

Houndhill as drawn for Joseph Wilkinson's *History of Worsborough* in 1872.

Evidence that I could ever yet see to have been the inheritance of any other family.[3]

He was a supporter of the Royalist cause and fortified Houndhill for the king in the Civil War. He planned to ring the house with a wall, but the physical remains of this work consist of just two cylindrical towers. He offered no resistance when Parliamentary troops arrived and he had to pay substantial fines to keep his property.

The man who was responsible for the new stone wing at Houndhill was another Richard Elmhirst (1640–73), the nephew of the Richard Elmhirst who died in 1654. The house has an H-plan, with two parallel wings joined by a narrow hall block, which contained the principal entrance. The hall block and the west wing, which consisted of a little parlour, a little dining parlour, chambers and closets above and a cellar below, were constructed with ashlar stone and supported by a king-post roof. In 1672 Richard paid tax on eleven hearths there, so it was completed before he died at an early age. In the following year the property passed to his youngest sister, Mary, whose second husband, Samuel Saltonstall, was described as a gentleman when his probate inventory was appraised at Houndhill in 1690.[4]

The rooms that were listed in the inventory correlate closely with the principal divisions of the present house. On the ground floor they consisted of a hall, parlour, little parlour, little dining parlour, kitchen, and a pantry with a cellar. The upper rooms were described as the red chamber, yellow chamber, stairhead chamber, kitchen chamber, little kitchen chamber, and a closet, and the outbuildings comprised a malt chamber, brewhouse, wainhouse, and stable. His farm stock at Houndhill consisted of four cows and a calf, 45 sheep and twelve lambs, three horses and a mare, a sow and three pigs, seven acres of oats and peas, two acres of hardcorn (a mixture of wheat and rye), and 4½ acres of barley. He also kept a large flock of sheep and a herd of heifers on the edge of the Pennine moors above Dunford Bridge, many miles to the west.

Swaithe Hall

Swaithe is a place-name of uncertain origin that was first recorded in the late twelfth century.[5] A family called Swathe paid poll tax there in 1379, but little is known of the history of this remote spot on the north-eastern edge of Worsbrough township until the Micklethwaites arrived in the sixteenth century. They had taken their name from the *mickel thwaite*, the 'great clearing' between Silkstone and Cawthorne that became known later as Banks Hall, and their main residence was at Ingbirchworth in the parish of Penistone. A James Micklethwaite (1509–47) was living at Swaithe in 1544, when he was mentioned in his cousin John's will. [6] He may have been the man who erected the timber-framed hall block with a king–post roof that has been dendro dated to sometime after 1522.[7]

Richard's son, William Micklethwaite (1532–95) was planning an update of the house just before he died. In his will he left 'all the slate stone which is provided towards my new kitchen ... all my timber which is felled towards building ... [and] all the glass standing in the windows about the house'.[8] Timbers in a north–south range have been dendro dated to 1597–8, but the process of rebuilding was a slow one. A Victorian drawing of Swaithe Hall shows a datestone over the front door, inscribed 'R 1618 M'.[9] This has since been removed, but the initials were those of Richard Micklethwaite.

This Richard Micklethwaite married Diana Wordsworth at Worsbrough church in 1605. They had two daughters, but no sons. The eldest daughter, Margaret, married Richard Elmhirst of Houndhill; their other

Swaithe Hall in 1972, showing the timber-framed house, Richard Micklethwaite's gabled wings of 1618, and Joseph Mitchell's Victorian hall to the left.

daughter married Henry Wordsworth of Penistone. The family ties with the Wordsworths continued when Elizabeth, the daughter of Richard Micklethwaite's second marriage, married Ralph Wordsworth of Water Hall, gentleman (1591–1663) at Penistone. Ralph Wordsworth built the present, gabled Water Hall and the barn, which has a 1641 datestone. Their eldest son, John Wordsworth (1626–90), moved to Swaithe, while their second son, Josias, inherited Water Hall.[10]

The Wordsworths had settled in Penistone in the late fourteenth century and had become a prolific family in the parish and at Lower Falthwaite, Stainborough (the home of the poet's ancestors). Meanwhile, Elias, son of John Micklethwaite of Ingbirchworth, had moved to York, where he became a successful merchant, twice lord mayor, and an MP, before he died in 1632. Twenty years later, his son, John Micklethwaite of York, gentleman, sold to John Wordsworth, for £2,600, 'the capital messuage of Swaithe Hall' and another house in Lower Swaithe.

John Wordsworth was taxed on nine hearths at Swaithe in 1672.[11] It was probably he who rebuilt the wings in stone. He married four times. His first wife was Mary, the daughter of Sir Edward Rhodes of Great Houghton. His second was Sarah, the daughter of William Spencer, esquire, of Bramley Grange; the third was Deborah, the daughter of Robert Hyde of Denton, near Manchester; and the fourth was a daughter of Richard Micklethwaite, the former owner of Swaithe Hall. All these families were Puritans in the early seventeenth century, Parliamentarians during the Civil War, and fervent Nonconformists during the reigns of Charles II and James II.

The famous Nonconformist preacher, the Revd Oliver Heywood, was a frequent guest at Swaithe Hall in the 1660s–80s and he led many services there. Swaithe, Great Houghton, and Water Hall and Bullhouse Hall in the parish of Penistone served as his headquarters when he visited South Yorkshire. Another regular visitor to Swaithe, the Leeds antiquary, Ralph Thoresby, regarded John Wordsworth as 'the good old gentleman'.[12]

John's religious zeal was reflected in the choice of name for his son and heir, Eliasaph, an obscure biblical name taken from The Book of Numbers, chapter 1, verse 14. When Eliasaph married Mercy Jackson of Leeds, they set up home at Lower Swaithe Hall, known later as Swaithe House, on which they inscribed their initials and the date 1681. Eliasaph died young and Mercy returned to her native district. In 1690, shortly before his death, John Wordsworth sold Swaithe Hall to Captain Rhodes of Great Houghton, for £1,640. Nearly two centuries later, a large Victorian mansion was added to the old Swaithe Hall by Joseph Mitchell, a local colliery owner.

Rockley Hall

Rockley, the 'clearing noted for its rooks', was first recorded in a document that can be dated between 1185 and 1215.[13] This secluded estate on the western edge of the chapelry of Worsbrough belonged to a family that was descended from Robert of Rockley, who seems to have been the son of William, the younger son of the Fitzwilliams, the knights of Emley and Sprotbrough. The Rockleys lived in the predecessor of the present Rockley Old Hall, which in their time seems to have been surrounded with a moat. About 1280, however, the Rockley estate was acquired by John de Everingham, who had moved from the place of that name in the East Riding about thirty years earlier when he had inherited Stainborough through marriage.[14]

A younger branch of the Rockleys was seated a little higher up the valley in a house that they called Rockley Hall and which became known much later as Rockley Abbey. In 1379 the poll tax returns for Worsbrough township were headed by the two knights, Adam de Everingham and Robert de Rockley.[15] The two families quarrelled violently over Rockley Old Hall, including an ugly brawl in Worsbrough church, but neither physical force nor litigation changed the situation. The Everinghams remained the owners of Rockley Old Hall for three centuries.

In the sixteenth and seventeenth centuries the younger branch of the Rockleys profited from ironstone mining and charcoal burning in their woods and the working of a water-powered bloomery at Rockley Smithies. They lived at Rockley Hall (known later as Rockley Abbey) until 1724, when large mortgages forced them to sell to Thomas, Earl of Strafford, of Wentworth Castle. As prominent local Royalists they had suffered heavy losses during the Civil War. Yet in 1660 Francis Rockley, esquire, was ranked with Thomas Edmunds, esquire, of Worsbrough Hall as the wealthiest payer of poll tax in the township.[16] By 1672, however, they had slipped down the league, for Mr Jarvis Rockley was taxed on only six hearths, compared with the thirteen hearths of Worsbrough Hall and five other houses in the township with more than six. Clearly, they had not been able to modernize and enlarge their house. By 1702 Catherine Rockley, the heiress, was beginning to mortgage Rockley Hall and its lands heavily and she was eventually ruined by reckless projects. The last of the Rockleys, Robert of Woodsome Lees in the parish of Almondbury, died in 1772.

The former prominence of the Rockleys is evident from their monuments in the parish church. In 1409 Sir Robert Rockley founded the chantry of St Ellen (later, re-dedicated to St Catherine) at the east end of the north aisle, where his tomb is built into the north wall. Through marriage, he or his namesake had also held the sub-manor of Bolsterstone within Hallamshire. Between this chapel and the chancel a tomb chest commemorates Thomas Rockley, who died in 1503. The most eye-catching of these monuments, however, is found on the south side of the church, where Roger Rockley, who died in 1534, is represented in a timber monument as a knight on the upper level and as a skeleton below.

In 1573 financial extravagance by Henry de Everingham forced him to sell Rockley Old Hall to William Walker. Nothing is known about the purchaser's background, except that he also farmed at Kendal Green near by, but his descendants lived at the Old Hall for over a century. An *inquisition post mortem* of another William Walker of Worsbrough, yeoman, in 1641 recorded '1 messuage called the Old Hall alias Rockley Old Hall alias Rockley manor house'. [17] His son, Dr Obadiah Walker, became a famous theologian and Master of University College, Oxford. The Walkers built the earliest parts of the present hall, which was much enlarged later by George Milner, the son of William Milner of Burton Grange.[18]

Rockley Hall as drawn for Joseph Wilkinson in 1872.

Rockley Old Hall has no datestone and its details are sober and conservative, but it was evidently built in stages. The second and third gables from the left are smaller and of a different pitch from the other three, and the central door lintel is much larger than the rest. At the rear, this part of the house is marked by a string course and an eight-light mullioned-and-transomed window and it does not extend as far as the wings. Traces of the medieval house of the Everinghams can be found inside, but the yeoman Walkers must have rebuilt it sometime after 1573. They were probably also responsible for the gabled wing to the left, for such single projecting wings were in vogue in South Yorkshire during the first half of the seventeenth century.[19]

The property eventually passed to the Milners, who late in the Stuart era added the two-bay wing on the other side. By the 1740s Rockley Old Hall formed two separate dwellings, one the home of a clergyman and the other that of a gentleman.[20] Later still, it was made into three houses and by the nineteenth century it had degenerated into an ordinary farmstead. Joseph Wilkinson, the Victorian historian of Worsbrough, wrote:

> The situation is a very secluded one, and not near any public line of road, being almost lost among the woods and solitude in which it is situated.[21]

In the 1970s, the Old Hall and its outbuildings were converted into modern residences.

Worsbrough Hall

The hearth tax returns for the township of Worsbrough in 1672 began with Henry Edmunds, esquire, who was taxed on thirteen hearths. The large stone hall that his father had built dominated the village that clustered around the church and the grammar school. In contrast to the scattered settlements of the outlying parts of the township, Worsbrough was a typical estate village.

Thomas Edmunds (c.1596–1662), the man for whom the hall was built, was a newcomer to Worsbrough. He was the son of John Edmunds of Dalton and his wealth came from his position as Secretary to Sir Thomas Wentworth of Wentworth Woodhouse, the Earl of Strafford. Thomas Edmunds became a considerable landowner in various parts of Yorkshire, but chose Worsbrough as his main residence because it was close to Wentworth. After the execution

Samuel Buck's sketch of Worsbrough in 1719 or 1720, entitled 'The North Prospect of Worsper Village'. Worsbrough Hall is to the right of the tree on the left of the drawing.

of the Earl of Strafford, he continued to champion the Royalist cause from the garrison in York and so, when the Parliamentary forces triumphed, he was fined heavily. The Restoration of King Charles II two years before his death enabled him to recover his losses.[22]

Worsbrough Hall was built entirely in ashlar stone. No trace of a previous building survives. We have no records about its construction, but we can date it with reasonable confidence to the 1630s, before the outbreak of Civil War. It has a three-bay central block, with large mullioned-and-transomed windows in the upper storey and smaller mullioned windows below the string course. A three-storeyed porch provides the main entrance between two of the bays. The west wing was probably the service end, for it is of simpler construction than that to the east, which seems to have contained parlours and chambers.

Thomas's son, Henry Edmunds, JP, married Jane Robinson from the East Riding, but she died and so did their infant child. His second wife was Elizabeth, the daughter of Sir Gervase Cutler of Stainborough. She was the widow of Sir Thomas Herbert of York, baronet, traveller and man of letters, and very well connected to gentry families. Henry died in 1709, about twelve years after his wife. His brother, Thomas, who lived with him, died the same day. Henry had no children, but Thomas's son continued the line. Upon the death of Francis Offley Edmunds in 1831, Worsbrough Hall passed to his nephew, William Bennet Martin, Esquire, of Colston Bassett, Nottinghamshire, who built a large extension to the hall, in a similar style, and landscaped a small park, which involved the diversion of the turnpike road away from the village. His descendants profited greatly from the coal mines that were sunk on their Worsbrough estate, but the spoiling of the environment led them to move out of the district. The hall survived because it was converted into offices for the National Coal Board. It now stands amidst a modern housing development.

The family backgrounds of the owners of these four halls in Worsbrough township differed considerably. The Rockleys started off as medieval knights, the Elmhirsts as peasants. The Wordsworths were ardent Nonconformists, while the Edmundses and the Elmhirsts benefited from the fruits of political office under their mighty neighbour, the first Earl of Strafford, championing the Royalist cause. It is remarkable that all four houses survive.

Chapter 11

Bricks and Pantiles

B rick is such a common building material throughout South Yorkshire that it is hard to realize that, before the seventeenth century, it was used here only in prestigious buildings. Indeed, it was well into the eighteenth century before bricks became widely accepted in the west. The baptism and burial registers for the large parish of Sheffield between October 1698 and September 1703 noted just one brickmaker amongst the 1,149 men whose names were recorded. The first public building in the town that was built of brick was the Upper Chapel in 1700.[1]

The eastern parts of England were short of both timber and stone and so brick was used there in the late Middle Ages. The rich merchants of the East Riding led the way with such notable buildings as Holy Trinity church, Hull, and Northgate Bar, Beverley. No other part of England used brick on such a scale at so early a date. Then, during the fifteenth century, brick began to be favoured for prestigious buildings, such as the castles at Tattershall (Lincolnshire) and Kirby Muxloe (Leicestershire), houses such as that of the abbot of St Mary's, York, which became known later as the King's Manor, and for colleges and schools, notably Eton.

Archbishop Thomas Rotherham (1423–1500), a native of Rotherham who rose to be Archbishop of York and Chancellor of England, was one of the greatest builders and benefactors of his age. His palace at Bishopthorpe on the outskirts of York was built of brick and so was the College of Jesus that he founded in his native town, close to the parish church, in the early 1480s. This was the first brick building in South Yorkshire and 'as red as Rotherham College' became a local saying. When John Leland visited the town about 1540 he saw 'a very fair college sumptuously buildid of brike for a provost, v prestes, a schole-master in song, and vi chorestes, a schole-master in grammer, and a nother in writing'.[2] The college lasted just 64 years before it was dissolved by King Edward VI in 1547. A former pupil wrote in 1591 that it was:

A fair house, yet standing; but God knoweth how long it shall stand; for certain brick chimneys, and other brick walls (for it is all made of brick) is decayed and fallen down for lack of use; for there hath been few persons, and sometimes none at all, of long time dwelling therin.[3]

The ruins are incorporated within a modern department store, but only a few features are displayed.

Brick was not used again in a major South Yorkshire building until the 1570s, when George, the sixth Earl of Shrewsbury and his wife, Bess of Hardwick, were given the daunting task of holding Mary, Queen of Scots in custody for fourteen years. The old hunting lodge in the deer park that stretched from the River Sheaf up the hillside to the east of the castle and town, had already been converted into a country house in the 1520s and 1530s. Now, it was made into a much more splendid residence that was largely built of local stone, but with the main entrance framed by two octagonal brick towers. One of them was still standing when S. H. Grimm painted a view of the ruins about 1790.[4]

Low Grange at Thurnscoe was re-fashioned in Georgian times, but its walls retain Tudor blue brick patterns set amongst the red. The original house was built for John Constable, a Nottinghamshire gentleman.

More substantial remains of an early brick building can be seen at Low Grange, Thurnscoe. The Cistercian monks of Roche Abbey had erected a grange there, but the sole reminder of their presence is part of a fourteenth-century cross-slab grave cover that bears a worn cross head with 'ivy-leaf' terminals and which is built into the south-east face of the garden wall. After the dissolution of the abbey, John Constable, a gentleman from Nottinghamshire and a younger son of an East Riding family, bought the grange. He seems to have built the earliest part of the present house. Was he, perhaps, familiar with brick buildings before he settled in South Yorkshire? No other brick houses were built within many miles of Thurnscoe until long after his time. It remains a remarkably early example.

Peter Ryder's survey of the building in 1979 showed that part of Constable's house forms the south-eastern section of the long block that comprises the main front and which is entirely built of brick.[5] The three exposed walls all show remains of diaper work, that is a pattern of lozenge designs set out in blue brick on the red in the late-medieval and Tudor manner. This decoration indicates an early brick house of some social standing. In the eighteenth century it was given a pediment and new sash windows, but an earlier two-light mullioned window, now much decayed, can still be seen at the head of the south-eastern gable.

In the seventeenth century both the extension at the north-western end of the original building and the wing to the rear were built of brick with stone quoins and with stone surrounds to the door and windows, probably by Thomas Sheircliffe, a younger son of the family at Whitley Hall, Ecclesfield. Various mullioned and mullioned-and-transomed windows survive, together with two four-centred doorheads. The stone plinth of the north-eastern gable of the rear wing bears the incised date '1664'. Close by, is a fine barn of seventeenth-century date, whose brick walls, with stone quoins at the angles, mask a timber arcade of nine bays.

John Constable was a relatively small landowner to choose brick for his house at Thurnscoe. In the western half of South Yorkshire, beyond the magnesian limestone belt, brick remained an unusual building material throughout the seventeenth century. The only other example that is known to us was the great house that Sir Thomas Wentworth, first Earl of Strafford and King Charles I's leading minister, built at Wentworth Woodhouse. It served a household of 64 persons, including 49 servants, and it was taxed on 43 hearths in 1672.[6] Some of the fabric is incorporated in the great eighteenth-century house, but neither the remains nor a plan of c.1725 fit the drawing of a building that appeared in Hunter's *South Yorkshire* in 1831.[7] We cannot be certain that this etching of a large, symmetrical house of three storeys, with two detached lodgings connected to the main building by covered galleries, is indeed a view of the old house at Wentworth.

In 1696 the Wentworth estate passed to Thomas Watson-Wentworth, the nephew of the second earl. When his son and namesake inherited the property in 1723 he set about building a new house in the Baroque style, facing the village. This building remains in private ownership in a secluded position behind the later Palladian range, so it is not well known. It is largely built of pink brick but with a liberal amount of stonework on the gaily decorated façade. The Palladian building, which was begun soon after this west range was completed, did not use brick and thereafter stone was favoured for the country houses of South Yorkshire.

Meanwhile, however, the use of brick had spread down the social scale to the ordinary farmhouses and cottages in the lowlands around Doncaster, where suitable building stones were not available when the old tradition of timber-framed houses came to an end. References to Brickhill Carr and

When Thomas Watson-Wentworth II inherited the Wentworth Woodhouse estate in 1723 he built a house in the Baroque style, mostly of brick. Both the style and the use of brick soon went out of fashion, so he then built the huge Palladian range in stone that faces the other way.

Tylehouse Kilne in a 1607 survey of Hatfield show that bricks were being made locally by the beginning of the seventeenth century.[8] The Dutch and Flemish families that settled in Hatfield Chase after Vermuyden's drainage scheme in the 1620s had long been familiar with brick houses roofed with pantiles in their native lands. During the late 1690s one of their descendants, Abraham de la Pryme, wrote in his unpublished history of the village of Hatfield:

> The manner of the building that it formerly had were all of wood, clay, and plaster, but now that way of building is quite left of, for every one now, from the richest to the poorest, will not build except with bricks: so that now from about 80 years ago (at which time bricks was first seen, used, and made in this parish), they have been wholly used, and now there scarce is one house in the town that dos not, if not wholy, yet for the most part, consist of that lasting and genteel sort of building; many of which are also built according to the late model with cut brick and covered over with Holland tyle, which gives a brisk and pleasant air to the town, and tho' many of the houses be little and despicable without, yet they are neat, well furnished, and most of them ceiled with the whitest plaster within.[9]

The gypsum plaster was 'digged up in great Quantity and plenty' near by in the Isle of Axholme. A few undated examples of these seventeenth-century houses survive in Hatfield, but the earliest brick house that can be dated precisely is one that was built near Sykehouse in 1702. Occasionally, a building in the Yorkshire countryside bears the name 'Red House' to remind us that its builder was the first to use bricks in his locality. One of the best known stands north-west of Adwick-le-Street, near the A1 motorway.

Surviving probate inventories that were attached to the wills of lowland farmers provide occasional evidence of individual enterprise. In 1719 Thomas Wilson of Trumfleet in Kirk Sandal parish had a brick kiln valued at £5 and he was owed a guinea by John Revell for supplying 3,000 bricks. In the same year, Thomas Mallinson of Kirkhouse Green in the parish of Kirk Bramwith had bricks in his yard that were priced at £3.15s.0d., and in 1727 Francis Shepherd, a Stainforth husbandman, had 'a Brick Hill' worth £5.[10]

These new brick houses were roofed with pantiles in the Dutch manner. 'Pan' is a Dutch word for curved red tiles. They were commonly brought from Holland to Hull as ballast in the seventeenth century before they were

From the seventeenth century onwards brick buildings with pantile roofs became the common style in the eastern lowlands around Hatfield.

first manufactured locally. An early record tells us that in 1704 Doncaster corporation built two new houses at Rossington that were covered in pantiles that had been made in Hatfield.[11]

In earlier times, thatch had been the usual roofing material in both the countryside and the towns. A survey of the main street of Wombwell in 1516 recorded 40 houses that were roofed with straw, fourteen roofed with stone, and one that was half-roofed with stone and half with thatch.[12] Other surveys provide glimpses of the same practice. In 1611 William Fenton of Wadsley had a dwelling house, a parlour, and a barn 'all covered with straw in great decay'; Philip Asburrie of Owlerton rented '1 dwelling house and Kitchin 3 baies and an outshutt thatch saveing the Kitcin [which] is nue and slated and an old barn of 3 baies thatcht'; and George Oxspring of Sheffield had 'A Thatcht house of 3 baies butting west on the street … alsoe a new dwelling house slated of a bay and a halfe, A Stable 1 bay, and an outshutt thatch, a barn 2 baies slated'.[13] In 1616 Richard Archdale of the Brushes had merely a 'Dwelling house and mistall [cowshed] of 2 Baies Thatcht', but a note was added in 1672 to say, 'now 7 Bay all slated'.[14]

During the late seventeenth and eighteenth centuries pantiles became very fashionable in many parts of eastern England. In South Yorkshire their use soon spread from the lowlands on to the magnesian limestone. For example, in 1694 Ralph Thoresby, the Leeds antiquary, noted in his diary a journey through Stapleton, to the north of Campsall, which he described as 'a pretty village, where the Dutch tiles are much used'.[15] Converting the roofs of old thatched houses was a straightforward job, for the pitch did not have to be altered, but pantiles were easily lifted by the wind and so rain percolated the interior rubble of the walls. The new stone houses that were erected in the villages on the magnesian limestone belt therefore adopted the practice whereby a bottom course of heavy stone slates kept the roof secure. Another change that was often made in brick buildings was the replacement of mullioned windows by sliding-sashes, which were an innovation of the 1680s that combined practical value with aesthetic appeal. An early example is Grange Farm, Moss, which is dated 1705.

Brick was adopted much more slowly at the vernacular level in the western parts of South Yorkshire, though they were used for industrial buildings,

The villages on the magnesian limestone were built in local stone, but pantiles replaced thatch as the roofing material. These nineteenth-century houses in the lower part of Hooton Pagnell are typical in their use of a course or two of heavy coal-measure sandstone slates to prevent wind and rain from penetrating the roof space.

such as the Catcliffe glasshouse and the pottery kiln that survives on the outskirts of Swinton. The change occurred more quickly in Sheffield than in the surrounding countryside. Once the new fashion was accepted, rich and poor families alike saw the cost advantages in turning from stone to brick, for brick-making earths were plentiful on the edges of the town. By 1764 the Reverend Edward Goodwin could write that, 'The buildings are in general of brick', and in 1819 Joseph Hunter observed that, 'A few of the old stone buildings remain: but brick, as being the much cheaper material is now chiefly in use for dwelling-houses and manufactories'.[16]

The bricks that were used in these early centuries were hand made. In Yorkshire, they vary in colour from the orange-red of Burton Agnes Hall, near Bridlington, to the dull browns of the central Vale of York, depending on the nature of the local clays and the methods used in the firing process. They gave each district a distinctive character. With the coming of the canals and the railways all this changed. The new rows of terraced houses that were uniformly built with machine-made bricks and Welsh blue slate roofs looked much the same wherever they were erected.

Chapter 12

On the Limestone North of the Don

Running up through the centre of South Yorkshire, a narrow band of magnesian limestone, never more than five miles wide, forms a distinctive landscape that is utterly different from the moors and the coal-measure sandstones to the west and the lowlands to the east. It provides a welcome stretch of countryside, many of whose villages have a decidedly old-fashioned air and a character that is very different from the neighbouring pit towns and villages on both sides. Some of the old settlements, such as Conisbrough, Dinnington and Maltby to the south of the Don and Adwick-le-Street to the north, were altered radically by coal-mining in the twentieth century, but others were preserved by great lords or village squires, who benefited from the royalties that came from the coal seams under their estates but who kept the colliers' houses well out of sight.

The special character of this district goes back thousands of years, for the fertile soils that overlie the limestone attracted settlers from very early times. Aerial photographs have revealed a remarkable series of crop marks, which show that the cornfields were farmed during the Iron Age and the Romano-British period.[1] A prehistoric and Roman ridgeway that ran all the way along the magnesian limestone belt can be recognized by numerous 'street' names, some of which are marked on large-scale Ordnance Surveys maps, and by its continued use as a boundary between ancient parishes. This ancient route crossed the River Don between Conisbrough and Mexborough at Strafford Sands - the 'street ford' where the wapentake of Strafforth met from Viking times onwards - and continued north as Street Lane dividing the parish of Barnburgh from High Melton and that of Hooton Pagnell from Brodsworth, then as Old Street dividing Hooton Pagnell from Hampole. A Bronze Age barrow once marked the junction between the parishes of Barnburgh, High Melton and Marr.[2]

Such was the intensity of the farming in early times that nearly all the local woods had been cleared before the Norman Conquest. The few woods that remained provided timber for building and underwood for a whole host of purposes. One rare survival is Hampole Wood on the borders of Hampole, Brodsworth and Hooton Pagnell. In the Middle Ages it belonged to the nuns at Hampole Priory, which had been founded by 1156. Nothing remains of the priory, north of the present village, though a few architectural fragments can be seen in some of the local gardens, yet the wood survives. When the sixteen nuns were forced to leave in the late 1530s, a survey of their properties included a 120-acre wood, 'in which are 18 coppices called haggs, viz. 1 of the age of 18 years another of the age of 17 years and so in succession from year to year'. The wood had been carefully managed.[3]

In the Middle Ages the farming families of this district lived in compact villages, which were surrounded by arable land that was worked on the open-field system. The quality of the soils attracted a relatively dense population and so the parishes were similar in size to the small ones of Midland England and unlike the large, rambling ecclesiastical units that characterized the rest of South Yorkshire. Yet, on the whole, the parish churches in this fertile area have remained modest in size, for the district was badly affected by the Black Death and other disasters during the fourteenth century, when the population shrank dramatically.

Late Medieval Decay

In 1253 Geoffrey Luttrell, lord of Hooton Pagnell, obtained a royal charter to hold a Thursday market and a three-day fair during the feast of St Lawrence. The stump of a medieval market cross still stands on a firm base in the village street. Hundreds of village markets and fairs such as this, up and down the land, came to an end during the long economic depression of the late Middle Ages. Amongst the 40 married couples and 29 single persons who paid poll tax at Hooton Pagnell in 1379, only two tailors and a smith were taxed at more than the basic rate of fourpence.[4] The traders had gone.

A similar fate befell the Thursday market and annual four-day fair that Henry de Laci, lord of the honour of Pontefract, founded in 1293–94 at Campsall, though the initial prosperity of these events is evident from the 1334 taxation returns, when the inhabitants of Campsall made the fourth highest contribution in the whole of South Yorkshire.[5] The 1379 poll tax returns record a chapman (or middleman) and twelve craftsmen there, but in 1627 a survey reported that 'The towne of Campsall had in tymes past the priviledge of a markett, which is now decayed and lost by discontinuance'.[6]

The medieval church of All Saints, Frickley, stands alone in the cornfields. The village had decayed by the seventeenth century, but the church continued to serve the inhabitants of nearby Clayton and in Victorian times the squire of Frickley Hall restored it.

This general decline of the population and economy caused some settlements that were weakened by pestilence to disappear altogether, though they often survived in reduced form for decades or even centuries. Most of the deserted villages and hamlets of South Yorkshire are to be found in these central parts, on or just off the magnesian limestone. The classic example is Frickley, where All Saints church stands alone amidst the corn fields, below the escarpment to the west of Hooton Pagnell. The village was never large, but it was not killed off by the Black Death, for in 1379 six married couples and eleven single persons over the age of sixteen paid poll tax there and in 1436 a rental named three open-fields: Mill Field, Clough Field and Kirk Field, 'the field by the church'. Two centuries later, however, a parliamentary survey of 1650 reported that 'there are inconsiderable numbers in this Parish'. [7]

All traces of the village of Frickley disappeared during the eighteenth-century landscaping of the squire's estate, although some ridge and furrow patterns associated with the old strip system in the communal open fields are visible in the pastures to the north. The hearth tax returns of 1672 [8] recorded a 'Widdow Jackson' with ten hearths, but her house was demolished in the mid eighteenth century and the surrounding moat became a landscaped feature of the gardens of the Georgian hall that Anthony Wharton erected on a new site a little further to the west.

Close by, two ancient settlements that were recorded in Domesday Book in the southern quarter of the parish of Hooton Pagnell were gradually reduced to one or two farms. Both were granted relief from tax payments in the 1350s, so they must have been badly affected by the Black Death. In 1379 Bilham still had fifteen inhabitants over the age of sixteen, but Stotfold had only three. The ridge and furrow patterns that locate the former open arable fields provide the only physical evidence of these medieval settlements. Other nearby examples of deserted sites include Stubbs Hall, near Hampole, where nine married couples and seven single persons were taxed in 1379, and Deightonby and Milnthorpe in the parish of Thurnscoe, just below the limestone escarpment.[9]

Estate Villages

The character of the villages that survived the late-medieval fall in population gradually underwent profound changes of ownership and therefore of character. In the seventeenth century, a prolonged national slump in the prices for corn ruined many small farmers and forced them to sell. The small farming families on the magnesian limestone that managed to survive turned much of their arable land to pasture, either by converting strips in the open fields into grass leys or by enclosing whole blocks of furlongs. Villages that became dominated by squires include Hickleton, High Melton and Marr to the north of the Don and Loversall, South Anston and Thorpe Salvin to the south. They enclosed their open arable fields long before the age of parliamentary enclosure in the late eighteenth and early nineteenth centuries.

Owston's decline came much later. In 1343 nearly 50 freeholders held land there and in 1379 as many as 90 people over the age of sixteen paid the poll tax, including twelve men who were rich enough to be assessed at more than the basic rate. By 1545, however, the village was dominated by William Adam, who was taxed on goods worth £12, and who farmed the Duchy of Lancaster lands, together with another 184 acres and the pasture rights in the park. Nevertheless, in 1672 the village had 41 houses, a mill and a forge, and the village was still quite large when Thomas Jeffreys made his map of Yorkshire in 1772. Soon afterwards, however, the Owston estate was landscaped by Humphrey Repton for the squire of the new hall and the village was reduced to a few houses and cottages.[10]

Hooton Pagnell took its name from its prominent position on the magnesian limestone escarpment, the 'farm on the spur of land'. It was distinguished from Hooton Levitt and Hooton Roberts by the name of its Norman lords, the Pagnells, who were succeeded through marriage by the Luttrells and in 1605 by Sir Richard Hutton, which is why the local pronunciation of the village name became Hutton Pagnell (or Pannell). [11] In 1548 the lord and his eleven tenants farmed a third of the cultivated land

Hooton Pagnell Hall, the Vicarage and the parish church stand together at the southern end of the village. The gable ends of the farmhouses front the village street and their crofts extend to a back lane, with the former open fields beyond. *Photo: The Royal Commission on Historical Monuments, now English Heritage*

and nineteen freeholders owned the remaining two-thirds. By 1763 the lord had acquired all but thirteen acres of glebe land and the 70 acres that were divided between the three surviving freeholders.[12]

In 1704 the Warde family, subsequently known as the Warde-Aldams, became lords of the manor of Hooton Pagnell. Their hall is a large and complex building of several different periods, starting with the fourteenth-century west range that rises high above the road along the escarpment and the gatehouse with its oriel window, though much of this 'medieval' appearance is the result of major restoration work between 1894 and 1900. Next to the hall stand the Victorian parsonage and the Norman parish church, whose ungainly appearance before it was much altered and 'restored' in 1876 is revealed by a painting that hangs in the church.

Some of the foundations of the farmhouses and cottages that stretch along both sides of the village street stand on the natural rock. A planned development of a nineteenth-century group of houses in traditional vernacular style below the escarpment can be viewed from near the market cross. As is usual on the magnesian limestone belt, no timber-framed buildings survive; the earliest houses date from the seventeenth-century. The use of local stone allows the village to blend perfectly into the landscape.

The best example is Home Farm, built largely of limestone rubble but with ashlar quoins, lintels and window frames, chamfered mullioned windows and drip-moulds, and a stone-slated roof, whereas most of the other houses have pantile roofs with a bottom course or two of sandstone slates. The three rooms on the ground floor of Home Farm have the typical seventeenth-century arrangement of an off-centre entry leading to the chimney that serves both the kitchen and the hall, with a parlour beyond. These rooms have chambers above them, but they are only one bay deep. Home Farm has its gable end (with just an attic window) facing the street, so that livestock and carts could reach the farm buildings and crofts at the rear and go along the Back Lane to the former open arable fields to the east. The villagers' common occupied inferior, low-lying ground to the west.

Gentry Halls

Sprotbrough Hall, which was built about 1685 for Sir Godfrey Copley in the new French style that he had seen on his travels, with grounds laid out in the contemporary French manner, was demolished in the 1920s and the site is now covered with modern houses.[13] Elsewhere on the magnesian limestone, several neighbouring halls, dating from the middle decades of the eighteenth century, still dominate their villages.

One of the best known is Cusworth Hall, which is now a country house museum. In 1669 Robert Wrightson, an attorney from Hemsworth, bought the earlier, gabled hall that stood further down the hill, near the old village. In 1740, his son, William Wrightson (1676–1760), a former MP and the steward to the Duke of Norfolk's South Yorkshire estate, commissioned George Platt of Thrybergh to build the present house. Then, in 1749, prompted by his son-in-law, John Battie of Warmsworth Hall, Wrightson turned to James Paine, who had acquired a reputation from his work at Nostell Priory and the Doncaster Mansion House, to re-model the south front, including the removal of the pediment, and to add two small wings, one for a chapel, the other for a library. The interior decoration was mostly by Joseph Rose, the plasterer, and Francis Hayman, the painter. In the 1760s Richard Woods, who was working at that time at Cannon Hall, landscaped the grounds in the present style.[14]

Hickleton Hall was built by George Platt to similar designs a year or two later for Godfrey Wentworth, and in the late 1740s James Paine designed Wadworth Hall for Josias Wordsworth, a Penistone man who had made his fortune in London as a merchant trading with Russia. Paine went on to design a Palladian villa for the Earl of Scarbrough at Sandbeck Park and to build the enormous stable block and the elegant bridge over the River Derwent at Chatsworth.

In the eighteenth and nineteenth centuries some of the villages on the magnesian limestone acquired their present character when many small farms were engrossed within a squire's large estate. By Victorian times, the 'estate villages' that were owned by great landowners had an immediately recognizable appearance. At Hickleton, for instance, in the 1840s Sir Francis Wood rebuilt the homes of his tenants in the vernacular style of the Elizabethan and Stuart age, with local limestone walls and red pantile roofs, all tastefully assembled along the village street beyond the grounds of the hall. A sign on the village green once read: 'The Earl of Halifax invites you to rest awhile and enjoy Hickleton'. The village had neither a Nonconformist chapel nor a pub, and even today the only shop is tucked discreetly away. Hickleton Hall stands aloof from the village, in spacious grounds behind by a forbidding wall. It was bought in 1829 by Sir Francis Wood and sold by his descendant Edward Wood, Earl of Halifax, in 1947. It now houses a Sue Ryder home for disabled people.

This detail of Thomas Jeffreys's map of Yorkshire (1772) shows that the villages in this district were dominated by their squires.

Neighbouring villages such as Sprotbrough and Cusworth were also rebuilt in traditional styles by their squires during the reign of Victoria. The vicar of Sprotbrough praised the comfort of the new cottages and thought that 'the poor now enjoy houses not to be excelled by the poor of any parish around'.[15] The farmworkers and craftsmen who were tenants of estate cottages undoubtedly had better accommodation than similar families who lived beyond the reach of a squire. Yet some labourers preferred inferior housing, job insecurity and a long walk to work to the deferential life-style of the estate village, where a man had to doff his cap and his children were taught to curtsy whenever a member of 'the family' passed by.

The character of these estate villages was also 'improved' by the squire's restoration of the parish church. In the 1870s and 1880s the second Viscount Halifax, the lay leader of the Anglo-Catholic Unity Movement, rebuilt much of St Wilfrid's church, Hickleton. Such was his standing in the neighbourhood that the neighbouring gentry followed his example. All the surrounding parishes became (and remain) High Church, though none matched Hickleton in the number and quality of its statues, religious paintings, Bodley screen, choir stalls and gilded reredos. The squires also built new parsonages in Gothic styles to allow the incumbent and his family to live in comfort in a house that was second in importance to that of the lord of the manor.

Coal Mining

In the late Victorian and Edwardian era deep mines were sunk on the concealed coalfield under the magnesian limestone escarpment and many of the old farming parishes of the Doncaster district were altered beyond recognition. Only the squires of the trim estate villages managed to preserve their rural surroundings whilst benefiting from the royalties acquired from the mining of coal below their land. Yet these squires were far from being remote county gentry with limited horizons. William Aldam of Frickley Hall (1814–90), for example, was an entrepreneur who invested in canals and railways.[16] Nevertheless, the names of new collieries, such as Frickley, Brodsworth Main and Hickleton Main, were deceptive, for the squires took care to preserve their own environment by insisting that the mines were sunk out of sight of their halls and that new pit villages should be built beyond their parish boundaries. The Frickley miners were housed in South Kirkby and South Elmsall, the Hickleton men in Thurnscoe and Goldthorpe, whilst the estate villages remained unaffected.

Brodsworth parish, bounded on both the east and the west by former Roman roads, provides the best example of this new trend. St Michael's church stands amongst woodland on a brow, near the hall but high above the few houses and cottages that are strung out along the dry valley below. The earliest parts of the church date from the late Anglo-Saxon or early Norman period. Brodsworth Hall is a remarkable house of the 1860s that was designed in an Italianate style by Casentini of Lucca for Charles Sabine Augustus Thellusson and surrounded by formal gardens. [17]

Wealthy families such as the Thellussons spent only part of the year in their country houses, yet their halls dominated many parts of the countryside before the First World War, especially during the shooting season. Brodsworth had once belonged to the Archbishop of York and the Earl of Kinnoul before it was bought by Peter Thellusson, an immensely rich City of London merchant and speculator of French-Swiss extraction. Charles Sabine Augustus-Thellusson, who was born in Florence in 1822,

Brodsworth Hall has been restored to its former glory by English Heritage. It was built in an Italianate style in the 1860s. The quarry that provided the building stone has been converted into an attractive landscape feature within the grounds.

was the heir to his great-grandfather's fortune. Upon his death in 1885, he was succeeded by the last of his four sons, a man who combined the role of squire of Brodsworth with the more glamorous world of international yachting. English Heritage has thoroughly restored the house and gardens.

When Brodsworth Main colliery was sunk to the Barnsley seam in 1905–8 in a joint operation between Hickleton Main Colliery Company and the Staveley Coal and Iron Company, no coal miners were housed in Brodsworth village. Instead, in 1907, Arthur Markham, Liberal MP and one of the owners of Hickleton Main, persuaded the company to commission Percy Houfton of Chesterfield to design a new model village immediately north of the grounds of 'Woodlands' house in the neighbouring parish of Adwick-le-Street. The density of housing, set amidst large greens, was kept as low as six houses per acre and all the houses were provided with at least three bedrooms, a bathroom and hot water. A full-time social worker helped to run the various clubs and societies and the two Methodist chapels that opened immediately were followed in 1913 by All Saints church.

Woodlands was perhaps the most ambitious mining village ever built in Britain, a planned community that was very different from the cramped, terraced houses of the normal pit village at that time. It set the standard for the council estates that were constructed after the First World War. In 1920 another village known as Woodlands East was built, then in the late 1920s a third estate was added to the north, but neither of these was as spacious as the original village.[18]

The new coal mining communities of the late nineteenth and early twentieth centuries have lessened the sense of contrast between the neat estate villages on the magnesian limestone escarpment and neighbouring parts of South Yorkshire, yet even now, when we climb the hill from Goldthorpe and Thurnscoe to Hickleton or cross the River Dearne on our way from Mexborough to High Melton we get a sense of entering a different world.

Chapter 13

Cannon Hall and its Park

The Spencer Family

Although Cannon Hall and its park now dominate the landscape around Cawthorne, this was not the most important site in the parish during the Middle Ages. The original house stood apart from the village, in a woodland grove that was known in 1323 as Cannon Greve. The place-name appears to have been derived from a family name, for in the early thirteenth century the owner was Gilbert Canun of Birthwaite, whose wife had inherited the estate. Their son Adam Canun of Cawthorne witnessed local deeds in 1286 and 1294.[1] In 1342 the Bosville family, knights of Ardsley and New Hall, Darfield, started to buy parts of this estate and eventually they acquired the whole of it. In 1381 Thomas de Bosville had a royal grant of free warren that allowed him to enclose a deer park there, the predecessor of the present landscaped one. John Bosville was the owner of Cannon Hall in 1445, but it is not known when he or his descendants sold this estate.[2] It eventually passed to the Hewett family.

In 1650 William Hewett sold Cannon Hall and its 233-acre estate to Robert Hartley, whose family had long been tenants there, but in 1656 Hartley died at the early age of 28, leaving a widow, Margaret. Amongst the heirlooms that he left her was 'one long table standing in the hall at Cannon Hall'.[3] On 31 March 1658 Margaret married John Spencer, a new resident of Cawthorne parish who soon arranged to buy Cannon Hall from his wife's daughter by her first marriage. John was a 29-year-old widower, whose first wife, Sara, had died the previous year, leaving him with one son, also called John, and three daughters.[4]

The Spencers were a gentry family from Criggon, Montgomeryshire. They seem to have been a junior branch of the Spencers of Huntingdon Hall, Cheshire, who had been active Royalists in the Civil War and whose fortunes had suffered from the king's defeat and execution. It is not known what connections enabled them to move from Criggon to South Yorkshire in the

1650s, except that they became involved in running the local iron industry. In 1658 Randolph Spencer was buried at Cawthorne and his brother John was buried at Wortley, where he had been in charge of the forge. Randolph's son, John Spencer (1629–81), who took Margaret Hartley as his second wife in the same year, ran an iron business at Barnby furnace on the eastern edge of Cawthorne parish.[5]

Barnby had taken its name from a man with the Old Norse personal name, Bjarni. It was recorded in Domesday Book as a separate small manor within the township of Cawthorne and in 1649 it contained only 349 acres.[6] The hall was the ancient seat of the Barnby family, whom Joseph Hunter ranked amongst the principal gentry of South Yorkshire from the fourteenth to the seventeenth century. They had also been the medieval lords of Midhope and Langsett on the edge of the Pennines, a few miles away.[7] The family's ancient home was replaced in the 1820s by the present 'Tudor Gothic' Barnby Hall, but a medieval arch was re-set in the garden wall and slight earthworks in the surrounding fields suggest that the settlement was once larger than it is now. A barn belonging to Barnby Hall Farm is of particular interest, for it was built as a late-medieval timber-framed house, originally of four bays, with an aisle on the north side. The house was converted into a barn in the late-eighteenth or early-nineteenth century.[8] Did John Spencer live here when he first came to the district to run the business at Barnby furnace?

The last of the male line of the Barnby family was the Thomas Barnby, esquire, who died at Barnby Hall in 1663. He had been the leading landowner in Cawthorne parish and in the previous decade he had been fined £188 for his active support of the Royalists in the Civil War. In 1652 his daughter, Mary, one of two co-heiresses, had married Nicholas Bowden, a gentleman of Bowden, near Chapel-en-le-Frith in Derbyshire. Their sons, Barnby and Thomas were baptized at Chapel-en-le-Frith in the next two years, but the family later moved to Barnby Hall, where Thomas Bowden died in 1681. In 1701 a half share of the hall was bought by John Spencer, then in 1755 the other half was purchased by William Spencer, so the whole of the Barnby estate became incorporated within that of Cannon Hall.[9]

John Spencer's fortunes improved when he moved to Cannon Hall upon his second marriage. The hearth tax returns for Cawthorne in 1672 reveal that he and his wife lived in a middle-sized house with five fireplaces. The largest house in the parish was that of Mrs Allott with nine hearths, followed by two others with six hearths and three (including Spencer's) with five hearths. Clearly, Cannon Hall did not yet dominate the local scene.[10]

In 1719 or 1720 Samuel Buck sketched Cannon Hall as part of a projected volume of Yorkshire houses. As the house was symmetrical, he did not need to sketch all the windows in this preliminary view. This is how the house looked until his grandson converted it into the present building. The outbuildings stood close by.

The main block in the centre of the present Cannon Hall was built in the late seventeenth century by the son of John Spencer's first marriage. This John Spencer II (1655–1729) married Anne, the daughter of John Wilson of Broomhead Hall in the chapelry of Bradfield. A preliminary sketch of the new hall by Samuel Buck, on his tour of Yorkshire about 1720, shows a five-bay building, three bays deep and 2½ storeys high, which was designed in the fashionable classical style of the time, with several outbuildings to the rear.[11]

The Charcoal Iron Trade

Ironstone had long been mined and smelted in Cawthorne township. In 1343 Nicholas Costnought had a forge there, and other documents refer to Cawthorne Smithies until well into the seventeenth century.[12] The foundations of Cinder Hill Farm, north of Cawthorne village, rest on extensive cinder banks, some of which were used to repair the local highways in the mid eighteenth century. But the great era of the charcoal iron trade was from the 1650s to the 1750s.

John Spencer II greatly improved his family's fortunes by his involvement in the iron trade. He bought a half share of Wortley forge for £2,000; he bought a share in the former Sitwell ironworks in Derbyshire and Nottinghamshire (Foxbrooke and Staveley furnaces, Staveley and Carburton forges, and Renishaw slitting mill); and he purchased shares in the Yorkshire forges at Attercliffe, Kirkstall, Wadsley and Wortley, together with the slitting mills at Kirkstall, Masbrough and Wortley, which supplied the local nailmakers. Historians refer to the group of gentlemen-ironmasters who controlled the West Riding and Derbyshire iron trade as the Spencer Syndicate, because of the leading role of the Spencer family. They were referred to in the trade as 'the Gentlemen', the wealthy men who invested in a complicated system of shareholding in ironstone mines, charcoal woods, furnaces, forges, and slitting-mills. By 1720 no less than 29 undertakings were financed by this group.[13]

Ironstone continued to be mined in shallow bell pits in the traditional manner, but the medieval smithies had long since been replaced by charcoal blast furnaces that were worked by water wheels. These furnaces were sited alongside streams that were dammed within a mile or so of the ironstone pits, often in an isolated place in the countryside. The outstanding survivor from this era is the furnace at Rockley, which was built in 1723 for Samuel Shore, a Sheffield merchant who was not a member of the Spencer Syndicate. Furnaces such as this one produced on average 300–400 tons of pig iron per annum and they needed 1,000 to 1,200 horse loads of charcoal each year. Between 1699 and 1705 Rockley furnace was supplied with charcoal from 43 different coppice woods within a fifteen-mile radius on the coal-measure sandstones and the magnesian limestone belt to the east. The demand for fuel for the furnaces transformed the character of the ancient deciduous woods of South Yorkshire.[14]

The pig iron that was smelted at the furnaces was taken several miles overland to the forges that had been built alongside the local rivers. One of the major forges of the Spencer Syndicate was that which was known later as Wortley Top Forge on the River Don. The site had been used as a bloomery from at least 1600 but the first clear evidence of its use as a forge for refining pig iron from blast furnaces is the Spencer lease of 1658. In the 1690s it received pig iron from the furnaces at Barnby, Bank (near Emley), Chapeltown and Rockley. John Spencer II was a partner in a lease of 1707

Wortley Top Forge on the River Don was at the heart of the Spencers' iron trade. A mill for slitting iron into rods for the local nailmakers stood near by.

and he was mentioned as the sole lessee in 1713, 1723 and 1738. His son, William, was the last of the family to take a lease, for a six-year term in 1746. A datestone reveals that the present building was erected in 1719, but it was much adapted in the later eighteenth and nineteenth centuries and the main drive shaft has been dated by dendrochronology to after 1833.[15]

John Spencer's elder son, William Spencer (c.1690–1756), who bought the remainder of the Barnby estate, married Christiana, the daughter and sole heiress of Benjamin Ashton of Hathersage Hall in Derbyshire, a wealthy owner of millstone quarries. Upon his death in 1725, Ashton left William his Derbyshire estates and £14,000. The Spencers were now wealthy landowners.[16]

Much of the iron that was produced locally during the charcoal era was made into nails. Two-thirds of the iron that was forged at Wortley was cut into rods in the adjacent slitting mill for the large body of local nailmakers. About 100 nailmakers' smithies were recorded in the hearth tax returns for South Yorkshire and north Derbyshire in 1672 and other nailers were probably unrecorded because they were exempt from payment because of their poverty.[17]

All the iron that was forged at Wortley in the 1690s was sold in fairly small quantities to local customers, but from 1725 onwards the gentlemen in charge of the charcoal woods, furnaces, forges and slitting mills became directly involved in the nail trade. William Spencer became the leading figure in this lucrative business. Between 1742 and 1747 he employed 120 nailmakers in a district that stretched southwards from Staincross and Mapplewell in the parish of Darton to the northern parts of the parish of Ecclesfield. His diary and letter books show that great quantities of nails were exported to London and were shipped from there across the Atlantic to Virginia, Jamaica, the Leeward Isles, Newfoundland and Philadelphia. Production expanded rapidly when demand exceeded supply. The 210 masters who signed an agreement at Ecclesfield in 1733, which tried to insist that apprentices should serve a full seven-year term instead of leaving after only two years service, fought a losing battle.[18]

The charcoal blast furnace at Rockley supplied Wortley Forge with iron. The photograph shows the excavation of the casting pit, led by David Crossley in 1978–82.

William Spencer employed John Dearden of Howbrook as his 'taker in of nails'. He also used the services of local chapmen, who between 1742 and 1748 delivered 4,465 bags of nails to the wharf at Rotherham on the Don navigation. Invoices mention at least ten different types of nails, which were valued collectively at nearly £10,307.[19]

William died on 30 January 1756 and was succeeded by his son, John Spencer III (1719–1775). The era of the charcoal iron trade was coming to an end in face of competition from coke-fuelled furnaces. In 1765 John withdrew from the business in order to spend the rest of his life as a country gentleman. In that year he commissioned John Carr, the famous York architect, to design two wings to the house, one to serve as a dining room, the other as a library. At first, these wings were just one storey high. By then, John Spencer had already started on an ambitious scheme to landscape the old park and to create new gardens.

In 1760 Richard Woods of Chertsey (Surrey), a landscape gardener with a national reputation, was commissioned to design a new scheme, and John Marsden, a local mason, was put in charge of the practical work. John Spencer took an active part in all the activities during the next few years. He often noted in his diary that he was 'busy planting' or 'busy amongst the workmen'. The first year was spent on improving the immediate surroundings of the house. A pinery was planted with Scots pine and Weymouth pine from Canada, and other trees and shrubs were planted elsewhere in great numbers. Full use was made of the timber that was already standing, but some clumps were thinned and trees were moved to more desirable situations. They consisted mainly of elm, beech, oak, chestnut and ash, but they comprised 217 varieties altogether. Some were brought from Whitby, Scarborough, Pontefract and Wakefield in order to create new clumps. Most of them matured in the nineteenth century.[20]

By the end of 1761 the New Kitchen Garden, the Hothouse and the Shrubbery had already acquired 188 different species of flowering shrubs, 57 store plants and six fruit trees. The Kitchen Gardens were not hidden in the manner that was favoured by 'Capability' Brown, but were placed prominently alongside the Hall. John Marsden then constructed the park wall and ha-ha on lines set out by Richard Woods. The wall was 3,220 yards long and had five gateways. The route to Cawthorne was altered and a new road was constructed from the Smithy to Beet House. The park was now secure enough to keep 94 deer within its bounds.

On 26 October 1761 Spencer and his workmen 'began making new bridge … most of the materials from the old bridge were used in the new one'. This is the main bridge on the road to the south-east side of the house. Between 1762 and 1764 three lakes were constructed and on 23 February 1764 Spencer 'signed a contract with Mr. Woods whereby he engages to complete my next piece of water … to make a Palladian bridge and a head at the Park Walls, to raise the water for 330 feet, to be completed in twenty weeks' time'. The lakes and cascades were in full view in the middle distance from the house, and the river banks were adorned with trees.

The landscape that we see today at Cannon Hall was created during the early 1760s. It soon attracted the attention of other Yorkshire gentlemen,

J. P. Neale's engraving of 1821 shows Cannon Hall and its landscaped park as they were designed during the ownership of John Spencer III, by the architect, John Carr, and the landscape gardener, Richard Woods.

notably John Battie Wrightson, who in December 1761 commissioned Richard Woods to landscape his park at Cusworth Hall.

John Spencer III died unmarried and was the last of his line. His principal heir was his sister Mary's son, Walter Stanhope of Horsforth and Leeds, who, in honour of his uncle, prefixed the name Spencer to his own. An engraving of Cannon Hall about the time of his death in 1821 shows that the wings had been raised to two-storeys and that a parapet adorned the entire house. From 1778 onwards Walter Spencer-Stanhope had regularly commissioned John Carr to make these additions, which harmonized well with the original hall, and to make many internal improvements.

Cannon Hall remained with the Spencer-Stanhope family until 1951, when it was sold to the County Borough of Barnsley. It was opened as a Country House Museum in 1957. Much of the eighteenth-century landscape has been preserved, but the park beyond the lakes has suffered from the activities of the war-time camps and by later opencast mining and housing development.

Chapter 14

Wentworth Castle

Wentworth Castle is a name that was invented about 1730. It puzzles us today because the building is a country house rather than a castle and it stands at Stainborough, a few miles away from Wentworth. It is often confused with the great house at Wentworth Woodhouse, for after the Second World War both buildings were converted into teacher-training colleges. The name was coined in the early eighteenth century by Sir Thomas Wentworth, the first Earl of Strafford of the second creation, who had recently rebuilt Stainborough Hall in a spectacular Baroque style and who had erected a mock medieval castle on the highest point of his estate on the site of an earlier fortification known as Stainborough Low. Stainborough takes its name from this 'stone fort' and Low is derived from the Anglo-Saxon word for a hill or burial mound. The mock castle has removed all trace of the 'castle ruins' that were mentioned in seventeenth-century manorial records and which were highlighted as a prominent feature in a view taken in 1714. This earlier earthwork may have been an Iron Age hill fort that was converted into a Norman motte-and-bailey castle, but on this we can only speculate.[1]

Back in the Middle Ages the Wentworths of Wentworth had built a house in the wood to the east of the village. Sir Thomas Wentworth, King Charles I's chief minister, was rewarded with the title of Earl of Strafford (the name of the wapentake, a sub-division of the West Riding, in which Wentworth lay), and upon his execution in 1641 this title passed to his son, William, who died childless in 1695. The earldom thus became extinct, but the next male heir, Thomas Wentworth of Wakefield, inherited the lesser title of Lord Raby. To his distress, however, the estate at Wentworth Woodhouse was bequeathed to his cousin, Thomas Watson, who thereupon adopted the name of Watson-Wentworth. This was the beginning of great rivalry between the two branches of the family, made worse by their different political attachments.

This view of the Baroque range at Wentworth Castle, designed by Johannes von Bodt for Thomas Wentworth, Lord Raby, was produced by the London firm of Jones and Co. in 1829.

During the reign of Queen Anne, the new Lord Raby rose to high positions in the army and the diplomatic service. He served as the British Ambassador in Berlin and he was one of the signatories to the Treaty of Utrecht (1713), which ended the long War of the Spanish Succession. He was determined to regain the title of Earl of Strafford and, as he needed a country seat to support his claim, Stainborough Hall provided a good opportunity, for it lay only a few miles from Wentworth. His political opponents described him as a persistent supplicant for favours from the Queen, an endless complainer and a downright snob. Jonathan Swift thought him 'infinitely proud and illiterate', and Lord Hervey described him as 'a loquacious, rich, illiterate, cold, tedious, constant haranguer in the House of Lords, who spoke neither sense nor English'.[2]

Dating evidence for the hall that had been built at Stainborough by Sir Gervase Cutler II (now the north range) is provided by tax returns of 1672, which noted that five of the eleven hearths were 'not yet finished'.[3] Sir Thomas Wentworth bought from the hall from the Cutlers in 1708 and immediately began to enlarge it in a spectacular Baroque style to the designs of the Berlin architect Johannes von Bodt. This new Baroque range is the only surviving English example of this famous continental architect's work. Lord Raby's marriage in 1712 to a wealthy London heiress meant that he had the means to pay for his project. In the previous year, Queen Anne had granted him the title of the first Earl of Strafford of the second creation.

The new range took many years to build and furnish, but the earl was often away in London or abroad and he had other houses to live in. The exterior was finished in 1713 but the interior was not completed until well into the 1720s. Not everyone was impressed. A young woman wrote to her aunt in 1717:

> I have been to visit Stars and Garters … There was not a suit of hangings, looking–glass or cabinet that was not adorned with those emblems of honour … He met us upon a fine prancing horse.[4]

The house now faced in a different direction and so the Italianate gardens of the Cutler mansion, which had stretched from behind the building up to the present rose garden, had to be redesigned on a new axis, probably by George London, the royal gardener, or one of his pupils. The new scheme is illustrated in a bird's eye view of 1714 by the Dutch artists, Kip and Knyff, and by a Badeslade print of 1739. The old public highway, up the hill from the crossroads at the Strafford Arms, behind Home Farm and along the line taken later by Lady Lucy's Walk, past Stainborough Low to Hood Green, was diverted to the present route along the northern edge of the park. The two views show a series of formal gardens in the French or Dutch style that was fashionable at the time, with waterworks, parterres, a wilderness, bowling green, lawns, tree–lined avenues, a deer park and woods intersected by radiating paths. Very few of these features can now be traced on the ground, for they were swept away in the landscaping undertaken by the next generation.

When Queen Anne died in 1714, the Tories lost all their influence at the Royal Court and the earl retired to Stainborough, where he occupied himself with building and laying out gardens and a park, which he stocked with over 300 deer. He planted Menagerie Wood and made a lake and cascade there (now gone); he planted or improved Ivas, Broomroyd and Lowe woods; he erected a number of statues and the garden building that was later converted into the Gun Room; he constructed an Orangery; his head gardener created the new kitchen and fruit gardens in the area beyond Home Farm that is

This old postcard shows the entrance to the mock castle on Stainborough Low and Rysbrack's statue of the first Earl of Strafford of the second creation in its original position there.

enclosed by a brick wall; in 1734 he built an obelisk and lodge near Round Green in honour of Queen Anne; and in 1739, the year of his death, he started to build the Rotunda on a knoll at the edge of Ivas Wood.

His major project, begun in 1727, was the construction of a mock castle on Stainborough Low. Four embattled towers marked the entrance through the vaulted archway of a sturdy gatehouse into a circular earthwork that was enclosed by a rampart and surmounted by a battlemented wall and four turrets; two of the towers have since fallen and a third has lost its top. The 'castle', inscribed 'Rebuilt in 1730', is a very early example of romantic medievalism. Upon its completion, the name of the Stainborough estate was changed to Wentworth Castle.

Meanwhile, the Whig family that had inherited Wentworth Woodhouse enjoyed the fruits of political victory under Kings George I and II. Thomas Watson-Wentworth, junior, succeeded his father and immediately began to rebuild Wentworth Woodhouse in Baroque style to match the hall of his cousins at Stainborough; it was finished by 1728. Sir Robert Walpole, the first man to be known as Prime Minister, rewarded him for his support in the House of Lords by creating him first a knight, then a baron, then an earl; in 1745 King George II made him Marquis of Rockingham, a higher rank than that of the Earl of Strafford at Stainborough.

The rivalry between the cousins was reflected in their buildings, as they strove to outdo each other. When Thomas Watson-Wentworth completed his Baroque range, he found that the style was now considered out of date and that the orthodoxy of the Whig nobility, headed by the Earl of Burlington, was the severe classical style known as Palladianism. He immediately set about building an immense Palladian range, which at 606 feet was eventually to have the longest front of any country house in England. Wentworth Woodhouse and its enormous landscaped park clearly outshone the Earl of Strafford's house at Stainborough.

The Second Earl

The second Earl of Strafford of the new creation, another William Wentworth, never became involved in politics and spent much of his life on his country estate. Though he did not have the wealth to compete with his cousin at Wentworth Woodhouse, he too built a Palladian range between 1759 and 1764, which he and his friends considered more aesthetically pleasing in its restraint than the overpowering, grandiose 'Whig palace' at Wentworth. At the same time, he destroyed the formal gardens that his father had constructed so lovingly, for the new fashion was for rolling parkland. Clumps of trees replaced straight avenues, lakes and serpentines were preferred to geometrical stretches of water, and classical temples and Gothic follies were placed at strategic points to catch the eye.

In 1789 Horace Walpole wrote that Wentworth Castle was 'my favourite of all great seats: such a variety of ground, of wood, and water; and almost all executed and disposed of with so much taste by the present earl'.[5] The visual impact of this new landscape has faded with the crumbling of some of the monuments and the decay of the serpentine, but much of their original appeal is still there.

The entrance to the estate from the public highway was marked by the Gothic Steeple Lodge, which was built about 1775. Just inside the grounds, the pillared 'Dutch barn' is one of the earliest of its type in the country. The drive continues past Home Farm and the former stables, towards a statue of the first earl in haughty pose and dressed in Roman garments. It was carved by Rysbrack, the Flemish sculptor, in 1743 and was originally placed

Jones and Co's view of the Palladian range built between 1759 and 1764 for the second earl, set amongst landscaped gardens.

by the entrance to the mock castle. The eastern entrance to the estate was marked by a tall stone arch near the Strafford Arms and the rear entrance by Archer's Hill gate. A Palladian bridge (which has since lost its balustrade) took the drive from the hamlet of Stainborough across the three-quarter-mile-long Serpentine, a series of ponds that gave the illusion of a winding river whose ends were masked by trees. Ha-has were dug to prevent livestock from grazing too close to the house.

Inspired by the landscape paintings of Claude Lorraine and Poussin, the earl erected several monuments at strategic points in the grounds. He completed the Rotunda on fourteen Ionic columns at the edge of Ivas Wood, which his father had begun on the model of the Temple of the Sibyl at Tivoli (Rome). In 1744 he built a tall column topped with a statue of Minerva, goddess of wisdom, to commemorate his father-in-law, the Duke of Argyll and Greenwich. Three years later, he placed an obelisk close to the mock castle in honour of Lady Mary Wortley-Montagu who had introduced smallpox inoculation into this country from Turkey; it is claimed to be the only garden monument in England that celebrates the intellectual achievements of a woman.

In 1756 an 'Umbrello' in the style of the Chichester market cross, perhaps designed by Walpole and Bentley, was erected in Menagerie Wood, but it has

The principal entrance to the estate is now via the Gothic Steeple Lodge that was built about 1775 in a similar design to that at the family's country house at Boughton (Northamptonshire). The 'Dutch Barn' cannot be dated precisely, but it is one of the earliest in the country, with sixteen pillars supporting a stone slate roof.

since collapsed. In the same year, a (demolished) pavilion was constructed at Rockley Woodhouse, by Rockley dam. Ten years later, on completion of the Palladian range, a Corinthian temple was built to overlook the south lawn and John Platt was commissioned to carve four Corinthian columns to match those of the house. Then in 1775, a third obelisk was raised to mark the way to Wentworth Castle from the Sheffield–Leeds turnpike road, on the edge of the estate three miles away at Birdwell. Meanwhile, beyond the park, the earl rebuilt a farm in an ecclesiastical style and gave it the unwarranted name of Rockley Abbey, and he constructed some mock, ruined fortifications on the crest of the hill at Worsbrough Common.

Visitors were unanimous in their praise of the new park and gardens. In 1770 Arthur Young was struck by:

the beauties of the ornamented environs … The water and the woods adjoining are sketched with great taste. The first extends through the park in a meandering course, and wherever it is viewed the terminations are nowhere seen, having everywhere the effect of a real and very beautiful river; the groves of oaks fill up the bends of the stream in the justest style … The shrubbery that adjoins the house is disposed with the utmost taste. The waving slopes dotted with firs, pines, etc. are pretty, and the temple is fixed on so beautiful a spot, as to command a sweet landscape of the park and a rich prospect of adjacent country.[6]

He remarked on the bowling green, 'thickly encompassed with evergreens; with a very light and pretty Chinese temple on one side of it', a statue of Ceres in a retired spot, the surprising prospect from the mock castle and the view of the extensive valley from in front of the Baroque range, down to the menagerie, well-stocked with pheasants, and the shrubbery spread over two fine slopes, together with the oak woods and a Gothic temple.

The Vernon-Wentworths

When the second Earl died childless in 1791 he was succeeded by the son of his cousin, then in 1802 by an even more distant relation, Frederick Thomas William Vernon, who assumed the surname of Vernon-Wentworth. Frederick was still a child at the time of his inheritance and he lived until 1885. He rebuilt the church in 1835 and was responsible for the remarkable conservatory, without which no great Victorian house could be considered complete. Lit by electric light, it contained orange, lime and palm trees, a variety of exotic plants and a range of mosses and ferns. The gardens on the slopes beyond were altered once again by the planting of foreign trees and rhododendrons. Additional greenhouses were constructed in the kitchen gardens and new plantations on the edge of the estate provided extra cover for pheasants.

   In 1897 his son, Thomas Vernon-Wentworth, built a final wing, containing an enlarged kitchen, a servants' hall and extra bedrooms and bathrooms, on the northwest side of the Cutler house and installed electric light throughout the building. Thomas's son, Captain Bruce Vernon-Wentworth, who succeeded to the estate in 1902, was responsible for some of the most attractive features of the present garden. In 1912 he built the terrace from which to view the park from the front of the Baroque range and enclosed it with ironwork gates and a new balustrade. Seven years later, he planted the avenue of trees known as Lady Lucy's Walk. But in the first half of the twentieth century heavy death duties and falling rents made it increasingly difficult to maintain a country house in good repair and in 1948 the Captain, who was a bachelor, sold the house, outbuildings and sixty acres of the garden and park to the Barnsley Education Committeee.

The Present Day

The house and gardens at Wentworth Castle are listed as of Grade 1 historical importance and the gardens are rated as of outstanding botanical as well as historic interest and are a refuge for wildlife. The unity of the old estate has been destroyed but in recent times great efforts have been made to restore the buildings and gardens whenever funds have been available. *Rhododenron Ponticum* has been vigorously cleared and national collection status has been granted to the *Species Rhododenron*. Most of the woods are still managed for pheasant shooting and timber, but opencast mining has destroyed Broomroyd Wood and a variety of crops are grown in the former park. The kitchen gardens have been adapted as the Nursery for Barnsley Metropolitan District Council. The 500+ acres of Wentworth Castle Gardens and Stainborough Park have been opened to the public, with a car park and a children's adventure playground. The Rhododendrons, Camellias and Magnolias have been enhanced, over 100,000 bulbs have been planted, and the historic parkland can be explored from three Parkland Trails, which link several restored follies and native woods, where red and fallow deer graze peacefully.

A press release in 2011 announced that a project had been created with three partners: Wentworth Castle Heritage Trust, Steel Valley Project, and Yorkshire Dry Stone Walling Academy Ltd, all helped by East Peak Innovation Partnership. Twelve conservation volunteers and staff have been trained to restore the East Ha-Ha, which was an integral part of the eighteenth-century landscape of Menagerie House, Umbrello Monument, and ornamental lakes. In 2013 a major project to restore the Conservatory was completed. Other restoration plans include the repair of the Kitchen Garden; of the lakes or ponds so that water can be viewed from the house and gardens; and of the Serpentine Bridge, Tuscan Temple, and Rotunda Temple; together with the creation of wildlife habitats including breeding ponds for Great Crested Newts.

Chapter 15

Inland Waterways

Until the age of the railways, heavy, bulky goods such as coal or metalware were transported, wherever possible, by water. Whereas a packhorse normally carried a load weighing about 240 pounds, the same animal could haul up to thirty tons on a navigable river or canal. Water transport was therefore considerably cheaper than overland carriage, especially if the merchants could arrange to load their ships and boats on the return voyages with cargoes of such things as iron and steel for the cutlers, Norwegian deals for builders, hides from Smithfield market for the tanners, or groceries for the shopkeepers. Back in the Middle Ages, much of South Yorkshire's imports and exports came and went via the wharfs at Bawtry and Doncaster, the two inland ports that, like so many others in eastern England, were sited not only at the highest points of river navigation but on the major highway known as the Great North Road.

Bawtry and the River Idle

Bawtry's history as a port probably goes back to Roman times, for it stood at an important crossroads where a fort guarded the banks of the River Idle. Bawtry is still recognizable on the ground as a medieval planned new town, which was grafted on to a small riverside settlement in the late twelfth or early thirteenth century, at a time when many towns were being founded up and down the country by kings, bishops and barons. The grid pattern of the medieval streets and alleyways around the market place is still clearly defined, yet the church stands just beyond this grid, alongside the former wharf. Dedicated to St Nicholas, the patron saint of seafarers, who has many churches in his honour in England's eastern and southern ports, it served as a landmark for incoming traffic long before the new town was created alongside it.[1]

The old course of the River Idle can still be followed, with difficulty, as it winds its way to the churchyard; the Ordnance Survey map reveals that

This aerial view shows that the plan of the Norman town, centred on its market place, is still evident on the ground. In the mid nineteenth century the railway cut through the old wharf and the River Idle had to be diverted along a new straight channel. Bawtry remained an important inland port until the late eighteenth century.

it remains the ancient boundary between Yorkshire and Nottinghamshire. However, in 1857, long after the decline of the port in face of competition from other waterways, the Great Northern Railway Company diverted the river and pool away from the church along a new, straight channel on the other side of their viaduct. Much of the old wharf, where the lord of the manor and the town burgesses had separate quays, is now covered with modern housing.

In 1276 Bawtry was described as a port in the Hundred Rolls and in the early fourteenth century Derbyshire lead is known to have been taken from here down the River Idle to Stockwith, where goods were transferred to larger vessels for the voyage along the Trent and the Humber to Hull, and so on to the east coast ports, London and abroad.[2] Like many English towns, Bawtry declined in the late Middle Ages after the huge drop in the national population caused by the Black Death, but by Elizabethan times it was flourishing again. In the early eighteenth century Daniel Defoe observed that Bawtry wharf was:

> famous all over the south part of the West Riding of Yorkshire, for it is the place whither all their heavy goods are carried to be embarked and shipped off.[3]

Hallamshire cutlery and South Yorkshire metalware, Derbyshire lead and millstones, and some West Riding textiles were taken to Bawtry, for it was the nearest river port, some twenty miles to the east of Sheffield.

Bawtry remained a thriving river port until the River Don was made navigable in the second quarter of the eighteenth century. It declined rapidly once the opening of the Chesterfield Canal in 1777 provided the lead and millstone merchants with a cheaper route to the Trent at Stockwith. By 1822 the port had 'little or no trade',[4] yet the town continued to flourish as a stopping place on the Great North Road and as a market centre, and it was largely rebuilt in the late Georgian era. The road leading down from the northern edge of the market place to the church still bears the name Wharf Street, but otherwise there is now little sign of Bawtry's former prosperity as a river port. A walk from the former warehouses on Church Street alongside the pools that mark the old course of the River Idle, continuing past the viaduct to the new course of the river, provides views of the church tower, which remains a striking focal point in the landscape long after all the hustle and bustle has gone.

Doncaster and the Dun Navigation

Doncaster takes its name from the Roman town that was constructed on the southern banks of the River Don. The old pronunciation of the river name was Dun, as in the place-names Dunford Bridge, near its source, and Barnby Dun, downstream from the town. When the river was made navigable beyond Doncaster in the eighteenth century it was at first known as the Dun Navigation.

Doncaster was Bawtry's chief rival as a river port for South Yorkshire, though it lay too far north to benefit from the trade in Derbyshire lead and millstones. River-borne goods were loaded and unloaded at Docken Hill, right alongside the north-eastern edge of the large market place that was laid out in the Norman period. From the Middle Ages into the nineteenth century Doncaster was the wealthiest and most important town in South Yorkshire. Its corn market and livestock fairs enjoyed wide fame and in the seventeenth and eighteenth centuries its wool market was undoubtedly one of the largest in the kingdom. The Great North Road passed through the town alongside this market place, not far from the wharf.[5]

After Cornelius Vermuyden's company had cut off the southern arm of the Don in the 1620s and had channelled all the water into the 'Dutch River', in order to drain the Hatfield and Thorne Levels, the Don became navigable for small boats as far as Doncaster for nine months in the year. A sale of the manor of Barnburgh in 1692 noted that:

These Lands lye neere Doncaster where there is a Navigable River downe to Hull and soe for transport by sea.[6]

Large vessels could get as far upstream as the highest tidal point at Wilsick House in the parish of Barnby Dun, but their passage beyond was said to be 'uncertain and hazardous', except 'in times of rises and freshes'. Progress through Doncaster was prevented by the corporation's mills and beyond the town by the rocks, shallows, and banks of sand and gravel in the magnesian limestone gorge between Sprotbrough and Warmsworth.

Improved inland waterways were essential to economic progress long before the Industrial Revolution and the age of canals. In the late seventeenth and early eighteenth centuries a large number of private Acts of Parliament were obtained to improve the navigability of English rivers. These projects were inspired not by any great advances in technology but by the growing importance of industry. By 1730 about 1,160 miles of English rivers had been made navigable for light craft. In Yorkshire, river navigation had been improved on long stretches of the rivers Ouse, Aire, Calder, Derwent, Don and Hull.[7]

The Dun Navigation project got off to a faltering start. In 1698 Sheffield's leaders did not support Sir Godfrey Copley, MP, when he presented a bill to make the River Don navigable above Doncaster, about the same time that Leeds and Wakefield were successfully promoting the Aire & Calder Navigation. Nor were they enthusiastic when Doncaster Corporation sponsored another bill in 1704. In 1721, however, the Cutlers' Company of Hallamshire, at last persuaded of the advantages of better transport, sponsored a bill that was presented to Parliament, but which was bitterly opposed not only by Bawtry merchants and landowners below Doncaster who feared flooding on the epic scale that had accompanied Vermuyden's first drainage scheme a hundred years earlier, but also by the lord of Hallamshire, the Duke of Norfolk, who was concerned about the water supply to his grinding wheels and forges on the banks of the Don. The bill was defeated in committee, but five years later, a compromise was agreed with the Duke, whereby the proposed navigation would end at Tinsley, three miles east of Sheffield. The Cutlers' Company was authorized to make the river navigable from Doncaster to Tinsley for boats of up to twenty tons and to keep the road from Tinsley to Sheffield in good repair, by levying a toll of a penny per ton on vehicles that used the new wharf. The following year Doncaster Corporation obtained an Act to improve the navigation downstream to the

Tinsley Locks. The River Dun Navigation was completed as far as Tinsley in 1751, then in 1819 it was extended to the canal wharf in Sheffield.

point where the river was tidal. By 1740 the Don had been made navigable as far inland as Rotherham; the whole enterprise was completed in 1751.[8]

On the lower reaches of the Don, a link to the Trent via Thorne for craft up to 200 tons was provided by the Stainforth & Keadby Canal (1793–1802), most of which flows through Lincolnshire. In modern times, a marina and boatyards have grown up around the lock at Thorne.

Meanwhile, further up river, the extra few miles from Tinsley to Sheffield were made navigable in 1819, when a compromise solution was reached with the Duke of Norfolk. In order to preserve the water supply to his industrial works on the River Don, a canal was dug from a series of eleven locks at the western edge of Tinsley up to the confluence of the Don and the Sheaf at Sheffield. The new canal stimulated the industrial growth of Sheffield's east end. Coal was exported from the duke's Park Colliery, and at the terminus William Greaves founded his Sheaf Works, Sheffield's first factory for making cutlery, steel and edge-tools. In the 1990s, the canal basin was transformed into a business and heritage centre under the name of Victoria Quays.[9]

The Dearne & Dove and Barnsley Canals

The South Yorkshire coalfield was landlocked and so was unable to compete against Britain's major coalfield in Northumberland and County Durham before the age of canals and railways. Once the River Don had been made navigable the next step was to dig artificial channels linking it with the heart of the coalfield where the Barnsley and Silkstone seams were mined. The first project was a relatively modest one in 1779–80, when the Marquis of Rockingham of Wentworth Woodhouse employed the great canal engineer, William Jessop, to make the 'Greasbrough cut' down to the River Don, with four broad locks and a reservoir.

At a meeting on 20 October 1792 at the White Bear Inn in Barnsley representatives from the Dun Navigation and the Aire & Calder Navigation agreed to construct canals from the River Don at Swinton and the River Calder at Wakefield to meet just south of Barnsley at Hoyle Mill. The two Acts for these canals - the Dearne & Dove and the Barnsley - were passed by Parliament in June 1793. The Dearne & Dove Canal began by climbing four locks at the transhipment wharf by the Ship Inn at Swinton, before passing through a 472-yard tunnel into the Dearne Valley and continuing through

The overgrown and drained Dearne and Dove Canal is seen on this photograph taken in 1970 near Swaithe, where it was crossed by the railway from Sheffield to Barnsley.

Wath, West Melton, Wombwell and Stairfoot on a ten-mile journey with eighteen locks. It reached the junction with the Barnsley Canal in 1804.[10]

A 2-mile branch to Elsecar with six locks and a reservoir was vital to Earl Fitzwilliam's development of a model industrial village, where only a farm had been before, as we shall see in chapter 17. Another two-mile branch, along the Dove Valley to Worsbrough, managed without locks, but it needed a much larger reservoir to feed the summit. Its opening in 1804 transformed the wooded countryside of the picturesque Worsbrough Dale. By 1838 White's *West Riding Directory* could report that here were:

> extensive iron, coal, lime, chemical, and flint glass works, with wharfs, boat-yards, a paper mill, and a large assemblage of houses, presenting a scene of bustle not often excelled in market towns.

Stone quarries, a glue manufactory and a gunpowder works were soon added. The Wesleyans, the Wesleyan Reform movement, and the Primitive Methodists each built a chapel, the choice of denominations reflecting the basic differences of outlook between the inhabitants of this new industrial community and those who resided in the old estate village, dominated by its hall, church and grammar school at the top of the hill.[11]

The enclosure of the commons of Worsbrough between 1817 and 1826 freed further land for building at the extremities of the parish. Pit villages were founded at Birdwell and Blacker and a colony of linen weavers was established at Worsbrough Common on the Barnsley boundary.

The Barnsley Canal needed fifteen locks between the River Calder at Heath and the summit at Walton, a further five locks to lift the canal to the terminus at Barnby Basin, and a reservoir at Wintersett; an extra reservoir was added at Cold Hiendley in 1854, but water supply was always a great problem. About a mile of the canal survives near Monkton as an elongated pond that is used by the local fishing club. Finally, the River Dearne was crossed by a spectacular five-arched aqueduct, which has since been demolished. This section of the canal was opened in 1799, but that from Barnsley to Barnby Basin was not completed until 1802.[12]

The main traffic down the canal was, of course, the coal that was mined in and around Silkstone. In 1808 the Barnsley Canal Navigation Company obtained an Act of Parliament to allow the construction of a railway to take horse-drawn waggons loaded with coal along a 2½-mile level stretch from Silkstone Cross to Barnby Basin. Some of the original stone sleeper blocks remain in situ. When the waggonway was completed in the following year it soon encouraged the building of furnaces at Low Mill and Barnby and the opening of the Waterloo Colliery.[13]

In the 1830s the coal owner, R. C. Clarke of Noblethorpe Hall, extended the waggonway up to Silkstone Common by an inclined plane worked by the Black Horse steam engine and then on to his pit at Huskar by a self-acting inclined plane. The main item of back carriage on the canal was limestone that had been quarried

Some of the stone sleeper blocks that carried the tramway from Barnby Basin to Silkstone Cross remain in position to this day.

at Cadeby and which was converted into lime in furnaces that were erected at the basin. Cart loads of lime were taken on the turnpike roads and local lanes to spread on newly enclosed fields as far away as the moorland edges in the Penistone-Holmfirth district.[14]

The prosperity of the Dearne & Dove and Barnsley canals lasted only until the railways that were built from the 1840s onwards provided fierce competition, though they survived in modified form into the twentieth century. Subsidence caused by mining also affected them adversely. In 1906 the Worsbrough branch of the Dearne & Dove Canal was the first to close, followed in 1928 by the Elsecar branch and in 1934 by most of the line from the Don to Barnsley. It was not until 1961, however, that the entire canal was abandoned except for the last half-mile and the four locks at Swinton, which were maintained to supply materials and water to the nearby glassworks. Meanwhile, in 1893, the section of the Barnsley Canal above Barugh Locks had been closed as most of the trade here had been lost to the railways, but the rest of the canal survived until 1953.[15]

In 1984 a Barnsley Canal Group was formed to campaign for the preservation and restoration of both canals and in 1991 they began to restore the part of the Elsecar branch that adjoins the Elsecar Heritage Centre. The group was re-formed in 2000 as the Barnsley, Dearne & Dove Canals Trust. A feasibility study concluded that the restoration of that section of the canal would be possible, though expensive. Because of their rural nature, the two branches of the Dearne & Dove Canal to Worsbrough and Elsecar have fared far better than the main line since its closure. Parts of the canal, such as the top of the Worsbrough branch, have remained in good condition despite years of neglect. On the Elsecar branch, funding from the Yorkshire European Community Trust has enabled the restoration of the top two pounds and lock and the addition of a launch ramp. The reservoir that fed the Elsecar branch has been designated a local nature reserve by Barnsley Council and the area surrounding the reservoir at the top end of the Worsbrough branch has become the Worsbrough Country Park.

Chapter 16

Wentworth and Elsecar

Wentworth

The estate village at Wentworth is largely nineteenth century in
appearance, but it was recorded in Domesday Book and its name has
an Anglo-Saxon origin. By 1303 the lords of the manor, who took
their surname from the village, were living at Wentworth Woodhouse, the
house in the woods to the east. They were of modest gentry status before
the sixteenth century, but the quality of the alabaster monument to Thomas
Wentworth, who died in 1588, and his wife, Margaret, née Gascoigne, in the
Old Church at Wentworth, demonstrates their rise in society. In 1601 their
son, William Wentworth, was appointed sheriff of Yorkshire and, ten years
later, he was made a baronet. He was a rich man with an estate worth over
£6,000 per annum.[1]

The Renaissance monument to Sir William (died 1614) and his wife,
Anne (died 1611), in the same church is attributed to Nicholas Johnson,
a Flemish sculptor who had settled in Southwark.[2] Their son, Sir Thomas
Wentworth, became one of South Yorkshire's most famous national figures.
In 1628 King Charles I appointed him President of the Council of the North
and in 1632 Lord Deputy in Ireland, a post that enabled him to acquire
substantial properties in the counties of Kildare and Wicklow, which
covered almost 90,000 acres. In 1640 he was elevated in rank as the first Earl
of Strafford in recognition of his services to the Crown, but soon afterwards
the king's control of national affairs broke down and, by order of Parliament,
Wentworth was executed on Tower Hill in 1641, shortly before the outbreak
of the Civil War.

The enormous house that he had built at Wentworth Woodhouse was left
intact for the next two generations under the second earl and his nephew, the
first Thomas Watson-Wentworth, but when Thomas Watson-Wentworth
II (1693–1750) inherited the estate in 1723 rebuilding began almost
immediately. This Thomas was a strong supporter of the Prime Minister,

Sir Robert Walpole, in the House of Lords and so he was rewarded regularly with honours. In 1725 he was created a Knight of the Order of the Bath, in 1728 he was elevated as Baron Malton, in 1733 as Earl of Malton, and in 1745 as Marquis of Rockingham, titles that indicated his other possessions in Yorkshire and Northamptonshire.[3]

Wentworth Woodhouse consists of two country houses that were built on different levels. They face in opposite directions, without direct means of access, and they differ in their style of architecture, the west range being English Baroque and the enormous east range Palladian. Nevertheless, they were both built for the same owner, Thomas Watson-Wentworth II. His accounts for the Baroque house record the millions of bricks that were made on the estate, stone from Hooton Roberts (another of his properties in South Yorkshire), and glass from the Bolsterstone works. He began this first house in 1724 and by 1728 all the external work had been completed.[4] A substantial amount of the first Earl of Strafford's house was retained behind the facade. This west range remains in private ownership and cannot normally be seen from close quarters. Its secluded position means that it is not well known.

Soon after the new Baroque house been completed, the style fell out of fashion amongst the Whig aristocracy and the strict Palladianism that was promoted by the Earl of Burlington and his followers came into favour instead. In the 1730s Thomas Watson-Wentworth turned to Burlington and his architect, Colen Campbell, for advice on a new range facing east. They approved a plan that was a bigger version of Wanstead House in Essex, which Campbell had designed for Sir Richard Childe. In 1734 Sir Thomas Robinson of Rokeby Hall, North Yorkshire, enthused:

> When finished 'twill be a stupendous fabric, infinitely superior to anything we have now in England; the front of the house and offices (exclusive of the stables) being a line of 606 feet built of the most beautiful hewn stone and the best masonry I ever saw … The whole finishing will be entirely submitted to Lord Burlington, and I know of no subject's house in Europe [which] will have seven such magnificent rooms so finely proportioned as these will be.[5]

Meanwhile, the grounds were altered to provide a suitable setting for the great house. Back in 1711, Ralph Thoresby, the Leeds antiquary, had found that the old gardens were 'large and noble, with delicate walks and groves', and with curious fishponds and a tower, though he did not mention the Gothic

The Palladian front at Wentworth Woodhouse is the longest of any country house in England. It was designed for Thomas Watson-Wentworth II by the Earl of Burlington's team of architects.

'bear pit' that dates from about 1630.[6] Watson-Wentworth's detailed records show that in 1726 Morley pond was enlarged, the following year 250 acres of Greasbrough common were taken into the park, 'The Ha, Ha, Levelling and Obelisks in the Garden were Articled for in 1728 and finished 1729', and by 1733 work was completed on new folds, water engines, a keeper's lodge, a greenhouse stand, and an early Gothic folly known later as the Needle's Eye, but originally as 'the obelisk in Lee Wood'. The major project for 1735–36 was the building of a terrace designed by the Earl of Carlisle, the owner of Castle Howard. His brother-in-law, Sir Thomas Robinson, wrote that the terrace was:

> 1,500 feet long, that next the wall 50 feet wide, and the lower one to that (which has a fall of 2 feet) 40 feet wide; at one end it terminates in a fine rotunda of the Ionic order, and at the other end a bastion. The terrace is the fence to that side of the garden towards the great woods and piece of water and [has] fine views from it.[7]

When the original terrace wall collapsed, the local architect, Ralph Tunnicliffe of Dalton, was held responsible, for failing to use 'cramps or throughs'. Tunnicliffe had once been in charge of the whole building programme, but by 1736, if not before, the Earl of Burlington's protégé, Henry Flitcroft, had been appointed above him. In Watson–Wentworth's words:

> In the Year 1737 the new Parlor and Drawing Room below Stairs were finished furnished and used, the Great Hall and Portico begun, the Cellars, Rustick Story completed and the great Hall erected to the Heigth of the first Window … 1738 The Great Hall was built and covered in, The Supping Room finished, the Place for a Stair Case erected … 1739 The great Porticoe was built which considering the Size of the Stones and the Quantity of Carving etc was done in one Year … 1740 the Two Windows joyning to the great Hall Northward were built and the supping room was first used and the rooms over it were wainscoted and the Ceiling Joyce put into severall of the Rooms, also the Carving of the Arms and other Ornaments of the great Front … 1741 and 1742 The old Gallery was rebuilt, and the North Wing erected … the Carpenter's Work of the Ceilings of the Great Hall, Dining Room and Portico were finished and a rough Coat of Plaster laid on … 1743 the new Gallery was fitted up and the masonry of the whole House, except some of the Ornaments, Paving etc. finished.[8]

The common entrance into the house was through the door in the rusticated basement into a hall that is divided into five low aisles by Tuscan columns. The entrance for the family and their visitors was far more imposing. Flights of steps approach the majestic portico with direct entrance into the marble saloon on the first floor, Palladio's *piano nobile*. Six enormous Corinthian columns support the pediment, which is adorned with a heraldic device and the motto, *Mea Gloria Fides*, 'My Faith is My Glory'. The marble saloon is a larger version of Inigo Jones's Queen's House at Greenwich; it covers sixty square feet and is forty feet high, with galleries ten feet wide. The marble was scagliola from Siena and much of the ornamentation was the work of James Stuart. Henry Flitcroft was also responsible for the arrangement and decoration of the principal apartments.[9]

After a visit in 1769 Arthur Young wrote that he 'never saw the advantages of a great fortune applied so nobly to the improvement of a country'.[10] The first Marquis was proud of his achievements and advised his son that 'If you

This detail of Thomas Jeffreys's map of Yorkshire (1772) shows the great house and park of the Marquis of Rockingham to the east of Wentworth village. 'Elsekers' is shown as a single farmstead.

lay out your money in improving your seat, lands, gardens, etc. you beautifye the country and do the work ordered by God himself'.[11]

The family's South Yorkshire estate virtually doubled in size between 1695 and 1782, from 9,420 acres to 17,200 acres. Melvyn Jones has shown how 96 separate land purchases added almost 4,500 acres to the South Yorkshire estate at the cost of more than £78,500. Most of these new properties formed an arc around Wentworth, stretching from Hoyland, Wombwell, Brampton, Wath, Swinton and Hooton Roberts to Greasbrough, Kimberworth and Tinsley.[12]

By 1750 the park had been extended to over nine miles in circumference. Humphrey Repton was commissioned to redesign it with monuments and follies on the most striking points in the landscape. Henry Flitcroft designed Hoober Stand, one of South Yorkshire's most prominent landmarks, in honour of King George II, after Thomas Watson-Wentworth had been created the first Marquis of Rockingham for standing firm in his role of Lord Lieutenant when Bonnie Prince Charlie's Highlanders invaded England in 1745. The stand is a curious, three-sided structure with 155 steps, reaching about 100 feet high; it was finished in 1748. The Marquis wrote:

> 1747 … began a large Pyramid on Hoober Hill in Honour to the most worthy King to whom I owed all Gratitude as being Personally my Patron & Friend without Ministerial Interposition.[13]

Two years later, the tower or stand on Hoyland Law was built, with a bowling green close by. A generation later, other striking follies were designed by John Carr and placed on prominent points of the landscape. They include Keppel's Column, which was built as an obelisk in 1773–36 and re-named upon Admiral Keppel's acquittal in 1778, the Mausoleum that was built between 1785 and 1791 by Earl Fitzwilliam in memory of his uncle, the second Marquis, the North Lodge (1793), Rainborough Lodge (1798) and Lion's Lodge (1804).[14] The brick school and almshouses at Barrow date from 1745–46, and of the many estate houses and cottages that survive from this period the most noteworthy is the former windmill in Clayfields Lane, which was built in 1745 and converted by Anthony Boulby, a bricklayer, into domestic accommodation in 1793 with a castellated top and the name 'Saxon Tower'. A new stone windmill replaced it, across the fields in the hamlet of Barrow.[15]

Work on the house and the outbuildings went on for years. The grounds do not have an imposing entrance, but on the long approach from the village the colossal scale of the buildings and the park is immediately evident in the stable block that was built to John Carr's designs between 1766 and 1789. The final version of the house also owes much to Carr, who in 1782–4 was commissioned by the second Marquis of Rockingham to design alterations to the original wings, which were only one-and-a-half storeys high and had plain, broad pediments. These plans were put into effect in 1806 by William, the fourth Earl Fitzwilliam, when the wings were raised to their present height, the pediments were reduced to three bays, and giant Corinthian columns were added.

Charles Watson-Wentworth (1730–82), the second Marquis of Rockingham, leader of the Whig party and for a brief time Prime Minister, had acquired an additional 3,000 acres at Badsworth, Ecclesall and Billingley upon his marriage to Mary Bright, the heiress of a baronet family. They had no children and so the Wentworth, Malton and Irish estates, with a London town house in Grosvenor Square, passed to his nephew, William, the fourth Earl Fitzwilliam (1748–1833), who in 1756 had succeeded to a large estate at Milton, near Peterborough.[16]

The present village of Wentworth is largely built of local coal-measure sandstone and is strung out along the street between the ruined medieval church at the west end and the grounds of the great house at the other. James Pigott Pritchett (1789–1868), best known as the architect of Huddersfield Railway Station (1847), was architect and surveyor to the Earls Fitzwilliam for over fifty years and was responsible for the churches, parsonages, schools, and lodges on the Wentworth estate.

The old church at the west end of Wentworth village was a chapel-of-ease in the parish of Wath. The tower looks stark without its battlements. John Skires left a bequest towards it when he made his will in 1497, so it was probably completed soon afterwards. The nave was rebuilt in 1684 but is now ruined, as are the former chancel and north chapel. The alabaster monuments of four generations of the Wentworth family are contained within what is now known as the Wentworth chapel at the east end.[17]

In 1885 J. L. Pearson, a leading Victorian architect, was commissioned to design Holy Trinity church to replace the old one. Sir Nikolaus Pevsner described it as, 'A very fine, sensitive and scholarly piece of Gothic Revival' in the thirteenth-century style.[18] It took two years to complete and in size it resembles a town church. The village also contains a Wesleyan Chapel that was built in 1834 in Clayfields Lane. Industry was kept out of sight.

Elsecar

William, the fourth Earl Fitzwilliam, and his son, Charles, the fifth earl (1786–1857), were paternalistic landowners whose tenants enjoyed better working conditions and more home comforts than most families of their rank elsewhere in South Yorkshire. Their view was that the ruling classes should accept their responsibilities and work to promote God's kingdom upon Earth. When Charles spoke out against the massacre of Peterloo, he lost his posts of Lord Lieutenant of the West Riding and of Ireland. Like their predecessors, they were keen to exploit the mineral resources on their estates, especially their coal reserves at Elsecar, Park Gate and Stubbin. Eventually, their income from coal and ironstone greatly exceeded their revenue from agriculture.

At the end of the eighteenth century, Elsecar began to grow from a single farmstead to a model industrial village. Old Row (seen here) was designed by John Carr for Earl Fitzwilliam to house his miners. It was completed by 1801.

When Earl Fitzwilliam sunk his Elsecar New Colliery to the Barnsley seam he installed a Newcomen-type beam engine to pump out the water. It is the only engine of its kind that still stands on its original site. Arthur Clayton showed that, despite the 1787 date on a lintel, records prove that the engine was built in 1794–5, when the colliery was opened. A new cylinder (1801), an extra boiler (1803–4), and a new wooden beam (1811–12) that was replaced by an iron beam (1836) enabled the engine to keep working until 1923, when electrical pumps were installed.[19]

The opening of a branch of the Dearne and Dove canal in 1799 was a great boost to the local economy. Lime kilns, coke kilns and a tar distillery were opened at the canal basin and John and William Darwin, who leased ironstone and coalmining rights from the Fitzwilliams, had two furnaces in Elsecar by 1800. Their firm prospered by making pig iron, domestic ranges, spoutings and rails for colliery tramways. Less than a mile away, the Walkers of Masbrough, South Yorkshire's leading ironmasters, established the Milton ironworks in the last decade of the eighteenth century and the reputation of the works grew after 1824 when William and Robert Graham arrived from London to manufacture pig, rod, hoop and sheet iron, castings, steam engines and boilers, suspension and other types of bridges, iron boats and general millwork.[20]

In 1850 the South Yorkshire railway provided access to the London market via Doncaster. The Elsecar ironworks and the Milton ironworks were both acquired by George and William Dawes from the Black Country, who ran a successful business until 1884. In 1870 their business comprised blast furnaces, puddling furnaces and rolling mills, which employed about 400 men. Barrie Trinder has calculated that one in four of these workers was born in the Black Country, including puddlers, shinglers and sheet-iron rollers from Tipton, Oldbury, West Bromwich and Bradley.[21]

Elsecar, or 'Elsekers', was the name of just a single farm when Thomas Jeffreys published his map of Yorkshire in 1772, but it grew rapidly after the opening of the new colliery in 1795. John Carr was commissioned to design colliers' houses at Elsecar, which compared most favourably with contemporary farm labourers' cottages or the typical one-storeyed miners' cottages that were found elsewhere. Between 1796 and 1801 Station Row and Old Row were built to Carr's designs, then in 1837 the long, curving terrace of 28 houses that the earl named Reform Row in honour of the passing of the Parliamentary Reform Act of 1832 provided much extra accommodation.

One of the most substantial buildings in the model village of Elsecar is the former lodging house, which the earl opened in 1854 to accommodate his young coal miners.

In 1854 the Miners' Lodging House in Fitzwilliam Street was opened for 'young colliers' who worked at the Simon Wood colliery. The 1850s and 60s also saw the provision of good quality housing, built with ashlar stone, in Cobcar Lane and Fitzwilliam Street. The fifth earl presented this new model community with a Wesleyan Methodist chapel (1842), Holy Trinity church (1843), and a Church of England school (1852), which replaced the 1836 National School. All these buildings, together with the flour mill (1842) and the sixth earl's private railway station (1870), survive in a designated conservation area alongside workshops that once formed part of the Elsecar Ironworks. They are eloquent testimony to the entrepreneurship and paternalism of the wealthy owners of the great mansion just out of sight at Wentworth Woodhouse.

Chapter 17

The Rivelin Valley

The Rivelin Valley was a remote and tranquil part of the city of Sheffield before the invention of the motor car. It was not until 1905 that a road was constructed from Malin Bridge up the valley to the Post Office, where it joined the 1818–21 turnpike road from Sheffield to Glossop via the Snake Pass. In earlier times, the valley was accessed only by steep, zig-zagging lanes such as the Racker Way which connected Stannington and Walkley. This track, which took its name from the old dialect word rakes for a path, was mentioned in John Harrison's survey of the manor of Sheffield

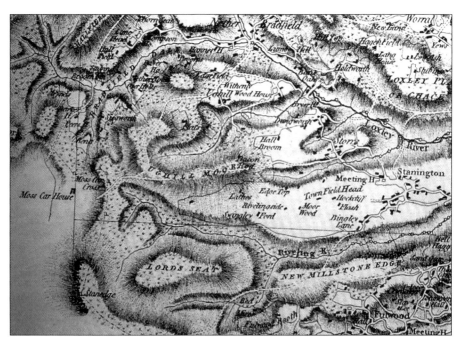

This section of Thomas Jeffreys's map of Yorkshire (1772) shows most of the area covered by the former Rivelin Chase, extending up both sides of the river valley and up on to the moors.

in 1637, our best source for the early history of the Rivelin Valley. Harrison also mentioned Coldwell Lane.[1]

Rivelin took its name from the small river that descended the steep-sided valley to its confluence with the River Loxley at Mousehole Forge and so on to the River Don, for it was simply a variant of rivulet. John Harrison's survey described the river in the old manner as Rivelin Water. It formed the boundary between the township of Stannington in the chapelry of Bradfield to the north and the townships of Upper and Nether Hallam in the parish of Sheffield to the south. All these places lay within Hallamshire, the ancient territory that was administered from Sheffield Castle.

Rivelin Chase

The medieval lords of Hallamshire designated the whole of the Rivelin Valley and the surrounding moors as a chase for hunting deer. The *chace of Riveling* was first recorded in 1383 but its history goes back much further than that.[2] The Norman lords created an enormous deer park on the opposite side of the River Sheaf from Sheffield Castle, as well as three adjoining chases or 'firths' at Rivelin, Loxley and Hawkesworth, in Bradfield Dale, which stretched over thousands of acres of bleak moorland. Harrison's survey of the manor of Sheffield in 1637 measured that part of 'Rivelin Firth that lyeth in the parish of Sheffield' at 5, 531½ acres, Stannington woods within Rivelin Firth at 217 acres, and 'the other part of Rivelin Firth lying … in the parish of Bradfield' at 1,114½ acres, making 6,863 acres in all.

Hunting was only an occasional activity, however, so these chases were put to other uses. A quarry was recorded in Rivelin in 1268,[3] and near the end of the thirteenth century Thomas de Furnival, lord of Hallamshire, confirmed the grazing rights of the inhabitants of Stannington, Moorwood, Hallam and Fulwood within the chase. The boundary started at the confluence of the rivers Loxley and Rivelin at Malin Bridge and went up to the ridge above Bell Hagg and Whiteley Wood before ascending Porter Brook and winding across the moors to Stanage. It then returned along Long Lane, 'the common way which leads from Sheffield towards the Derwent'.[4] Most of the township of Upper Hallam and much of the township of Stannington lay within the chase. In the 1440s the accounts of Henry Wrasteler, the forester of Rivelin, show that the inhabitants also had grazing rights for their swine in the woods and that outsiders paid rents for pasturing their plough oxen and bullocks on the moors.[5]

The starting point for hunting parties was Rivelin Lodge, high above the southern side of the valley; a later building occupies this site on the edge of Lodge Moor. The lord also had a cattle-rearing farm at Fulwood Booth, recorded in 1184,[6] and he had presented the canons of Beauchief Abbey with a farm at Fulwood Grange.[7] His deer keepers were based at Redmires, though Harrison noted that they also had grazing rights for their horses in the 62 acres of 'the Old Laund reserved for the Deare being Invironed with Rivelin Firth' and similar rights for two cows and a horse each in The Coppice. He observed that the lords of Hallamshire hunted not only red, fallow and roe deer but hares, pheasants, partridges, moor game - the old term for grouse - and wildfowl, and that they fished for salmon, trout, chevens and eels in the rivers, principally the Don.

The Woods

The Rivelin Valley was also famous for its timber. A manorial survey of 1624 noted the 'great store of timber' there,[8] and thirteen years later Harrison waxed lyrical about the enormous height and girth of the oaks in Hall Park, which stretched up the present Liberty Hill towards Stannington, covering 75 acres:

> There are alsoe within this Mannor very stately Timber especailly in Haw Parke, which for both straitnesse & bignesse there is not the like in any place that you can heare of being in length about 60 foot before you come to a knot or a bow, & many of them are two Fathams & some two fathams & a halfe about & they grow out of such a Rocher of stone that you would hardly thinke there were earth enough to nourish the rootes of the said trees.

In 1662 the Rivelin oaks were referred to in John Evelyn's book on trees, *Sylva*. He noted that in 'the upper end of Rivelin stood a tree, called the Lord's Oak, of twelve yards about, and the top yielded twenty-one cord; cut down about thirteen years since'. (A cord measures four feet by four feet by eight feet.) But Mr Halton, auditor to the Duke of Norfolk, told him that 'Rivelin itself is [now] destitute of that issue she once might of glorified in of Oaks, there being only the Hall Park adjoining, which keeps up with its number of Oaks'.[9]

Great changes were underway at this time. The Dukes of Norfolk, who had inherited the lordship of Hallamshire through marriage, did not live in Sheffield and so the Manor Lodge within Sheffield Park was allowed to decay and was largely demolished in the early 1700s. The deer were removed from the park and the chases, and the moors were largely given over to the grazing of sheep and cattle by tenant farmers. By the early eighteenth century the Rivelin oaks had been felled and the timber sold. Neither Hall Park nor Rivelin appeared in a list of the Duke's woods in 1720.[10] John Wilson of Broomhead Hall noted in his journal later in the century that, 'This Riveling was formerly full of wood and a chace of Red Deer therein'.[11] By then its character and appearance had changed considerably. The only wood to survive was The Coppice, which stretched down the hillside from Rivelin Lodge and was measured by Harrison at 225 acres. The small part that survives has not been coppiced for a century or so.

The removal of the deer brought another significant change to the wooded landscape. Holly trees had long been prized as winter fodder for deer and sheep. In 1441–2 the accounts of the forester of Bradfield had recorded 'holly sold there for the fodder of the animals in winter'. Small woods known as 'hollin haggs' were carefully managed and some of them were leased to tenants. In 1574 'one hage of hollen at Bell hagg' was let to Philip Morton of nearby Clough Field for five shillings a year, and in 1637 John Harrison recorded 28 'Hollin Rents' in the manor, including the £1.2s.2½d. paid by both Thomas and Rowland Revell for haggs in Rivelin; another 'Hagg of Hollin' stood in the Wood banke & under the Toft ends' at Stannington.[12]

The use of holly declined after the removal of the deer, though sheep continued to be fed in this way during winter. In the late 1690s Abaraham de la Pryme, the minister of Thorne, beyond Doncaster, noted in his journal that:

In the south west of Yorkshire, at and about Bradfield, and in Darbyshire, they feed all their sheep in winter with holly leaves and bark, which they eat more greedily than any grass. To every farm there is so many holly trees; and the more there is the farm is dearer; but care is taken to plant great numbers of them in all farms thereabouts.[13]

A member of the Earl of Oxford's party that passed through Sheffield Park in 1725 observed:

the greatest number of wild stunted holly trees that I ever saw together. They extend themselves on the common, on each side of the brook ... for a considerable way. This tract of ground they grow upon is called the Burley Hollings ... having their branches lopped off every winter for the support of the sheep which browse upon them, and at the same time are sheltered by the stunted part that is left remaining.[14]

New fodder crops gradually made this old practice redundant. In 1710 the Duke of Norfolk's bailiff noted that several holly haggs were 'unlett but most of them destroyed'. Yet two years later his woodward paid four shillings to Henry Broomhead for going on horseback for two days 'in the Great Snow to see if anyone Cropped Holling'. The final reference in the manorial records came in 1737, when a Bradfield man agreed 'to take all that hag of Hollin called Ugghill Wood'.[15]

The rugged slopes of the lower Rivelin Valley that were not occupied by holly haggs or coppices were used as commons for grazing. In 1637, for example, Harrison recorded:

a tenement called Bellhagg farme with a dwelling house a Barne a Smithy & a Close called the meadow thereto adjoyning ... & next unto a Common called the Hagg North East & Bell hagg greene South west & Cont[aining] 4 acres 2 roods 28 perches.

The hillsides ascending from the Rivelin Valley were well wooded and included haggs of holly for feeding the deer in winter time. Later, the woods were turned into coppices.

After the deer had been culled, the moors at the upper end of the valley were used for sheep and cattle grazing, for digging peat as a winter fuel, for burning bracken to make potash, and in some scattered places for mining shallow coal pits. Harrison also noted that 'very good Millnstones are hewen out in Rivelin or stone edge'. Millstone Hole survives as a minor place-name near Wyming Brook.

Water Mills

All these industrial activities were minor ones compared to the development of the river as a source of power for the Sheffield cutlers to grind their knives and edge tools. In 1637 Harrison observed that Sheffield's five rivers - the Don, Sheaf, Porter, Loxley and Rivelin - were:

> very profitable to the Lord in regard of the Mills and Cutler wheeles that are turned by theire streames, which weeles are imployed for the grinding of knives by four or five hundred Master Workmen that gives several marks.

He recorded a corn mill and four cutlers' grinding wheels in the Rivelin Valley.

Sheffield's national pre-eminence in this industry was based on the superiority of its water-powered grinding facilities. The rivers were small but they fell quickly and could be dammed at frequent intervals, and the local sandstone was ideal for grinding sharp edges. By 1660 at least 49 sites on its rivers, with a few others near by on the Blackburn Brook and the Moss Beck, had been provided with dams and buildings for grinding cutlery, milling corn, forging iron, smelting lead, and other industrial purposes. This provision multiplied dramatically in the next three generations, so that by 1740 at least 90 of the 115 places where water mills were constructed on the five rivers at one time or another were already in production. Two out of every three of these sites were used for grinding cutlery and edge-tools. At several of these sites, moreover, existing provision was expanded by enlarging the buildings and by installing more grinding wheels. This enormous growth in capacity took place before Benjamin Huntsman invented crucible steel and Thomas Boulsover invented Old Sheffield Plate, the traditional starting points of the local industrial revolution. The availability of so much water power was crucial to Sheffield's industrial development and its triumph over its rivals.[16]

In the more remote valleys much of this activity took place in the first half of the eighteenth century. Just six sites in the Rivelin Valley are known to have been occupied by 1700, and only Hind Wheel and perhaps Grogram Wheel were Elizabethan foundations. The Rivelin fell 280 feet in its last three miles and powered twenty mills from Uppermost Wheel in the west to its confluence with the Loxley in the east. Nine of these mills can be dated firmly to between 1719 and 1752 and another three were probably erected during that time. The comparative lateness of this development, compared with Sheffield's other rivers, is explained by the narrowness of the steep-sided valley and its remoteness beyond the high ground of Crookes and Walkley. If the distance from the centre of Sheffield had been shorter, further mills and dams might well have been constructed higher up the Rivelin Valley.[17]

All but two of the wheels were sited on the duke's estate, the exceptions being the ironworks at Walkley Bank Tilt (from 1762) and the much earlier Mousehole Forge. Mousehole's nickname was derived from its secluded position between the Rivelin and the Loxley rivers. In 1628 the site was being used as a lead smelting mill, but by 1664 it had been converted into an iron forge. The Bamforth family owned it for three generations, then in 1757 it was leased to John Cockshutt of Wortley Forge. Under the Armitage family, who took it over in the late eighteenth century, Mousehole became world-famous for its anvils. The forge closed in 1933 and is now a private residence.[18]

Most of the men who took out 21-year leases of grinding wheels from the Duke of Norfolk's estate were working cutlers whose weirs, goits, dams and buildings varied considerably in size. Some wheels (as the whole complex was called) had two ranges known as ends, each of which had perhaps four or more grinding troughs. The ancient system whereby cutlers rented space at a trough to do their own grinding continued in the eighteenth century, but the considerable growth in production meant that specialist grinders were increasingly able to find regular employment at their craft.

Today, the sites of the cutlers' grinding wheels in the Rivelin Valley are amongst the most accessible of those on Sheffield's five rivers. Just three are on private ground while the rest can be reached along public footpaths. Weirs, goits and dams can readily be identified at most sites, but the remaining buildings were cleared in the mid-twentieth century.[19]

Swallow Wheel is a typical example. It was in use by 1692 when Hugh Lockwood was the tenant. Seven years later, 'Lockwood Wheel' was

The second edition of *Water Power on the Sheffield Rivers* informs us that the Nether Cut Wheel on the River Rivelin was erected in 1719 and completely rebuilt about 1777. The grinding of cutlery continued here until 1939 and the shell of the building was still standing in 1954.

occupied by Joseph Swallow, a Stannington cutler whose probate inventory in 1709 recorded his tenant right of a cutler's wheel, a modest house, and personal estate valued at only £16.2s.6d. His son and namesake fared much better. In 1723 the younger Joseph agreed to make a new dam 'with good hewn stone and to make a good stone race and floor', then in 1737 he and Thomas Bower replaced the wheel. Eight years later, the buildings consisted of just one end and four troughs, but this was enough to make the lessees moderately prosperous.[20]

When Joseph Swallow died in 1755, he was described as a Stannington yeoman. His probate inventory listed the contents of his house, parlour, pantry, kitchen, scullery, cellar and the chambers over the house, parlour and kitchen. Like many of the rural metalworkers, he had a small farm with a cart house, corn chamber, stable and barn, and a smithy with tools valued at £5.14s.0d. The appraisers of the inventory also recorded 'The benefit of 3 apprentices, £40, Bills & Notes £36, Book Debts £158.5s.7d., Houses in Sheffield £220, Leases £298.18s.0d.', so he must have had a shrewd eye for business.

The contents of his grinding wheel in the Rivelin Valley were listed in detail:

3 Rough Stone Axletrees 15s.0d., a Whining Stone 5s.0d., 3 Glaziers £1.4s.0d., 17 pullies £1.6s.0d., 3 Stone Chains £1.10s.0d., 9 Horsing 15s.0d., 3 lesser axletrees 7s.6d., 2 of the largest axletrees £1.8s.0d, 3 pulley evens & 11 planks 6s.6d., 8 New Stones & 8 Colks £3.1s.6d., 3 Hack Hammers & 2 pickers 2s.0d., Wheel Bands £1.5s.6d., a Hatchet Drivel Hammers Chizel & Stedy 1s.6d., a Gavelock 2s.5d., a Range 1s.6d., a Ladder 4s.0d., 7 Glaziers £1.6s.0d.

The total value of his personal estate came to £918.7s.2d.[21]

By the beginning of the twentieth century Swallow Wheel lay in ruins, and in 1936 the *Sheffield Daily Independent* reported that 'nothing remains of the building'. A recent survey reported that the weir, constructed of large pitched stones, was in poor condition; the iron staple for the head goit shuttle survived, but the dam was overgrown; the ironwork of the pentrough could be seen in the wheel pit; the foundations of the buildings could be traced; and the tail goit which formerly fed directly into the head goit of Plonk Wheel downstream was overgrown.[22]

Parliamentary enclosure

Between 1791 and 1805 the 'Black Moors' within the former Rivelin Chase, together with the commons and wastes on the steep slopes of the Rivelin Valley, were enclosed by a private Act of Parliament. As lord of the manor, the Duke of Norfolk received large 'allotments' because of his previous ownership of the chase and in lieu of the great and small tithes, which Francis, fifth Earl of Shrewsbury, had acquired at the dissolution of the monasteries.[23] Some of the moorland edges were now cultivated for the first time, but most of the wastes in the upper part of the valley, extending to the county boundary at Stanedge Pole, were converted by the duke's estate into a grouse-shooting moor. Between 1830 and 1854 the Sheffield Waterworks Company constructed three reservoirs at Redmires and two in the Rivelin Valley to supply the needs of the rapidly expanding town. The water flowed by gravity along conduits to Crookes and thence by pipes into central Sheffield.[24]

High up the valley, the former Auley Meadows, which had taken their name from the Hawley family of Fulwood but which had become corrupted to Hollow Meadows, became the site of a distinctive new community, known by the ironic nickname of New England. In 1844 the Duke of Norfolk let much of his land there on long leases with nominal rents to small occupiers. Houses and cottages were built and crofts and gardens were brought 'into a good state of cultivation'. Three small cottages that were nicknamed 'Sparrow Barracks' were erected by a blade and scissor forger and a file forger and were occupied until the end of the century. A 'Truant School' that was built about 1871 by able-bodied paupers, who walked three to five miles from Sheffield each morning to be there by eight o'clock, lasted until 1922. Mark Firth, the Sheffield steelmaster, built a tiny Methodist chapel at Moscar and a burial ground for Sheffield's small Jewish community was enclosed nearby.[25]

Under the terms of the Enclosure Act, the inhabitants of Hallam, Fulwood, Stannington and Moorwood were allotted land in lieu of their ancient right of herbage in Rivelin, but the claims of 70 other men, including 35 cutlers, eighteen grinders, seven husbandmen, two shoemakers, a gentleman, a schoolmaster, a tailor and a wheelwright, were not allowed. Their solicitor claimed that 1,000 acres on the Black Moors were 'Rocks where the Poor burn Fearne and raise £120 by the Ashes' and that that the poor kept flocks of geese and 'many Galloways for Grinders to carry goods'.[26]

Rock House Farm, Stannington, was once typical of the small farms in and around the Rivelin Valley in having a cutler's smithy attached, seen here to the left of the farmhouse.

These claims were dismissed by the lawyer whose opinion was sought by the enclosure commissioners, as being 'most of them Wheelfellows – probably many not Inhabitants'. He judged (correctly) that the late thirteenth-century charter did not include the poor but allowed grazing rights only to the inhabitants who were freeholders. The grazing of geese and galloways and the burning of ashes were not customary rights but were practices that had arisen with laxer manorial control after the removal of the deer and because of the spread of cutlers' grinding wheels up the Rivelin Valley as trade and population increased.

The Bradfield militia return of 1821, which records the names and occupations of men aged between 18 and 45 who were liable to be called up for military duty, reveal just how important the grinding wheels along the Rivelin and Loxley valleys had become as a source of employment.[27] Of the 98 Stannington men in the list 46 were grinders and fifteen were cutlers. If we add the four filesmiths, three razorsmiths, two scissorsmiths, and a forge man, a button maker, a fork maker, a tilter and a blacksmith, the total number of those employed in the local metal trades comes to 75, or about three-quarters of the male workforce. These rural crafts have long since vanished, but the pleasure of a walk along the Rivelin Valley is enhanced by the knowledge of their former existence and the visual evidence on the ground.

Chapter 18

Nonconformist Chapels

A Nonconformist or Dissenter was originally someone who refused to conform to the Act of Uniformity of 1662 and other legislation that was passed after the Restoration of King Charles II in 1660. Over 2,000 clergymen, about one-fifth of the entire body of ministers in England and Wales, were ejected from their livings for refusing to conform to the Established Church, but many of them became private chaplains to gentry families and small congregations. A new era of toleration began in 1689, after King James II had been deposed, when the meeting places of Protestant Nonconformists were licensed for public worship by JPs meeting at quarter sessions.

Places of worship in remote areas that were distant from a parish church had been known as chapels during the Middle Ages, but during the first half of the seventeenth century the term became associated with the puritan form of religion. These chapels were plain, rectangular structures in vernacular styles, whose interiors were focused on the pulpit. One of the earliest in South Yorkshire was the Great Houghton chapel in the parish of Darfield, which was built about 1650 by Sir Edward Rodes. His crest above the east window is now unrecognizable, for the soft sandstone has crumbled badly. The chapel has mullioned-and-transomed windows and is crowned by rounded battlements, known as merlons, which rise in crow-stepped formation in the gables. The original pulpit and box pews with finials shaped like acorns remain in place. The Rodes family long remained dissenters, but in 1743 the archbishop's visitation reported that, 'This Chapel is now united to the Church of England'. The Elizabethan hall, in whose grounds the chapel was erected, was gutted by fire about 1960.[1]

Personal religious belief was obviously of prime importance in determining where chapels were sited, yet a wider explanation is needed for the striking geographical patterns in the strengths and weakness of each of the dissenting sects. Some estate villages on or close to the magnesian limestone belt have never had a chapel, for resident lords such as the Fountaynes and Montagus of High Melton and the Copleys of Sprotbrough ensured that these villages remained small and wholly agricultural in character, so that their inhabitants were entirely dependent upon the estate for their tenancies and employment. Nonconformity was easily suppressed in these circumstances. By contrast, it is the continuity of dissenting traditions that is striking in certain other communities, where there was no single dominant lord, particularly those in and around Sheffield, in the large parishes on the Pennine foothills, and in the isolated communities in the eastern lowlands.[2]

In 1669, during a brief period of toleration, thirteen dissenting chapels were recorded in South Yorkshire; two each in Sheffield and Rotherham, and one each in Attercliffe, Handsworth, Shirecliffe Hall, Penistone, Swaithe Hall, Great Houghton, and Hickleton, with two Quaker meeting houses at Balby and Darfield. Three years later, South Yorkshire had 22 'conventicles', which were mostly in the same places, with the addition of two in the lowlands at Kirk Sandall and Hatfield West Hall.[3] Between 1690 and 1692 the dissenters made their own enquiries to see which bodies needed financial support.[4] The reports confirm the early returns and show the importance of the recently established Attercliffe Academy, which educated Nonconformist ministers and the sons of prominent dissenters, and served as a mission headquarters for South Yorkshire.

A more accurate record of the extent of Nonconformity is provided by the Compton ecclesiastical census of 1676, which lists the number of dissenters in each parish.[5] These figures can only be regarded as rough estimates, but they show that Nonconformists formed a small minority of the population, probably about four per cent of the nation as a whole. In South Yorkshire just 736 dissenters of sufficient age to receive communion were recorded, that is only 3.1 per cent of the 23,497 inhabitants who were enumerated. The 65 Roman Catholics formed an even smaller group. Numbers and percentages, of course, do not tell the whole story, for the dissenters were often influential people who were committed to their cause.

The differences in their strengths and weaknesses across South Yorkshire were pronounced. Sheffield had about 300 dissenters – ten per cent of its communicants – whereas Doncaster had only eight amongst a population of similar size. The highest percentages of dissenters were in the eastern lowlands. In the parish of Fishlake, including the chapelry of Sykehouse, 136 dissenters formed 24.3 per cent of the communicants and in Thorne the 103 dissenters formed 20.6 per cent. Yet the large parish of Hatfield had only six dissenters among 642 communicants. The Thorne and Fishlake congregations must have looked for spiritual support further down the River Don, along their trade routes, for the district around Hull was one of the country's leading strongholds of dissent.

The lowlands contained many Dutch and Flemish strict Calvinists whose immediate ancestors had settled in the area after Vermuyden's company had drained Hatfield Chase. However, these immigrants only partly explain the high proportion of dissenters in this area. The ecclesiastical court books of the archdeaconry of York reveal that several people in Thorne who were prosecuted in 1664 for not attending church all had English names. In 1666 English 'quakers and sectaryes' of Fishlake were brought before the court, and Thomas Salten, gentleman, was charged with 'holding Conventicles at his own house'. Again, in 1680, numerous English people in Thorne were prosecuted 'for not being obedient to the Church of England in anything'.[6] Dissent had spread among the native population as well as among the immigrants.

Only a few Nonconformists were recorded in the Compton census in the remaining communities of South Yorkshire. In most places their numbers were negligible and in many parishes they were totally absent. On the magnesian limestone belt, thirteen of the twenty parishes with completed returns had no dissenters. Even in the villages that were not dominated by a gentleman's hall, the communal system of agriculture discouraged dissent. Parishes were small, isolated farmsteads were rare, and no industrial crafts that encouraged independence existed. In the whole limestone area only 49 dissenters were recorded, and 36 of these were listed in the market town of Tickhill or in the parish of Barnburgh, where the property was more divided than usual.

Six parishes on the coal-measure sandstones also had no dissenters. With the exception of Tankersley, they were all small places that lay just off the limestone belt to the east of Rotherham. They, too, were nucleated villages surrounded by arable fields and often dominated by the lord's estate. They were still unaffected by mining and quarrying and they had more in common with the limestone villages than with the larger parishes further west.

In 1676 the vicar of Penistone parish, the Reverend Henry Swift, ignored the Compton census. He had continued in his post after the Restoration, despite his refusal to conform to the Church of England, because he had the full support of the leading parishioners, all of whom were dissenters. Upon his death in 1689, however, the Crown appointed a new vicar who did conform, whereupon Elkanah Rich of Bullhouse Hall, two miles or so to the

Bullhouse Independent Chapel was built by Elkanah Rich in the grounds of his hall in 1692, three years after Nonconformist chapels were tolerated, following the Glorious Revolution of 1688. It remains independent of any religious denomination to this day.

west of Penistone, declared that as 'they had carried things so high and were so full of ceremonies' he would build a private chapel in his own grounds. This was opened in 1692 and it remains the oldest Nonconformist chapel with a continuous history in South Yorkshire. The first minister, the Revd Daniel Denton, was here until his death in 1721.[7]

'John Evans's List of Dissenting Congregations' in 1715 shows that the Old Dissent was still concentrated in the same places.[8] The largest congregation of dissenters in the whole of Yorkshire was at the Upper Chapel, Sheffield, where 1,163 people attended divine service. The terms by which the dissenters were described are puzzling at this time, for congregations sometimes changed their allegiances and the term 'Presbyterian' seems to have been a general one that occasionally included Independents and Unitarians. The Independent chapel at Bullhouse, which had an estimated congregation of 200, was labelled 'Presbyterian' in 1715, while the Presbyterian chapel at Underbank, Stannington, was recorded as 'Independent'. This latter chapel had been built in 1652 and by 1715 was attracting a congregation of 350. The congregation gradually moved from a Presbyterian to a Unitarian position. A new chapel was built on the remote site in 1742 and in the following year an estimated 250 families of

The Presbyterian Chapel at Underbank, near Stannington, was rebuilt in 1742 and long continued to attract a large congregation in this moorland district, far from the parish church at Ecclesfield and its Anglican chapel at Bradfield.

Nonconformists lived in the area. Its galleries and box pews were removed in 1867, but it remains one of the finest early chapels in Yorkshire.[9]

Meanwhile, the Quakers had grown in numbers from the time when George Fox had been active at Balby and Warmsworth. They were particularly successful among the poorer classes in the Sheffield area, though in the mid-1670s nearly 200 of them emigrated to America, and continued emigration helps to account for their eventual decline. Soon, the Quakers began to attract rich families as well. Their strongholds were the traditional ones of Sheffield, the moorland chapelries, and the lowlands in the east. In the rural areas, their most thriving congregation met at High Flatts in the parish of Penistone, where their meeting house at 'Quaker Bottom' is still the focal point of the hamlet. It served as a regional rather than a local centre, and the archbishop's visitation return of 1764[10] noted that 'many came out of different parishes' to swell the congregation to about 100. The Jacksons of Totties and Wooldale halls, near Holmfirth, were instrumental in the building of the High Flatts and Wooldale meeting houses, which later sponsored another at Lumb Royd, just outside Penistone. Men of this

The former Quaker meeting house at Warmsworth was built in 1706. The Friends had long been active in the Balby-Warmsworth district.

standing could dominate their chapels or meeting houses just as effectively as an Anglican squire could control the churches in their estate villages.

The former Quaker meeting house at Warmsworth, however, shows that even in a village on the magnesian limestone a determined family of yeoman freeholders could defy the Anglican squires who owned 75 per cent of the property. In 1706 Thomas Aldham opened this small building on his own land for Quaker meetings, not long after John Battie, a future Lord Lieutenant of the West Riding, had completed his new hall near by.[11]

A few new chapels were built during the first half of the eighteenth century, notably the one at Fulwood in 1729, with a minister's cottage alongside, but the old dissenting sects each suffered a decline during the middle decades of the eighteenth century, as they lost in fervour what they gained in respectability. The Presbyterians drifted into Unitarianism, whose rational approach attracted the ministers and the merchants, but which had little appeal to the poor. There was no 'enthusiasm' about it.

During these years, South Yorkshire was transformed by industrial developments and the population explosion. The old dissenting sects failed as badly as the established church in meeting this challenge. Both were unfitted to meet the spiritual and emotional needs of the masses. Into this vacuum stepped Methodism.

The Methodist preachers came into South Yorkshire from two different directions; from Epworth in the south-east, and from the Leeds circuit and Pudsey in the north. The Moravian colony that had been established at Fulneck, near Pudsey, by the Revd Benjamin Ingham and other followers of Count Zinzendorf, was much associated with Methodism in its early years and it supplied preachers to various parts of South Yorkshire. A list of 'Ingham Societies' in 1745 included thirteen members at Sykehouse and 22 at Ecclesall.

The list does not include the Wickersley society, but in 1764 the Moravians had some devoted followers there, many of whom were employed in quarrying grindstones. In 1676 Wickersley had been a small agricultural village with no dissenters, but now it had become one of those industrial villages that were to become so typically Methodist. In 1764 it contained thirteen Moravian families who met locally on three Sundays in the month and who made a round trip of 60 miles to Pudsey every fourth week. Only twenty people in Wickersley parish attended the communion services of the parish church and as few as eight received the Easter sacrament, but there were a further ten Presbyterians, four Quakers, two Baptists, 40 Methodists, about 70 who never attended any form of religious worship, and a further 70 who hardly ever went to church.[12]

Not all converts stood fast in their faith. At the same visitation in 1764 the vicar of Wickersley was:

> inclined to think that the Excess of preaching has almost extinguished Religion in this part; for those who were formerly the most zealous Dissenters (even amongst the Methodists and Moravians) are now become almost Infidels.

This sour opinion may not have been altogether valid, but indifference to all forms of religion was as characteristic of some communities as was the embracing of Dissent.

On their first visits to South Yorkshire, John and Charles Wesley and George Whitefield made their headquarters in rural places, especially in isolated farms and hamlets in semi-industrial areas on the edges of parishes, such as Thorpe or High Green. From these rural centres the preachers visited the surrounding villages and towns, where they at first met with violent opposition until landowners, including the Marquis of Rockingham, allowed them to preach. The visits of these famous preachers were highlights that encouraged local men to continue their efforts.

In some parts of South Yorkshire the connection between industry and Methodism was as striking as had been the links between industry and Old Dissent, but it was not just to the respectable artisans and new industrial leaders that Methodism appealed. Above all, its message was directed at the heathen poor, who had been left untouched by the Established Church and the old Nonconformist sects. But progress was slow and the Methodists had gained few proselytes by the time of the 1743 and 1764 visitation returns. The hostility of the established church is apparent in such comments as the one by the vicar of High Hoyland in 1764 (referring, presumably, to Clayton West, an industrial textile settlement at the edge of his parish):

> Some Interlopers from Places infected with Methodism are endeavouring to propagate their Notions, but gain few Proselytes. There is no licenced or other Meeting House, except a few private Houses may be called so; where the Above Crazy Visionaries sometimes assemble.

Membership of Methodist societies remained comparatively small until the 1830s. In 1773 there were only 910 members in the Sheffield circuit, which embraced North Derbyshire and most of South Yorkshire except the lowlands in the east. Nine years later, membership had risen a little to 1,070. Methodism had clearly not yet achieved the success that was to come its way during the nineteenth century.[13]

On Sunday, 29 March 1851 the first and only census of all those attending church services was taken by the state.[14] The most important fact that was revealed by this census was that well over half the population of the country did not attend any religious service at all. The second fact that emerged was that, of those who did attend services, about half (taking the country as a whole) were Nonconformists. The situation was very different from what it had been in 1676 when the Dissenters formed only four per cent of the nation. Now, the evangelical movement had triumphed and, far from being despised as a fanatical minority, the new Nonconformists were numerous and vociferous.

In 1851 the large parishes of the eastern lowlands were strikingly Nonconformist in sympathy, much more so than the rest of South Yorkshire. In every parish in these lowlands the various forms of Methodism were now the strongest form of dissent. In the large and populous parishes of the western half of South Yorkshire new Anglican churches had recently been built to serve smaller areas, but no such division of the ancient parishes had taken place in the agricultural and sparsely populated lowlands. Methodism was particularly strong in the outlying chapelries of Stainforth and Sykehouse and this tendency was reinforced by the fact that the Hatfield Methodists were mainly concentrated in Hatfield Woodhouse, by the drained area known as the Levels. The area that had once supported the Old Dissent was now predominantly Methodist.

The other ancient stronghold of Dissent had been Sheffield and the surrounding moorland area, but the Established Church had made a determined attempt at recovery in the town. In 1851 the proportion of Anglicans in Sheffield matched the rest of South Yorkshire, but Methodism was now much stronger. In Penistone parish, another old centre of Dissent, the Anglicans had two churches and the Bullhouse Independents and the High Flatts Quakers were still active, but the Quaker meeting-place at Lumb Royd had gone. In its place were three Wesleyan chapels and separate chapels for the Methodist New Connection, the Primitive Methodists, the Independents, and the Particular Baptists, all products of the Evangelical Revival.

The triumph of Methodism, however, was not limited to the older areas of dissent. The situation had been transformed so that nearly all areas had their Nonconformists now. The industrial poor turned increasingly to the Methodist New Connection (founded 1797) or to the Primitive Methodists (who broke away in 1812), while Wesleyan Methodism had become firmly established and respectable.[15]

Methodism had made a big impact in Barnsley, where little headway had been made by the Old Dissent, and it was particularly successful in the surrounding industrial villages, especially those that were secondary settlements away from the centres of their parishes, where neither squire nor vicar was able to exert much authority. Darton, for example, had only the Anglican church and a Wesleyan chapel in the central village, but further out in the parish the two nailmaking communities of Mapplewell and Staincross had three Wesleyan chapels. High Hoyland had only its parish church, but the new textile settlement down in the valley at Clayton West had chapels for the Wesleyans, Independents, Particular Baptists, Methodist New Connection, and Primitive Methodists, while the new Wesleyan Reform movement met in Aaron Peace's warehouse. To attend their services, the Anglicans had to climb the steep hill to the parish church in the old village.

On the coal-measure sandstones, only Stainborough, Tankersley and Thybergh continued to resist Nonconformity, but estate villages were not entirely immune for the Wesleyans had been allowed a foothold in Wentworth and they had also established themselves in Adwick-upon-Dearne, where the lord was non-resident.

On or just off the magnesian limestone, the estate villages of Hickleton, High Melton and Sprotbrough continued to resist Dissent, but elsewhere Methodism gained converts in the agricultural or quarrying communities. In this area, religious differences usually polarized to a choice between either the Established Church or Wesleyan and Primitive Methodism. Here, too, the Methodists were often strongest in the small secondary settlements that lay away from the parish church; for example, at Long Sandall, but not at Kirk Sandall; at Cadeby, but not in the estate village of Sprotbrough; and at Bentley (where they had three chapels), but not at Arksey. Although the Methodists had gained a foothold in this area, many of the congregations met in private houses and cottages, for they were too small and too poor to build a chapel.

The Unitarians and the Quakers were unmoved by the Evangelical revival, but the Independents (now often referred to as Congregationalists) and the Baptists joined in the new religious fervor. By 1851 the Quakers still had eight meeting places but had a total attendance of only 1,231. They were scattered and almost finished as a force to be reckoned with. The Unitarians had six chapels, with a total attendance of 1,282. They were only just managing to maintain their numbers and former influence. Other Nonconformist sects were by now much more important in the traditional strongholds of Old Dissent.

By 1851 the Wesleyan Methodists were easily the strongest Nonconformist sect in South Yorkshire, with 156 congregations and a total attendance of 29,183. They already had 131 chapels and a further 25 small groups met regularly in private houses. Everywhere, they were the chief alternative to the Church of England. They had broken down the old geographical barriers and flourished even in the arable limestone district. In addition, there were nineteen congregations, with a total attendance of 2,238, which belonged to the new Wesleyan Reform Movement, which had its headquarters in Sheffield.

Nonconformist chapels played a prominent part in the annual Whitsuntide processions. Here a group of Sunday School scholars and their families gather at Thurlstone in 1933 under their banner.

The Primitive Methodists were the second strongest Nonconformist sect in South Yorkshire, with 47 congregations and a total attendance of 8,365. The 'Ranters' as they were known were humble men and women in origin and they found a receptive audience amongst the poor, especially among the farm labourers of eastern England and in the new mining communities. In 1851 their main period of strength was still to come, for many of their meetings were small affairs.

The Methodist New Connection had become strong in the towns and industrial villages of the Sheffield-Rotherham-Barnsley district. In 1851 they had 24 congregations and a total attendance of 4,113. Taken together, the members of the various forms of Methodism outnumbered the congregations of the Church of England. The 'few crazy visionaries' of 1764 had, in less than a hundred years, become the most powerful body of all. The Methodists attracted people of all classes in almost every type of community.

As the British population soared in the later nineteenth and early twentieth centuries many more churches and chapels were built. They were as characteristic of the new pit villages as of the older settlements. By 1901

Nonconformists still outnumbered the members of the Established Church in the country as a whole. Millions of people attended a church or chapel every Sunday, often for two or three services a day. Those denominations that attracted wealthy congregations had rebuilt their chapels, first in classical and then in Gothic styles. But in the last third of the twentieth century large numbers of Nonconformist chapels became redundant. Many have been demolished; others have been taken over by different bodies, both religious and secular. The great age of religious Nonconformity has now passed.

Chapter 19

Coal Mining

The coal seams that outcropped near the surface in the western parts of South Yorkshire were being mined when records began. In 1293 an inquest heard that a man had been killed when he was digging coal near his home at Bull Haw, Silkstone. Soon afterwards, another inquest heard about the deaths of two men in a pit near Masbrough. Four deeds dated between 1370 and 1388 were concerned with shallow pits at Cortworth and Nether Haugh and another of 1397 referred to a 'colepitte' at Silkstone. Fifteenth-century records mention coal mining in Sheffield Park and at Grenoside, Greasborough and Rotherham. No doubt coal mining was much more widespread and of greater antiquity than the chance survival of these documents suggests.[1]

Before the Victorian era South Yorkshire miners did not form a special, easily recognizable group. Canals and navigable rivers had begun to open up distant markets during the eighteenth century, but it was only with the coming of the railways that the deep coal mines that worked the Barnsley and Silkstone seams were able to compete effectively with the coalfield of Northumberland and County Durham, which had ready access to markets by sea. In earlier times, coal miners were not a race apart that lived in 'pit villages'. They were no more different from their neighbours than were blacksmiths or quarrymen. They lived in similar houses to the farmers or craftsmen within a village or out in the countryside and they usually had a smallholding to farm.

Landowners with deposits of coal on their estates normally leased the mining rights to gentlemen or yeomen, who invested their capital in the necessary equipment and employed a team of miners for specified periods at agreed wages. In 1693, for example, William Greene, the owner of Thundercliffe Grange near Rotherham, had a complete set of mining equipment appraised in his probate inventory: three windlasses, a fire pan for ventilation, thirteen picks and three sinking picks, five coal hammers, a sledge-hammer and two other hammers, four wedges, two gudgeons, two shovels, a hatchet and a saw, and ten corves (trucks), hurry hooks for pulling them, a tub and a trunk. This was a considerable mining enterprise for its time in land-locked South Yorkshire.[2]

Once river and canal transport began to open up distant markets, miners were able to earn wages that were higher than those of most of the craftsmen and labourers. In 1771 Arthur Young reported in his *Tour through the North of England* that in the Rotherham district coal miners earned seven to nine shillings a week, near Wakefield they got 10 to 12 shillings, and on Tyneside they could earn as much as 15 shillings.[3]

In 1806 lists were made of all the men in the various townships of Staincross wapentake aged between 18 and 45 who were liable for military service if Napoleon's troops invaded England. Of the 1,734 men who were recorded in the return only 153 were described as miners or colliers, and some of these were ironstone miners and a few may have been wood colliers. Cawthorne township had 32, whereas Barnsley had only 25, Tankersley 13, Silkstone 11 and Wortley 10. At that time, the townships of Barugh, Carlton, Monk Bretton, Royston, Ryhill, Shafton and South Hiendley, which later in the century were to become pit villages, had no coal miners at all.[4]

In the early nineteenth century most pits were shallow and cool to work in, but they were sometimes wet. The seams of coal were often thin; indeed some were less than eighteen inches high. Even in the new, deep mines, which were opened in the middle decades of the nineteenth century, working space was limited and the hewers had to move about on their hands and knees. Only in the thick seams of the nine-foot 'Barnsley Bed' were miners able to stand up. The early method of getting coal was the bord and pillar system, where the hewer worked by himself in his own place. The coal that he cut was removed to the bottom of the pit shaft by children and youths and sorted at the surface by other youngsters, old miners and women.

An inscription on a stark Gothic monument in the churchyard at Silkstone commemorates a horrific accident in a local mine without a touch of human sympathy. It reads:

THIS MONUMENT was erected to perpetuate the remembrance of an awful visitation of the Almighty which took place in this Parish on the 4th day of July, 1838. On that eventful day the Lord sent forth his Thunder, Lightning, Hail and Rain, carrying devastation before them, and by a sudden irruption of water into the Coalpits of R. C. Clarke Esqr. twenty six human beings whose names are recorded here were suddenly Summon'd to appear before their Maker. READER REMEMBER! Every neglected call of God will appear before Thee at the Day of Judgement. Let this Solemn Warning then sink deep into thy heart and so prepare thee that the Lord when He cometh may find thee WATCHING.

George Birkinshaw 10, Joseph Birkinshaw 7, Isaac Wright 12, Abraham Wright 8, James Clarkson 16, Francis Hoyland 13, William Atick 12, Samuel Horne 10, Eli Hutchinson 9, George Garnett 9, John Simpson 9, George Lamb 8, William Womersley 8, James Turton 10, John Gothard 8.

Catherine Garnett 11, Hannah Webster 13, Elizabeth Carr 13, Ann Moss 9, Elizabeth Hollings 15, Ellen Parker 15, Hannah Taylor 17, Mary Sellars 10, Elizabeth Clarkson 11, Sarah Newton 8, Sarah Jukes 10.

The monument is inscribed on each of its four sides with biblical texts.

This grim Gothic monument in Silkstone churchyard commemorates the deaths of 26 children in the Huskar pit disaster of 1838.

Work had progressed normally for most of the day at the Huskar 'day-hole' pit, when a thunderstorm, which lasted from about 2.30 pm to 4 o'clock, caused the small stream that formed the township boundary to rise to a dangerous height. This stream was dry for most of the year and had never been known to overflow. However, on this occasion it rose so high that it eventually ran into the drainage sough by which the winding engine discharged its water. The winder warned the banksman, who in turn shouted down the pit telling the miners to come out. The men knew nothing of the storm and, thinking that an explosion had occurred, they extinguished their lights. They could not leave via the shaft as the rising water had stopped the engine, so they made their way in the dark to the other shaft. But here the water had entered the firing hole and had stopped the other winding engine. Had they stayed where they were, all would have been safe; indeed, the men left unharmed after the flood had subsided. But the nature of the trouble was not understood and the children pestered the men to let them leave by the 'day-hole'. This seemed a reasonable plan and eventually 40 children left together to what they thought was safety, but shortly after they had passed through one of the ventilation trap doors, flood water came gushing towards them. The fourteen children at the front were flung aside and managed to scramble into a side-passage, where they survived to tell the tale, but the other 26 were pinned against the trap door. The weight of the water prevented the door being opened and the children were drowned.

Three years later, the Reverend J. C. Symons, the commissioner enquiring into the employment of children in the mines, visited Silkstone to see 'some of the largest collieries in my district' and to interview a wide range of people. Most of his contacts agreed that the children's work was not unhealthy. The owner, R. C. Clarke of Noblethorpe Hall, made a point of having good ventilation in his pits; they were examined each morning before work began, and Davy safety lamps were used. Edward Ellis, a local surgeon, thought that mining was healthier for the children than was weaving or even farm labouring and he did not think that a reduction in hours of work or the abolition of child labour was required. Witnesses agreed that work began between five and six in the morning and, though it often continued until five in the afternoon, it sometimes ended as early as 2 o'clock. But a large gathering of miners at Barnsley Court House expressed an opinion different from that of Edward Ellis. They told Symons that eight hours work was enough for a child. However, as the parents could not support their children on reduced wages, legislation to limit the number of hours would have to be accompanied with some provision for maintenance.[5]

R. C. Clarke guardedly admitted that he did not think mining was suitable work for girls, but he did not know how the parents could support them otherwise. A total of 91 boys and 53 girls were employed in his pits. Matilda Carr, aged 12, said, 'I don't like it, but my father can't keep me without going', and Hannah Clarkson, aged 16, remarked, 'If I had a girl of my own I would rather send her to the pit than clam, but if I had the choice I would rather send her to some other work'.

The miners who met at Barnsley Court House resolved almost unanimously that, 'The employment of girls in pits is highly injurious to their morals', that it was no proper work for a female, and 'that it is a scandalous practice'. But if girls were not employed in some parts of the coalfield, why was it necessary for the Silkstone miners to send their daughters into the pits? They claimed that they had no alternative if the girls were not to starve, but three years after the passing of the 1842 Act forbidding the employment of women and girls in the mines and the use of boys under the age of 10, a commissioner reported that:

> The temporary privation occasioned to some of the females formerly employed in the pits has nearly passed away. Almost all have found other occupations. Several expressed to me their content at the alteration: 'they were glad to be out of the pit', 'it wanted doing most sadly', and 'it will be a deal better for all now it is done'.[6]

The Huskar pit disaster shook the nation's conscience and was instrumental in the production of the House of Commons *Report to the Commissioners on the Employment of Children* (1842). A particularly effective ploy of the reformers was to include drawings of children with chains attached to their belts, 'hurrying' or pulling loaded trucks of coal on their hands and knees, with others 'thrusting' behind. When the commissioner visited 'Mr George Chamber's Day-hole Colliery' at High Green and Newton and Chambers's ironstone pit across the parish boundary in Tankersley, he found 'a rather extensive' mine where asses were employed 'to draw the loaded corves from the dip banks to the main gates'. The seams of coal were very thin and black damp was a problem. Chambers contracted the work of 'getting and hurrying' to 'undertakers'.

The attitudes of the undertakers were often harsher than those of the owners. George Shaw, the steward to the Thorncliffe pit, said:

> Those colliers who have got their own children at work with them use them worse than the others ... There is no beating of the lads, except by their own fathers.

He claimed that:

> We were obliged to have doors put at the mouths of the foot rails, about five years ago, in order to prevent the undertakers working the lads

before six in the morning. Previous to that being done they used to come to work at three or four, or just when they had a mind.

Boys from these pits answered the commissioner's questions. George Brammit was:

about 10 years old. I hurry along the level, and up the board gates. There is always someone to help me. We go into the pit mostly at 5 in the morning and come out sometimes before 5 in the evening. We dine at 12, and stop a quarter of an hour and more sometimes, and then I go and help to fill a corve; but the pit stops an hour. I don't fill at other times. It isn't hard work hurrying, and it doesn't tire me at night. I like being there. I'd rather be at school. I don't know how long I have been in the pit. I go to Sunday School regularly every Sunday. I can read in 'Reading Made Easy'. They teach me to write. Jesus Christ came on earth to save sinners. I don't know what death he died. I know I must pray to be saved.

Henry Goddard was:

10 years old last Christmas. I attend a trap door. I sit in the dark generally, but sometimes they give me a light. Sometimes I get three bits of candle a day, sometimes more. The corves pass sometimes every five minutes. I sometimes walk about two or three yards. It doesn't make me tired. I like being down the pit, but I'd as lieve be at school. I can't read, but I have been at day-School once. I left off when I came to the pit two years ago. I don't go to Sunday School. I run about on Sundays I reckon. I've no mother, and my father never sends me to school. I go sometimes. I don't know my a, b, ab. I learnt a, b, c, at school. God made the world. I don't know who was the son of God. I am sure that I am not telling any lies.

Patrick Kiltride was 11 years old:

I'm a hurrier. I have been in the pit about a year. I used to go about begging before. I hurry along the maingate about 250 yards. It's level. Another boy hurries with me and I lather him sometimes. I sometimes get lathered myself. They wouldn't keep me if I went to school, but I'd rather go there than be in the pit. I can't read.

Daniel Drenchfield did not know when his birthday was, what 3 x 10 came to, the name of the biggest city in England, nor who Jesus Christ was. He had been to Sunday School at Wortley and knew that 'I sall go to hell if I am not a good boy'. He had learned his catechism off by heart but had no idea what it meant. He was typical of many others.

After a couple of years of 'trapping', that is opening and closing a ventilation door to allow the passage of the corves, a teenage boy usually moved to 'hurrying' and then to driving the pit ponies that pulled trucks of coal from the coal face to a collecting place called a pass-by. The coal was then hauled to the pit bottom by a steel cable, worked by an engine. The ponies trotted quickly along the level, rarely stumbling in the darkness, though they were pulling three or four trucks, each of which was loaded with between eight and ten hundredweight of coal. The accidents that occurred were usually because of the misbehaviour or irresponsibility of the boy drivers. They matured quickly when they became hewers in their teens.

Working Conditions in Coal Mines, 1850–1914

Most pit villages did not acquire their distinctive character until Victorian or Edwardian times, once railways had opened up new districts by transporting coal cheaply and quickly. As mines were sunk deeper and deeper, dust swirled about from the hewing and moving of coal, getting into the miners' lungs and blackening them from head to foot. The atmosphere was also poisoned by the smells from sweating miners and stinking ponies. Undergound sanitation facilities were non-existent. Even in the early twentieth century the use of electric light beyond the main roadways from the pit bottom was almost unheard of. Working conditions varied a great deal, not only from district to district, but also from pit to pit, and the nature of the seams was constantly changing. The risk of the roof collapsing was always present.

Every year between 1850 and 1914 an average of more than a thousand British miners were killed in accidents, many of them through indiscipline or indifference to safety rules.[7] The worst disasters were the terrible explosions of gas in which hundreds of miners died from the force of the blast. In the Dearne Valley 189 miners were killed in 1857 at Lundhill; 59 lost their lives at Edmunds Main in 1864; and 361 died in the Oaks Colliery explosion in 1866.[8]

Yet terrible events such as this were responsible for only about a quarter of fatal mining accidents in the Victorian and Edwardian era; most deaths came from isolated roof falls. We have no reliable statistics on the accidents that caused injuries rather than deaths, but John Benson has estimated that the proportion was almost 100 to one.[9] More working days were lost from injuries than from strikes and lock-outs.

The slag heaps, or muck stacks as they were generally known, that rose from the vicinity of a pit head were uncommon before the 1880s. Originally, the miners were paid by the number of corves of coal that they sent out of the pit, so riddling was done underground, but

This monument in Darfield churchyard commemorates the disaster of 1857, when 189 miners were killed in a gas explosion at Lundhill colliery, Wombwell.

increased competition and abuses by both workers and management meant that more efficient sorting methods were needed. Enormous, ugly slag heaps now began to dominate the new pit villages.

Britain's coal miners increased rapidly in number from about 50,000 in 1800 to over 1 million by the First World War.[10] Most of this increase occurred in the later Victorian and Edwardian era. Coal miners were amongst the most mobile sections of the population until they and their families settled down in the pit villages that became well-established in the late nineteenth century. News of a new pit opening spread quickly and men in search of employment sometimes travelled from far afield. Once they had become established in a coalfield, however, they rarely moved beyond other local collieries. Single men formed a minority amongst the immigrants; outsiders such as Irish labourers, tended to lodge with people whom they knew. As the immigrants clustered together, sometimes in the same row of

The old farming parishes of the Dearne Valley were transformed during the Victorian period. The Barrow colliery and coke ovens, shown here in 1969, were erected at Blacker on the southern edge of Worsbrough township, while the old estate village in the background remained unaffected.

terraced houses, new mining communities soon acquired a strong sense of community.[11]

Whole districts were changed beyond recognition by the deep mining of coal. Many of the 94,110 miners who were recorded in the 1901 census returns for the West Riding lived in new settlements such as Denaby Main or at places like Grimethorpe, which had only been hamlets before. In the Dearne Valley old settlements such as Darfield, Wath and Wombwell were transformed, then in the late Victorian and Edwardian era deeper mines were sunk on the concealed coalfield under and beyond the magnesian limestone and many of the old farming parishes of the Doncaster district were altered beyond recognition. Doncaster had become encircled by new pit villages.

The industry that defined South Yorkshire in so many ways during the nineteenth and twentieth centuries has now gone and the environment of the pit villages has been transformed. Looking back, we can now see that the dominance of coal mining lasted for only a few generations. This is a relatively short time in the long history of South Yorkshire.

The terraced houses of the pit village of Denaby Main were built to a density of 46 per acre. By 1868 the colliery was employing about 250 miners. In 1893 a new pit at Cadeby Main was opened on the other bank of the River Don and by 1901 the village contained houses for about 2,500 employees.

Chapter 20

A Miscellany

Much more 'history on the ground' remains to be discovered in the South Yorkshire countryside. This final chapter looks at a miscellaneous collection of buildings that have special stories to tell. Our understanding of their nature and purpose is enhanced when we are able to place them in wider historical contexts.

The Barnburgh dovecote

The earliest dovecotes or pigeon houses belonged to lords of the manor or to monasteries until their use began to spread in the seventeenth and eighteenth centuries. Pigeons were valued for their meat, eggs, feathers, down and dung. The cost of their upkeep was small, for they forage for food and have a strong homing instinct.

Dovecotes are difficult to date. Brian Elliott has recorded 26 surviving examples in the Rotherham Metropolitan District and 38 in the countryside around Doncaster.[1] The best surviving example in South Yorkshire is the one that once belonged to the More family of Barnburgh Hall. Its roof timbers have been dated by dendrochronology to between 1487 and 1523. Built of local magnesian limestone, the dovecote has a hipped roof, topped with a lantern,

The well-conserved Barnburgh dovecote now stands in a green area at the edge of a group of former outbuildings of the hall, which have been converted into domestic accommodation in modern times.

and is lit by four small, square windows half way up the walls, just above a stringcourse.

In 1692, when the dovecote was included in a sale of the manor of Barnburgh, it was described as:

> A very fair large Dove Coate built five square with eight fine large pillars to support the Arch. All the gudgeon holes of Free stone w[hi] ch are at least 1700. The whole Fabrick of Stone but only the Door, and being well looked after would be worth many pounds the yeare. [2]

The dovecote stands north-east of Hall Street on the edge of the former hall complex.

Village Schools

One of the best surviving examples of an old South Yorkshire village school that was built in the same vernacular style as the local domestic houses stands on the north-eastern side of the churchyard at Laughton-en-le-Morthen.

The early seventeenth-century village school at Laughton-en-le-Morthen still fulfills its original purpose across the road from the parish church.

Sometime between 1610 and 1619 two local landowners, Anthony Eyre and Edmund Laughton, donated the land on which to build the school, with a master's house attached on the east and a garden beyond.[3]

The school has been re-roofed with Welsh blue slates, but the rest of the building retains its original appearance. The walls were built of local magnesian limestone rubble with ashlar quoins and mullioned windows. Discreet additions to the rear have enabled it to continue as the village school at the present time.

The location of the school close to the parish church is typical of many early educational establishments. Penistone Grammar School, for example, was built in the Kirk Flatt, just across the road on the north side of the churchyard.[4] The Elizabethan grammar school at Worsbrough occupied a similar position on a green or common. A previous school that was associated with a chantry chapel inside St Mary's church, Worsbrough, had been closed in 1547 when chantries throughout the land were dissolved by an Act of Parliament, but in 1560 the parishioners were able to recover the endowments and William Wolley, the former chantry priest, was appointed as the schoolmaster.[5]

The early eighteenth-century village school at Harthill stands in the churchyard and now serves as a village hall.

In 1632 John Rayney, a native of Worsbrough who had prospered in the City of London and who was motivated by his Puritan beliefs, bequeathed property to the Worshipful Company of Drapers in order to pay £30 a year to a lecturer (a preacher) at the church and £13.6s.8d. to the master of the grammar school, who was to teach 'learning, writing, cyphering [and] the grounds of religion'. The school building appears to date from Rayney's time, but it is now a private house.[6]

Another old school stands in a corner of the churchyard in South Yorkshire's most southerly parish of Harthill. It dates from about 1720, the same time as the nearby rectory. The absentee lord of the manor, the Duke of Leeds, acted as patron and paid the master £12 per annum.[7] Like most of the other old buildings in the village, the school was constructed of local 'Rotherham red' sandstone. By the time of its foundation, even small village schools were beginning to look quite different from their predecessors. That at Harthill was built in a classical style, though with a projecting gable in the centre instead of a pediment. Light was provided by an oval window over the former entrance and the cross-windows that were fashionable at that time. The school now serves as the village hall.

Hellaby Hall

The site of the deserted medieval village of Hellaby Hall has been transformed in recent decades by a large industrial estate at the junction of the M18 motorway and the road from Rotherham to Maltby. Hellaby Hall, one of the most striking and unusual gentry houses in South Yorkshire, is now a hotel and conference centre at the edge of the estate, so it no longer catches the eye of drivers along the main road. The hall was in a sorry state in the 1970s and was badly affected by fire in 1980, but a public enquiry saved it from demolition.

Hellaby Hall was built by Ralph Fretwell on the site of his ancestral home.[8] He was a Quaker who had made his fortune producing sugar on a plantation in Barbados, where the highest mountain on the island is still known as Mount Hillaby. He returned to England in the late 1680s and began to build his new home. The Braithwell parish register records that his second daughter, Marafe, was baptized on 14 February 1690 (modern style) at a private ceremony in the home of Mr Eyre of Bramley, as Fretwell's house was not then finished.

The dramatic roofline of Hellaby Hall sets it apart from other houses. It was rescued from dereliction in the 1980s and now serves as a hotel.

The Dutch-style houses that Ralph Fretwell had seen in Barbados inspired him to attempt something similar in South Yorkshire. Hellaby Hall is in most ways a standard late-seventeenth century house. It still has some of the cross-windows that were fashionable at that time, and elsewhere we can see how sash windows have replaced the original ones. Three sides of the hall were built of coursed magnesian limestone from local quarries, but the front was faced with high-quality Roche ashlar and the roof was covered with pantiles. The hall stands on a slope, so the sides and the rear were given an extra storey to reach the same height of the front. Later, another wing was added at the rear.

Yet this is not how we see Hellaby Hall at first sight. Its appearance was transformed by an exotic Dutch gable that starts with big spiral scrolls at each end and which rises by slopes and curves to a flat top. This eye-catching gable is, however, purely decorative, for it has no third storey behind it.

When Ralph Fretwell died in 1701 the four appraisers of an inventory of his personal estate met in his kitchen and proceeded room by room to list all the furniture and utensils.[9] This is a valuable record of the original arrangements, for the interior of the house was totally altered in the nineteenth century and again in modern times. The appraisers went on to record his livestock, crops and farm equipment, and then they noted that eleven hogsheads of sugar worth nearly £200 had arrived at Hull. Finally, they made an account of the debts that were due to him (some of which were 'desperate'), and of 'Three bills of Exchange return'd from Barbados amounting in all to £2,700', with a further £2,000 forwarded by a Mr Mel. Holder. The source of the income that paid for Fretwell's new residence was made perfectly clear.

New Mill Bridge

Packhorse bridges are often thought to be medieval, for they seem so simple in style, but surviving examples are in fact much later. Where we have documentary evidence, we find that they date from the second half of the seventeenth century to the third quarter of the eighteenth. Earlier packhorse bridges were wooden ones. This should not surprise us when we remember that most houses were timber framed before the seventeenth century, when stone buildings became fashionable.[10]

The bridge that now stands in Glen Howe Park at Wharncliffe Side, north of Sheffield, provides us with a good example. A plaque claims that this is 'An Ancient Pack Horse Bridge' that was re-erected here by Joseph Dixon,

New Mill Bridge dates from 1734. It was moved from the Ewden Valley when the reservoir was built and re-erected in Glen Howe Park.

a local paper manufacturer, when the original site was flooded upon the creation of Ewden reservoir. It was known anciently as New Mill Bridge, for it stood by a corn mill of that name in the Ewden Valley. A New Mill Bridge was mentioned in a charter that dates from before 1279,[11] but we must not be misled into thinking that the present bridge dates from that era.

John Wilson, an eighteenth-century antiquarian who lived at the nearby Broomhead Hall, noted that in 1734 the ratepayers of Bolsterstone employed Benjamin Milnes, a local mason, to take down the old wooden bridge and to build a stone one in its place.[12]

New Mill Bridge was originally part of an ancient route from Bradfield to Bolsterstone and on to Silkstone and Wakefield. This highway crossed the Little Don at Unsliven Bridge and the River Don at Willow Bridge. Its line is marked by various guide stoops that Justices of the Peace at Quarter Sessions ordered to be erected between 1733 and 1738. The unusual six-sided stoop at Dyson Cote on the great ridge between the two rivers is inscribed 1734, the same year that New Mill Bridge was replaced in stone. It seems that a deliberate attempt was made to improve this old highway at that time.[13] The route was never important enough to become a turnpike road, however, so the bridges were not replaced later in the eighteenth century by new ones that were wide enough to take wheeled vehicles. Packhorse bridges survive only in remote places such as this moorland district, where travellers proceeded either on horseback or on foot.

Catcliffe glasshouse

This cone-shaped structure alongside the Sheffield Parkway that leads to the M1 motorway is the oldest surviving glassworks in western Europe. It was built as one of a pair in 1740 by William Fenny, a descendant of a family of skilled glassworkers in Lorraine, on the borders of France, Luxembourg and Germany, and the former manager of the Bolsterstone glasshouse. The Bolsterstone works belonged to his mother-in-law, Mary Blackburn, who was worried that after her death Fenny would build a rival works near by. In a codicil to her will in 1738, she therefore stipulated that Fenny's children would not receive their legacies unless he promised not to erect a glassworks within ten miles of Bolsterstone. Catcliffe lies 10½ miles away. Some of the Bolsterstone workforce accompanied Fenny in his move.[14]

The Tudor glass industry was located in woodland districts, notably The Weald in Kent and Sussex, where the Lorraine immigrants first settled to escape religious persecution, but in the early seventeenth century coal rapidly replaced wood as the fuel in glass furnaces and so the industry was re-sited in the coalfields by wealthy landowners.[15] The earliest of these new furnaces in South Yorkshire was erected in 1632 by Sir Thomas Wentworth, close to his stately home at Wentworth Woodhouse. It did not last long, but the place-name Glasshouse Green survives.

The glasshouse at Catcliffe is well known to travellers along the M1 motorway and the Sheffield Parkway. It dates from 1740 and is the oldest of its kind.

Later furnaces were owned or managed by descendants of the Lorraine immigrants, such as the Pilmays, who built a glasshouse at Silkstone by 1658. In the late seventeenth and early eighteenth centuries glass furnaces became more complex, particularly in their flue systems, which ended up as the great conical superstructures such as that at Catcliffe. The use of sophisticated technology at Silkstone is evident from the probate inventory of Abigail Pilmay, who died in 1698. High-quality sand was brought from Brierley in Staffordshire and used with red lead for the manufacture of crystal glass; rape ashes produced alkali for green bottles; 'bluepowder' and manganese were the main colouring agents; and salt petre was used to keep window glass clear.[16]

The Catcliffe works stayed in production until the early years of the twentieth century.

Thurlstone weaving

In the late eighteenth and early nineteenth centuries the manufacture of woollen cloth, an ancient speciality of the moorland townships on the edges of the Pennines, grew significantly. Thurlstone became an industrial village that spread northwards to 'Top o' th' Town' and along the valley of the

River Don to the south, in order to accommodate growing numbers of mill workers and handloom weavers.

The national population was rising rapidly at this time and that of the township of Thurlstone, which stretched across the moors to the county boundary at Saltersbrook and which included many hamlets and isolated farmsteads well beyond the village, almost doubled between 1801 and 1851. The 1806 militia returns for Thurlstone township [17] reveal that 68 of the 130 men who were aged between 18 and 45 and so liable for military duty were employed in the textile trades. They comprised 40 weavers, 21 clothiers, four cloth dressers, a slubber, a yarn maker and a dyer. A 'clothier' was a small manufacturer or someone who combined weaving with running a small farm, whereas a 'weaver' was a wage earner who worked full-time at his loom in an upstairs chamber of a cottage rented from a mill owner.

This weaver's cottage attached to the gable end of a seventeenth-century farmhouse in Thurlstone has a typical row of windows in its upper storey to allow the maximum amount of light to fall on the loom.

As the population grew, the opportunities to rent farm land dwindled, so the proportion of 'clothiers' declined while the number of 'weavers' increased to cope with the extra yarn that was spun, mainly by women and children in the new water-powered mills in the river valleys. Demand for men who could weave all the yarn that was produced in the mills soared, so Thurlstone soon acquired rows of cottages with characteristic ranges of upstairs windows where the handlooms were installed. The first edition of the six-inch Ordnance Survey map (1854) marks the tenters in the back gardens where cloth was hung and stretched on tenterhooks after returning from the fulling mill. A fine example of a row of weavers' cottages, lit by a row of windows in the upper storey, can be seen at Tenter Hill.

My great-great-grandfather, John Hey (1781–1855) came to live near 'Top o' th' Town' shortly after 1800. He was one of the weavers in the militia list of 1806. The 1841 census recorded him as a fancy weaver living at the first of eight households in 'New Street', which was recorded after the enumerator had visited 'Syke' and before he got to 'Green' at the top end of the village. Ten years later, the 1851 census named John as a 70-year-old widower who was still following the trade of fancy weaving. His home was recorded as the first of what had become ten households in New Street, after the census enumerator had finished with 'Top o' th' Town'. Some of the cottages in New Street (shown in the photograph) have a classic row of weavers' windows that provided ample light for upstairs chambers.

The name New Street was recorded in the nearby Providence Baptist Chapel records in 1824,[18] but it disappeared after the 1851 census. In 1861, three of the householders who had lived in New Street ten years previously were living in Royd Moor Lane, a name which had not been used in the village records before, though no doubt it had long been applied to the climb out of Thurlstone up to Royd Moor Farm. It is apparent that the weavers' cottages that were built in the early nineteenth century alongside a seventeenth-century farmhouse were at first called New Street, just as a similar group of dwellings that led off Town Gate was called New Row. At that time, houses were not numbered and rows and streets did not have name signs, so it was quite common for names to change. John Hey's dwelling was the first in the enumerators' list of the New Street households in 1841 and 1851, but as we do not know which way the enumerator walked along the street it is not certain that this was his cottage.

Notes

Chapter 1

1. P. Ryder, *Saxon Churches in South Yorkshire* (South Yorkshire County Council, 1982).
2. R. Morris, *Churches in the Landscape* (London, 1989), pp. 258–59 and 461.
3. J. Hunter, *South Yorkshire: The History and Topography of the Deanery of Doncaster*, I (London, 1828), p. 389.
4. J. E. Morris, *The West Riding of Yorkshire* (London, 1911), pp. 75–76
5. Hunter, I, p. 89.
6. P. F. Ryder: survey of Thorpe-in-Balne for the South Yorkshire Archaeology Service.
7. Sir N. Pevsner, *The Buildings of England: Yorkshire, the West Riding* (Yale, 2003), pp. 154–56.
8. R. Wood, 'The Romanesque Doorway at Fishlake', *Yorkshire Archaeological Journal*, 72 (2000), pp. 17–40; R. Wood, 'The Romanesque Memorial at Conisbrough', *Yorkshire Archaeological Journal*, 73 (2001), pp. 41–60.

Chapter 2

1. A fuller version appears in J. Rodwell and D. Hey, 'The King's Wood in Lindrick', *Landscapes*, X1: 1 (2010), pp. 47–66.
2. J. Hunter, *South Yorkshire: The History and Topography of the Deanery of Doncaster*, 1 (London, 1828), p. 267; S. O. Addy, 'Roche Abbey Charters', *Transactions of the Hunter Archaeological Society*, IV (1937), pp. 226–48; J. Aveling, *The History of Roche Abbey* (Worksop, 1870); D. Hey, *Medieval South Yorkshire* (Ashbourne, 2003), pp. 94–99.
3. I would like to thank the Earl and Countess of Scarbrough for their kind hospitality, for unrestricted access to King's Wood, and for the use of the Sandbeck Estate Archives; and Mr Richard Street, the estate forester, for his account of the recent management of King's Wood.
4. J. A. Newbould, 'Notes on the Distribution of Large-Leaved Lime (*Tilia platyphyllos. Scop*) on the Magnesian Limestone in South Yorkshire', *The Naturalist*, 126 (2001), pp. 139–50.
5. Aveling, pp. 130–31.
6. Sandbeck Estate Archives, MTD/B30/11, 12 and 13a.
7. G. C. Hopkinson, 'The Charcoal Iron Industry in the Sheffield Region, 1500–1775', *Transactions of the Hunter Archaeological Society*, VIII, part 3 (1961), pp. 122–51.
8. Sandbeck Estate Archives, MTD/B8/14.
9. A. Rodgers, 'Early Watermills of the Maltby Area' in M. Jones, ed., *Aspects of Rotherham*, 1 (Barnsley, 1995), p. 60.
10. Sandbeck Estate Archives, ETP/10.

11. Sandbeck Estate Archives, Timber Sales, 80/5.
12. Information from Ken Hawley; Kelham Island Museum, Sheffield, Hawley Tool Collection: sales catalogues.
13. Aveling, pp. 15, 17.
14. *Calendar of Charter Rolls, 1226–1257*, p. 146.
15. The National Archives, SC6/Henry VIII/4535; (*bosco voc' laghton lyndrek per est C acri*).
16. M. Gelling and A. Cole, *The Landscape of Place-Names* (Stamford, 2000), pp. 213–16.
17. R. White, *Dukery Records* (Worksop, 1904), pp. 361–64.
18. V. Watts, ed., *The Cambridge Dictionary of English Place-Names* (Cambridge, 2004), p. 116; White, pp. 110–11, 116, 367.
19. A. H. Smith, *The Place-Names of the West Riding of Yorkshire*, I (Cambridge, 1961), p. 150.
20. White, p. 309.
21. R. T. Timson, ed., *The Cartulary of Blyth Priory* (Thoroton Society, XXVII, 1973), p. 119.
22. Aveling, p. 152.
23. D. Hey, 'Yorkshire's Southern Boundary', *Northern History*, XXXVII (2000), pp. 31–47.
24. Hunter, 1, pp. 295, 303.
25. P. N. Wood, 'The Little British Kingdom of Craven', *Northern History*, XXXII (1996), pp. 1–20; Watts, pp. 166.

Chapter 3
1. J. Hunter, *South Yorkshire: The History and Topography of South Yorkshire*, I (London, 1828), p. 237.
2. A. H. Smith, ed., *The Place-Names of the West Riding of Yorkshire*, I (Cambridge, 1961), pp. 52–54.
3. D. Hey, *Medieval South Yorkshire* (Ashbourne, 2003), pp. 70–74.
4. R. Timson, *The Cartulary of Blyth Priory* (Thoroton Society Record Series, XXVII, 1973).
5. T. Beastall, *Tickhill: Portrait of an English Country Town* (Doncaster, 1995); Hunter, I, pp. 232–34.
6. D. Hey, *Medieval South Yorkshire*, pp. 135–40; M. W. Beresford, *New Towns of the Middle Ages* (1967).
7. W. Farrer, ed., *Early Yorkshire Charters*, III (1916), 1439.
8. Hunter, I, p. 237; Beastall, pp. 8–9.
9. The National Archives, E317 Yorks 58.
10. J. R. Magilton, 'The Topography of a Medieval Town', *Transactions of the Hunter Archaeological Society*, 10, part 5 (1979), pp. 344–49.
11. D. Hey, C. Giles, M. Spufford and A. Wareham, eds, *Yorkshire West Riding Hearth Tax Assessment, Lady Day 1672* (British Record Society, 2007), pp. 435–36.
12. Hunter, I, p. 14.
13. R. E. Glasscock, ed., *The Lay Subsidy of 1334* (London, 1975).
14. C. C. Fenwick, ed., *The Poll Taxes of 1377, 1379 and 1381*, part 3 (Oxford, 2005), pp. 336–38.
15. Beastall, pp. 54–56; Hunter, I, p. 245.
16. Beastall, p. 57.

17. Beastall, pp. 59, 61–62.
18. Beastall, pp. 67–69; Hunter, pp. 243–44.
19. B. Sprakes, *The Medieval Stained Glass of South Yorkshire* (Oxford, 2003), pp. 98–110.
20. L. T. Smith, ed., *Leland's Itinerary in England and Wales*, I London, 1964), pp. 35–36.
21. The National Archives, MPC/96.
22. J. J. Cartwright, ed., *The Travels through England of Dr Richard Pococke* (Camden Society, 1888), pp. 170 and 180.
23. C. B. Andrews, ed., *The Torrington Diaries*, II (London, 1935), pp. 20 and 343.
24. E. Baines, *History, Directory & Gazetteer of the County of York, I: West Riding* (Leeds, 1822), pp. 418–20.
25. Hunter, II (1831), p. 490.

Chapter 4
1. A. Rodgers, 'Archaeological Excavations at Roche Abbey' in M. Jones, ed., *Aspects of Rotherham*, 2 (Barnsley, 1996), pp. 95–114; P. Ferguson, *Roche Abbey* (English Heritage guide, 1990).
2. J. H. Aveling, *The History of Roche Abbey, from its Foundation to its Dissolution* (Worksop, 1870), pp. 97–160; J. Hunter, *South Yorkshire: The History and Topography of the Deanery of Doncaster*, I (London, 1828), p. 271.
3. Hunter, I, p. 186.
4. J. Burton, *The Monastic Order in England, 1069–1215* (Cambridge, 1999), pp. 263 and 275; J. Wilkinson, *Worsborough: Its Historical Associations and Rural Attractions* (London, 1872), pp. 74–75.
5. W. Farrer and C. T. Clay, eds, *Early Yorkshire Charters, 7, The Honour of Skipton* (Cambridge, 2013), pp. 202–11.
6. Hunter, I, p. 84.
7. W. Farrer, ed., *Early Yorkshire Charters*, III (Edinburgh, 1916), 1266 and 1273–1276; T. W. Hall, 'Thundercliffe and the Hermitage of St John' in *Sheffield Manorial Records*, II (Sheffield, 1928), pp. 220–37.
8. J. W. Walker, ed., *Abstracts of the Chartularies of the Priory of Monkbretton* (Yorkshire Archaeological Society Record Series, 82, 1924).
9. R. Graham and R. Gilyard-Beer, *Monk Bretton Priory* (HMSO, 1966).
10. J. Eastwood, *History of the Parish of Ecclesfield* (London, 1862), pp. 88–142; D. Hey, *Historic Hallamshire* (Ashbourne, 2002), pp. 27–43.
11. C. C. Fenwick, ed., *The Poll Taxes of 1377, 1379 and 1381*, part 3 (Oxford, 2005), p. 301; P. F. Ryder, *Medieval Buildings of Yorkshire* (Ashbourne, 1982), p. 84.
12. Fenwick, part 3, pp. 315 and 336.
13. D. Hey, *A History of the Peak District Moors* (Barnsley, 2014), pp. 64–67.
14. Hunter, I, pp. 83–85.
15. The National Archives, E317/15.
16. T. Umpleby, *Water Mills and Furnaces on the Yorkshire Dearne and its Tributaries* (Wakefield, 2000).
17. D. Hey, L. Liddy and D. Luscombe, eds, *A Monastic Community in Local Society: The Beauchief Abbey Cartulary* (Cambridge, 2011), pp. 17–19.

Chapter 5

1. S. Jones, 'Whiston Hall Barn', *Archaeological Journal*, 137 (1980), pp. 431–33.
2. I. Tyers and C. Groves, 'Dendrochronology and the Analysis of Whiston Barn, near Rotherham', *Yorkshire Buildings: The Journal of the Yorkshire Vernacular Buildings Study Group*, 30 (2002), pp. 72–84.
3. Vernacular Architecture Group: Dendrochronology Database (updated 2014): <archaeologydataservice.ac.uk/archives/view/vag_dendro/>.
4. D. Hey, *A History of Sheffield* (Lancaster, 2010), p. 16.
5. J. Hunter, *South Yorkshire: the History and Topography of the Deanery of Doncaster*, II (1831), pp. 181–82.
6. See note 3.
7. D. Hey, *Medieval South Yorkshire* (Ashbourne, 2003), pp. 84–85.
8. P. F. Ryder, 'Oxspring Lodge: reconstructing a Yorkshire hunting lodge', *Post-Medieval Archaeology*, 19 (1985), pp. 49–62.
9. S. Jones, 'Gunthwaite Barn'', *Archaeological* Journal, 137 (1980), pp. 463–66; P. F. Ryder, *Timber Framed Buildings in South Yorkshire* (South Yorkshire County Archaeology Monograph no. 1, undated), pp. 78–82; D. Hey, *A History of Penistone and District* (Barnsley, 2002), pp. 36–37 and 44–45.
10. N. Alcock and D. Miles, *The Medieval Peasant House in Midland England* (Oxford, 2013).
11. M. Habberjam *et al.*, *The Court Rolls of the Manor of Wakefield from October 1350 to September 1352* (Yorkshire Archaeological Society, 1987), p. 105. In 2014 Old Hall Farm at Brightholmlee produced a dendro date of 1484 for its cruck trusses.
12. P. F. Ryder, *Timber Framed Buildings in South Yorkshire* (South Yorkshire County Archaeology Monograph no. 1, undated), pp. 6–13.
13. Sheffield Archives, NBC 20.
14. See note 6.
15. See note 6.
16. C. Morris, ed., *The Illustrated Journeys of Celia Fiennes, c.1682–c.1712* (London, 1982), p. 103.

Chapter 6

1. A. H. Smith, ed., *The Place-Names of the West Riding of Yorkshire*, I (Cambridge, 1961), p. 331.
2. Nottinghamshire Archives, DD/SR/26/21; DD/SR/36/51.
3. DD/SR/36/52-53.
4. DD/SR/36/54-55.
5. W. Farrer, ed., *Early Yorkshire Charters* (Cambridge, 2013), 1798–1806.
6. West Yorkshire Archive Service, Bradford, Spencer Stanhope 4/11/95/1.
7. *Calendar of Charter Rolls*, I (Record Commissioners, 1837), p. 383.
8. A. H. Smith, ed., *The Place-Names of the West Riding of Yorkshire*, I (Cambridge, 1961), p. 332.
9. J. Hunter, *South Yorkshire: The History and Topography of the Deanery of Doncaster*, II (1831), p. 361; Nottinghamshire Archives, DD/SR/26/97.
10. D. Hey, 'Townfields, Royds and Shaws: The Medieval Landscape of a South Pennine Township', *Northern History*, L, no. 2 (2013), pp. 216–38.

11. Sheffield Archives, Crewe Manuscripts 680.
12. W. Paley, ed., *Court Rolls of the Manor of Wakefield, I, 1274 to 1297*, Yorkshire Archaeological Society Record Series, XXIV (1901), pp. 175, 193, 217, 225, 291.
13. Sheffield Archives, Crewe Manuscripts 957. See note 10, pp. 235–36.
14. Sheffield Archives, Crewe Manuscripts 670.
15. W. P. Baildon, ed., *Court Rolls of the Manor of Wakefield, I, 1274–97*, (Cambridge, 2013), p. 291; W. P. Baildon, ed., *II, 1297–1309*, p. 113; J. Lister, ed., *IV, 1315 to 1317*, p. 4.
16. Nottinghamshire Archives, DD/SR/209/158.
17. *Ancient Deeds*, II, p. 504; Hey, 'Townfields …', pp. 231–32.
18. *Ancient Deeds*, I, C1500.
19. Barnsley Archives, A/3204/Z, map 4.
20. J. N. Dransfield, *A History of the Parish of Penistone* (Penistone, 1906), pp. 178–79.
21. M. L. Faull and S. A. Moorhouse, *West Yorkshire: An Archaeological Survey to A.D. 1500: 3, The Rural Medieval Landscape* (Wakefield, 1981), p. 661.
22. G. Redmonds, 'Personal Names and Surnames in Some West Yorkshire Royds', *Nomina*, 9 (1985), pp. 73–79.
23. *Ancient Deeds*, I, C1575.
24. Hunter, II, pp. 194–96.
25. *Calendar of Charter Rolls, II, 1257–1300* (1906), 353.
26. Hunter, II, p. 196.
27. Hunter, II, p. 360–61.
28. J. Kenworthy, *Midhope Potteries* (Deepcar, 1928).
29. Sheffield Archives, Crewe Manuscripts 746.
30. J. Kenworthy, *The Lure of Midhope-cum-Langsett* (Deepcar, 1927) and *The Early History of Stocksbridge and District* (Deepcar, 1928).
31. Sheffield Archives, Elmhirst Muniments 778/1.
32. Sheffield Archives, Elmhirst Muniments 821.
33. Dransfield, pp. 51–52.
34. D. Hey, *A History of the Peak District Moors* (Barnsley, 2014), chapter 6: 'Grouse Moors', pp. 138–56.

Chapter 7
 1. D. Hey, 'The Parks at Tankersley and Wortley', *Yorkshire Archaeological Journal*, 47 (1975), pp. 109–19.
 2. T. W. Hall, *A Descriptive Catalogue of Charters and Manorial Records Relating to Tankersley'* (Sheffield, 1937), pp. 6–8; the 1772 map is reproduced opposite p. 6.
 3. H. E. J. le Patourel, *The Moated Sites of Yorkshire* (Leeds, 1973).
 4. Sheffield Archives, Talbot Letters 2/71 and 2/258.
 5. Sheffield Archives, Talbot Letters 2/44.
 6. J. Lister, ed., *Yorkshire Star Chamber Proceedings*, *IV* (Yorkshire Archaeological Society Record Series, 70, 1927), p. 49.
 7. W. Brown, ed., *Yorkshire Star Chamber Proceedings*, *I* (Yorkshire Archaeological Society Record Series), 41 (1909), pp. 48–52 and *III*, 51 (1914), pp. 154–55.

8. *Memoirs of Anne, Lady Halkett, and Ann, Lady Fanshawe*, ed. John Loftis (Oxford, 1979).

9. 'Depositions from York Castle', *Surtees Society*, XL (1861), p. 70 note.

10. D. Defoe, *Tour through the Whole Island of Great Britain*, (Everyman edition, 1962), II, p. 185.

11. Sheffield Archives, Wentworth Woodhouse Muniments, R 183.

12. R. Pococke, *Travels through England, 1750–51*, ed. J. J. Cartwright (Camden Society, 1888), p. 65.

13. A. K. Clayton, 'The Break-Up of Tankersley Park', *South Yorkshire Times*, 3 February 1962. The following paragraph is based upon the Wentworth Muniments quoted in this article.

14. Sheffield Archives, Wentworth Woodhouse Muniments, A 1273.

15. Sheffield Archives, Wentworth Muniments, box 36, no. 9.

Chapter 8

1. A fuller version appears in D. Hey and J. Rodwell, 'Wombwell: The Landscape History of a South Yorkshire Coalfield Township', *Landscapes*, 7: 2 (2006), pp. 24–47.

2. J. Hunter, *South Yorkshire: The History and Topography of the Deanery of Doncaster*, II (London, 1831), p. 122.

3. W. Page, ed., *Chantry Certificates*, Surtees Society, XCI (1892), p. 192.

4. British Library, Harley 4617.

5. J. S. Purvis, ed., *The Cartulary of the Augustinian Priory of St John the Evangelist of the Park of Healaugh* (Yorkshire Archaeological Society Record Series, XCVII, 1935).

6. Trinity College, Cambridge, archives: 17 Darfield, 1–142, especially 7 (1620 survey), 13 (1757 and 1795 surveys and map) and 19–21 (1772–3 exchanges and map).

7. Borthwick Institute for Archives, University of York, TA 647L.

8. A. H. Smith, ed., *the Place-Names of the West Riding of Yorkshire*, I (Cambridge, 1961), p. 105.

9. H. Cook, K. Stearne and T. Williamson, 'The origin of water meadows in England', *Agricultural History Review*, 51, part I (2003), pp. 155–62.

10. Sheffield Archives, WWM/C/2/256 and WWM/C/2/72-154.

11. Borthwick, RIIIF.XXIII.

12. C. C. Fenwick, ed., *The Poll Taxes of 1377, 1379 and 1381: part 3* (British Academy, 2005), p. 300.

13. D. Hey, *Packmen, Carriers and Packhorse Roads* (Ashbourne, 2001), pp. 60–61.

14. M. Gelling and A. Cole, *The Landscape of Place-Names* (Stamford, 2000), pp. 58–60.

15. Sheffield Archives, WWM/C/2/258.

16. Sheffield Archives, Fairbank DAR 6L.

17. Sheffield Archives, NBC 81.

18. Trinity College, Cambridge, Darfield 13.

19. The National Archives, MAF/32/1169.336 and MAF/32/1126.315.

Chapter 9

1. A. H. Smith, ed., *The Place-Names of the West Riding of Yorkshire*, I (Cambridge, 1961), pp. 3–4.

2. M. Beresford, 'Inclesmoor, West Riding of Yorkshire' in R. A. Skelton and P. D. A. Harvey, eds, *Local Maps and Plans from Medieval England* (Oxford, 1986), pp. 147–61.
3. The National Archives, Maps and Plans, MPC 1/56; reproduced in D. Hey, *A History of Yorkshire: 'County of the Broad Acres'* (Lancaster, 2005), pp. 162–63.
4. L. T. Smith, ed., *Leland's Itinerary in England and* Wales, I (London, 1964), pp. 36–37.
5. J. Hunter, *South Yorkshire: The History and Topography of the Deanery of Doncaster*, II (London, 1828), p. 157.
6. British Library, Lansdowne 897.
7. J. Tomlinson, *The Level of Hatfield Chase and Parts Adjacent* (Doncaster, 1882).
8. D. Hey, 'Yorkshire and Lancashire' in J. Thirsk, ed., *The Agrarian History of England and Wales, V:I, 1640–1750* (Cambridge, 1984), pp. 79–80.
9. Borthwick Institute for Archives, University of York, Doncaster deanery wills and inventories.
10. J. J. Cartwright, ed., *The Travels through England of Dr Richard Pococke* (Camden Society, 1888), pp. 184–85.
11. Hunter, II, p. 154.
12. J. Goodchild, 'The Peat-cutting Industry of South Yorkshire', *The South Yorkshire Journal*, part 3 (Cusworth, 1971), pp. 1–5 and part 4 (1973), pp. 11–19.
13. J. Murray, *Handbook for Travellers in Yorkshire*, (London, 1874), pp. 85–101.
14. See note 12.
15. R. Van de Noort, *The Humber Wetlands: The Archaeology of a Dynamic Landscape* (Bollington, 2004).

Chapter 10

1. E. Elmhirst, *Peculiar Inheritance: A History of the Elmhirsts* (privately published, 1951).
2. S. Jones, 'Houndhill', *Archaeological Journal*, 137 (1980), pp. 442–44. I am grateful to the late Mr A. O. Elmhirst for guiding me around his home, including his attic, on several occasions.
3. E. Elmhirst, p. 49.
4. Printed in D. Hey, *Buildings of Britain, 1550–1750: Yorkshire* (Ashbourne, 1981), pp. 152–53.
5. A. H. Smith, ed., *The Place-Names of the West Riding of Yorkshire*, I (Cambridge, 1961), p. 293.
6. Borthwick Institute of Archives, York University, Doncaster deanery wills.
7. Vernacular Architecture Group: Dendrochronology Database (updated 2014): <archaeologydataservice.ac.uk/archives/view/vag_dendro/>.
8. Borthwick wills.
9. J. Wilkinson, *Worsborough: Its Historical Associations and Rural Attractions* (Barnsley, 1872), opposite p. 197.
10. Wilkinson, pp. 197–98.
11. D. Hey *et al.*, eds, *Yorkshire West Riding Hearth Tax Assessment, Lady Day 1672* (British Record Society, 2007), p. 381–82.
12. Wilkinson, pp. 199–204.
13. A. H. Smith, ed., p. 293.

14. Wilkinson, pp. 59–99.
15. C. C. Fenwick, ed., *The Poll Taxes of 1377, 1379 and 1381*, part 3 (The British Academy, 2005), p. 340.
16. Sheffield Archives, Wentworth Woodhouse Muniments, Bright Papers 1–3319.
17. Sheffield Archives, Wharncliffe Deeds, 316.
18. 'The Journal of Mr. John Hobson, late of Dodworth Green', *Surtees* Society, LXV (1875), pp. 257–8, 30 September 1726: 'Mrs Milner of Old Hall at Worsborrow Dale, was buried at Worsborough. She died the Wednesday night of a feaver, and left a son and a daughter. It formerly belonged to the family of the Rockleys, and was called Rockly hall.'
19. S. Jones, pp. 23–30.
20. Borthwick wills and inventories: 5 January 1746/7 William Milner, Old Hall, gent.; 15 September 1746 David Travis, clerk, Old Hall.
21. Wilkinson, p. 72.
22. Edmunds, pp. 32–58.

Chapter 11
1. D. Hey, *The Fiery Blades of Hallamshire: Sheffield and its Neighbourhood, 1660–1750* (Leicester, 1991), p. 85.
2. L. T. Smith, ed., *Leland's Itinerary in England and Wales*, IV (London, 1964), p. 14.
3. J. Guest, *Historic Notices of Rotherham* (Worksop, 1879), p. 96.
4. D. Hey, *A History of Sheffield* (Lancaster, third edn, 2010), pp. 28–34.
5. South Yorkshire Archaeology Service report.
6. J. Hunter, *South Yorkshire: The History and Topography of the Deanery of Doncaster*, II (London, 1831), p. 84; D. Hey *et al.*, eds, *Yorkshire West Riding Hearth Tax Assessment, Lady Day 1672* (British Record Society, 2007), p. 442.
7. Hunter, II, p. 95.
8. A. H. Smith, ed., *The Place-Names of the West Riding of Yorkshire*, I (Cambridge, 1961), pp. 7–12.
9. British Library, Lansdowne MS 897.
10. Borthwick Institute for Archives, University of York, Doncaster deanery wills and inventories.
11. *A Calendar to the Records of the Borough of Doncaster*, IV (Doncaster, 1904), p. 162.
12. British Library, Harley 4617.
13. S. O. Addy, *The Evolution of the English House* (London, 1898), pp. 207–10.
14. Sheffield Archives, MD 456.
15. J. Hunter, ed., *The Diary of Ralph Thoresby*, I (London, 1830), p. 261.
16. E. Goodwin, 'Sheffield' in G. L. Gomme, ed., *The Gentleman's Magazine Library: Topographical History of Worcestershire and Yorkshire* (1902), pp. 325–33; J. Hunter, *Hallamshire: the History and Topography of the Parish of Sheffield in the County of York*, ed. A. Gatty (London, 1861), p. 13.

Chapter 12
1. D. N. Riley, *Early Landscape from the Air: Studies of Crop Marks in South Yorkshire and North Nottinghamshire* (Sheffield, 1980).

2. D. Hey, *Medieval South Yorkshire* (Ashbourne, 2003), pp. 15–17.

3. The National Archives, SP 5/2/f. 185.

4. A. Ruston and D. Witney, *Hooton Pagnell: the Agricultural Evolution of a Yorkshire Village* (London, 1934), pp. 213–28; C. C. Fenwick, ed., *The Poll Taxes of 1377, 1379 and 1381*, part 3 (The British Academy, 2005), p. 314.

5. R. E. Glasscock, ed., *The Lay Subsidy of 1334* (The British Academy, 1974).

6. Sheffield Archives, Bacon Frank Muniments 956.

7. M. Beresford, *The Lost Villages of England* (London, 1954), p. 334; M. W. Beresford, 'The Lost Villages of Yorkshire', part III, *Yorkshire Archaeological Journal*, XXXVIII (1955), pp. 238–40.

8. D. Hey *et al.*, *Yorkshire West Riding Hearth Tax Assessment, Lady Day 1672* (The British Record Society, 2007), p. 399.

9. D. Hey, *Medieval South Yorkshire* (Ashbourne, 2003), p 156.

10. The National Archives, DL 43/10/5; Fenwick, p. 360.

11. A. H. Smith, ed., *The Place-Names of the West Riding of Yorkshire* (Cambridge, 1961), p. 87.

12. See note 4.

13. D. Hey, *A History of Yorkshire: County of the Broad Acres* (Lancaster, 2005), p. 315.

14. Hey, *Yorkshire*, pp. 111–15.

15. J. G. Fardell, *Sprotborough* (Doncaster, 1850).

16. Doncaster Archives, DD/WA.

17. English Heritage guide, *Brodsworth Hall and Gardens* (2009).

18. D. Hey, *Yorkshire*, pp. 409–10.

Chapter 13

1. J. Hunter, *South Yorkshire: The History and Topography of the Deanery of Doncaster*, II (London, 1831), pp. 231–32.

2. D. Hey, *Medieval South Yorkshire* (Ashbourne, 2003), pp. 84–85.

3. C. T. Pratt, *History of Cawthorne* (Barnsley, 1882), pp. 49–67.

4. Hunter, II, p. 232.

5. D. Hey, *The Rural Metalworkers of the Sheffield Region* (Leicester, 1972), pp. 42–49.

6. A. H. Smith, ed., *The Place-Names of the West Riding of* Yorkshire, I (Cambridge, 1961), p. 323; see note 3.

7. Hunter, II, pp. 233–34.

8. P. Ryder, 'Five South Yorkshire Timber-Framed Houses', *Yorkshire Archaeological Journal*, 59 (1987), pp. 51–82.

9. Pratt, pp. 41–48.

10. D. Hey *et al.*, *Yorkshire West Riding Hearth Tax Assessment, Lady Day 1672* (British Record Society, 2007), p. 371.

11. *Samuel Buck's Yorkshire Sketchbook* (Wakefield Historical Publications, 1979), p. 128.

12. Sheffield Archives, SYCRO/630/Z1/1.

13. A. Raistrick and E. Allen, 'The South Yorkshire Ironmasters, 1690–1750', *Economic History Review*, Old Series, IX (1939), pp. 168–85; Hey, *Rural Metalworkers*, pp. 31–49.

14. D. Crossley, 'The Blast Furnace at Rockley, South Yorkshire', *The Archaeological Journal*, 152 (1996), pp. 291–380.

15. D. Crossley, 'Wortley Top Forge', *Archaeological Journal*, 137 (1980), pp. 449–52.
16. Hunter, II, p. 232.
17. Hey, *Rural Metalworkers*, pp. 10–13.
18. R. Butterworth, 'The Ecclesfield Nailmakers' Agreement', *Transactions of the Hunter Archaeological Society*, 2 (1924), pp. 114–19.
19. Hey, *Rural Metalworkers*, pp. 43–44.
20. B. E. Coates, 'Parklands in transition: Medieval Deer-park to Modern Landscape Park', *Transactions of the Hunter Archaeological* Society, 9, part 3 (1967), pp. 132–50; Metropolitan Borough of Barnsley, *Cannon Hall: A Country House Museum* (undated).

Chapter 14
1. J. Lees-Milne, *English Country Houses: Baroque, 1685*–1715 (London, 1970), pp. 236–42; D. Hey, *Buildings of Britain, 1550–1750: Yorkshire* (Ashbourne, 1981), pp. 95–98; D. Hey, *Wentworth Castle: A Short History* (Derby, 1991).
2. J. J. Cartwright, ed., *The Wentworth Papers, 1705–1739* (London, 1883).
3. D. Hey *et al.*, eds, *Yorkshire West Riding Hearth Tax Assessment, Lady Day 1672* (British Record Society, 2007).
4. See note 2.
5. J. Wright, ed., *The Letters of Horace Walpole, Earl of Oxford*, VI (London, 1840), p. 346.
6. A. Young, *Tour through the North of England*, I (London, 1771), pp. 139–48.

Chapter 15
1. D. Hey, *Packmen, Carriers and Packhorse Roads* (Ashbourne, 2001), pp. 77–80.
2. D. Hey, *Medieval South Yorkshire* (Ashbourne, 2003), pp. 143–48.
3. D. Defoe, *Tour Through the Whole Island of Great Britain* (Everyman edition, 1962) II, p. 181.
4. E. Baines, *History, Directory & Gazetteer of the County of York: 1. West Riding* (Leeds, 1822), p. 140.
5. D. Hey, *Medieval South Yorkshire*, pp. 130–35.
6. Sheffield Archives, NBC 20: 'Particular of Mr. Moore's Estate – part of Manor of Barnbrough 1692'.
7. T. S. Willan, *The History of the Don Navigation* (Manchester, 1965); Hey, *Packmen*, pp. 81–83.
8. D. Hey, *The Fiery Blades of Hallamshire: Sheffield and its Neighbourhood, 1660–1740* (Leicester, 1991), pp. 162–67.
9. D. Hey, M. Olive and M. Liddament, *Forging the Valley* (Sheffield, 1997), pp. 31–33.
10. R. Glister, 'The Dearne and Dove Canal' in B. Elliott, ed., *Aspects of Barnsley*, 3 (Barnsley, 1995), pp. 116–32.
11. D. Hey, 'Industrialised Villages' in G. Mingay, ed., *The Victorian Countryside*, I (London, 1981), pp. 353–62.
12. R. Glister, 'The Development and Decline of the Barnsley canal' in B. Elliott, ed., *Aspects of Barnsley*, 5 (Barnsley, 1998), pp. 41–55.
13. J. Goodchild, 'The Silkstone Railway' in B. Elliott, ed., *Aspects of Barnsley*, 2 (Barnsley, 1994), pp. 229–50.

14. H. Taylor, 'The Nineteenth Century Limekilns at Barnby Basin, South Yorkshire', *Yorkshire Archaeological Journal*, 81 (2009), pp. 311–27.
15. C. Richardson and J. Lower, *South Yorkshire Waterways* (2012).

Chapter 16
1. J. Hunter, *South Yorkshire: The History and Topography of the Deanery of Doncaster*, II (London, 1831), pp. 78–100.
2. S. Bennett and T. Dodsworth, 'Remembered in Stones: Church Monuments in the Rotherham Area' in M. Jones, ed., *Aspects of Rotherham*, 3 (Barnsley, 1998), pp. 60–79.
3. Hunter, p. 90.
4. Sheffield Archives, Wentworth Woodhouse Muniments, A 1273.
5. M. I. Wilson, *William Kent, Architect, Designer, Painter, Gardener, 1685–1748* (London, 1984), p. 166; C. Hussey, *English Country Houses: Early Georgian, 1715–1760* (London, 1955), pp. 147–54.
6. J. Hunter, ed., *The Diary of Ralph Thoresby*, II (London, 1830), p. p. 84–85.
7. See note 5.
8. See note 4.
9. J. Allan, 'Wentworth Woodhouse', *Archaeological Journal*, 137 (1980), pp. 393–97; D. Hey, *Buildings of Britain, 1550–1750: Yorkshire* (Ashbourne, 1981), pp. 104–10.
10. A. Young, *Tour through the North of England*, I (London, 1771), pp. 262.
11. Sheffield Archives, Wentworth Woodhouse Muniments, A 1273.
12. M. Jones, 'The Expansion of a Great Landed Estate: The Watson-Wentworth South Yorkshire Estate, 1695–1782' in M. Jones, ed., *Aspects of Rotherham*, 3 (Barnsley, 1998), pp. 80–98.
13. See note 4.
14. R. B. Wragg 'The Rockingham Mausoleum (1784–1793)', *Yorkshire Archaeological Journal*, 52 (1980), pp. 157–66; R. B. Wragg, 'Four Monuments at Wentworth', *Transactions of the Ancient Monuments Society*, 23 (1978), pp. 29–39.
15. A. K. Clayton, 'The Wentworth Round-Houses', *Transcations of the Hunter Archaeological Society*, 8, p. 229–33.
16. See note 12.
17. Hunter, II, pp. 97–99.
18. Sir N. Pevsner, *The Buildings of England: Yorkshire, The West Riding* (Yale, 2003), p. 538.
19. A. K. Clayton, 'The Newcomen-Type Engine at Elsecar, West Riding', *Transactions of the Newcomen Society*, 35 (1962), pp. 108.
20. A. K. Clayton, *Hoyland Nether* (typescript, Hoyland Library, 1973).
21. B. Trinder, *Britain's Industrial Revolution: The Making of a Manufacturing People, 1700–1870* (Lancaster, 2013), p. 331.

Chapter 17
1. J. G. Ronksley, ed., *An Exact and Perfect Survey and View of the Manor of Sheffield With Other Lands by John Harrison, 1637* (Hull, 2009).
2. D. Hey, *Historic Hallamshire* (Ashbourne, 2002), pp. 94–111.
3. D. Hey, *Packmen, Carriers and Packhorse Roads* (Ashbourne, 2001), p. 100.

4. Hey, *Historic Hallamshire*, p. 95.
5. T. W. Hall, *A Descriptive Catalogue of Sheffield Manorial Records* (Sheffield, 1926), p. 45.
6. D. Postles, 'Rural Economy on the Grits and Sandstones of the South Yorkshire Pennines, 1086–1348', *Northern History*, XV (1979), pp. 1–19.
7. D. Hey, L. Liddy and D. Luscombe, eds, *A Monastic Community in Local Society: The Beauchief Abbey Cartulary* (Cambridge, 2011), p. 15.
8. Sheffield Archives, Bright 24.
9. J. Evelyn, *Silva, or a Discourse on Forest Trees*, II, ed. A. Hunter (London, 1801).
10. Sheffield Archives. ACM S 284.
11. University of Leeds, Brotherton Library, Wilson collection, CLIX, p. 79.
12. Sheffield Archives, Ronksley, 159/12084, ACM S 158, 282, 376, 377.
13. C. Jackson, ed., *The Diary of Abraham de la Pryme* (Surtees Society, LIV, 1870), p. 165.
14. Historical Manuscripts Commission, 29: *Portland Manuscripts*, VI (1901), pp. 143–46.
15. M. Spray and D. J. Smith, 'The Rise and Fall of Holly in the Sheffield Region', *Transactions of the Hunter Archaeological Society*, 18 (1995), pp. 60–74.
16. D. Hey, *The Fiery Blades of Hallamshire: Sheffield and Its Neighbourhood, 1660–1740* (Leicester, 1991), pp. 179–83.
17. C. Ball, D. Crossley amd N. Flavell, eds, *Water Power on the Sheffield Rivers*, second edn (Sheffield, 2006), pp. 81–113.
18. R. A. Postman, *The Mousehole Forge* (Michigan, 2003).
19. See note 17.
20. Ball, Crossley and Flavell, pp. 90–91.
21. Borthwick Institute for Archives, University of York, Doncaster deanery wills and inventories.
22. Ball, Crossley and Flavell, p. 91: Fig. 103 'Swallow Wheel by R.F. Drury 1880'. The OS grid reference is SK 305875.
23. Hey, *Historic Hallamshire*, pp. 102–3.
24. J. Cass, 'Water Supply' in C. Binfield *et al*, eds, *The History of the City of Sheffield, 1843–1993*, II (Sheffield, 1993), pp. 118–29; J. Cass, 'The Rivelin Tunnel, 1903–1910', *Transactions of the Hunter Archaeological Society*, 18 (1995), pp. 60–74.
25. *Sheffield Clarion Ramblers' Handbook* (1948–49), pp. 86–93.
26. J. B. Wheat, 'Garret Gleanings', *Transactions of the Hunter Archaeological* Society, IV, part I (1930), pp. 50–51.
27. Bradfield Parish Archives.

Chapter 18

1. D. Hey, *Buildings of Britain, 1550–1750: Yorkshire* (Ashbourne, 1981), pp. 124–25.
2. D. Hey, 'The Pattern of Nonconformity in South Yorkshire, 1660–1851', *Northern History*, VIII (1973), pp. 86–118.
3. Printed in Revd. B. Dale, *Yorkshire Puritanism and Early Nonconformity* (Bradford, 1909), and J. G. Miall, *Congregationalism in Yorkshire* (London, 1868).
4. Printed in A. Gordon, *Freedom After Ejection, 1690–92* (Manchester, 1917).
5. A. Whiteman, ed., *The Compton Census of 1676: A Critical Edition* (London, 1986); Hey, 'The Pattern of Nonconformity', pp. 90–94.

6. Borthwick Institute for Archives, York University, R.VI.E.2.
7. D. Hey, *A History of Penistone and District* (Barnsley, 2002), pp. 79–97.
8. Dr William's Library, London, MS.34-4.
9. C. Stell, 'Underbank Chapel, Stannington', *Archaeological Journal*, 137 (1980), pp. 455–56.
10. Borthwick Institute, Archbishop Drummond's Visitation Returns, 1764.
11. Hey, *Buildings of Britain*, pp. 128–30.
12. Hey, 'The Pattern of Nonconformity', p. 97.
13. Hey, 'The Pattern of Nonconformity', p. 100.
14. The National Archives, H.O. 129/504–11.
15. Hey, 'The Pattern of Nonconformity', pp. 100–16.

Chapter 19

1. D. Hey, *Medieval South Yorkshire* (Ashbourne, 2003), pp. 181–82.
2. Borthwick Institute for Archives, University of York, Doncaster deanery wills and inventories.
3. A. Young, *Tour through the North of England*, I (London, 1779), p. 115.
4. D. Hey, ed., *The Militia Men of the Barnsley District, 1806: An Analysis of the Staincross Militia Returns* (Sheffield, 1998).
5. *Royal Commission on Children's Employment (Mines), 1st Report* (1842), parts I and II, Parliamentary Papers (380) XV and (381), XVI (Irish University Press).
6. See note 5.
7. J. Benson, *British Coalminers in the Nineteenth Century: A Social History* (London, 1989), pp. 28–63.
8. H. and B. Duckham, *Great Pit Disasters: Great Britain 1700 to the present day*, (Newton Abbott, 1973)
9. See note 7.
10. D. Hey, *How Our Ancestors Lived: A History of Life A Hundred Years ago* (London, 2002), pp. 100–2.
11. A. G. Walker, "Migration into a South Yorkshire Colliery District, 1861–1881', *Northern History*, 29 (1993), pp. 165–84.

Chapter 20

1. B. Elliott, 'Some Dovecote Sites in the Rotherham Area' in M. Jones, ed., *Aspects of Rotherham: Discovering Local History*, 2 (Barnsley, 1996), pp. 153–79; B.Elliott, A Field guide to Dovecotes of the Doncaster Area' in B. Elliott, ed., *Aspects of Doncaster: Discovering Local History*, 1 (Barnsley, 1997).
2. Sheffield Archives, NBC 20: 'Particular of Mr. Moore's Estate – part of Manor of Barnbrough 1692'.
3. D. Holland, ed., *History in Laughton-en-le-Morthen* (Doncaster, 1969).
4. D. Hey, *A History of Penistone and District* (Barnsley, 2002), pp. 110–14.
5. P. J. Wallis, 'Worsborough Grammar School', *Yorkshire Archaeological Journal*, 39 (1958), pp. 147–63.
6. See note 5; J. Wilkinson, *Worsborough: Its Historical Associations and Rural Attractions* (Barnsley, 1872), pp. 320–1.

7. S. L. Ollard and P. C. Walker, eds, *Archbishop Herring's Visitation Returns*, II (Yorkshire Archaeological Society Record Series, 1929), p. 39.
8. J. Hunter, *South Yorkshire: The History and Topography of the Deanery of Doncaster*, II (London, 1828), p. 260.
9. Transcribed in D. Hey, *Buildings of Britain: Yorkshire, 1550–1750* (Ashbourne, 1981), pp. 150–51.
10. D. Hey, *Packmen, Carriers and Packhorse Roads*, (Ashbourne, 2001), pp. 52–63.
11. J. Kenworthy, *Midhope Potteries* (Deepcar, 1928), p. 135.
12. See note 11; note by J. Kenworthy in *Transactions of the Hunter Archaeological Society*, II, 2 (1921), p. 203.
13. Hey, *Packmen*, pp. 31–32.
14. D. Ashurst, *The History of South Yorkshire Glass* (Sheffield, 1992).
15. D. Crossley, *Post-Medieval Archaeology in Britain* (Leicester, 1990), pp. 226–42.
16. D. Hey, 'The Use of Probate Inventories for Industrial Archaeology', *Industrial Archaeology*, X, no. 2 (1973), pp. 201–13.
17. John Goodchild Collection, West Yorkshire Archives, Wakefield, printed in D. Hey, ed., *The Militia Men of the Barnsley District, 1806: An Analysis of the Staincross Militia Returns* (Sheffield, 1998).
18. Barnsley Archives, Thurlstone Providence Particular Baptist Chapel registers.

Index